D0579980

# INSIDE
# TALK
# RADIO

ALSO BY PETER LAUFER

*Iron Curtain Rising: A Personal Journey Through the Changing Landscape of Eastern Europe*
Mercury House, 1991

*Nightmare Abroad: Stories of Americans Imprisoned in Foreign Lands*
Mercury House, 1993

*A Question of Consent: Innocence and Complicity in the Glen Ridge Rape Case*
Mercury House, 1994

*Neon Nevada*
University of Nevada Press, 1994 (coauthor with Sheila Swan Laufer)

*When Hollywood Was Fun*
Birch Lane Press, 1994 (collaborator with Gene Lester)

# INSIDE TALK RADIO

*America's Voice or Just Hot Air?*

# PETER LAUFER

A Birch Lane Press Book

Published by Carol Publishing Group

A Birch Lane Press Book
Published by Carol Publishing Group
Birch Lane Press is a registered trademark of Carol Communications, Inc.
Editorial Offices: 600 Madison Avenue, New York, N.Y. 10022
Sales and Distribution Offices: 120 Enterprise Avenue, Secaucus, N.J. 07094
In Canada: Canadian Manda Group, One Atlantic Avenue, Suite 105, Ontario M6K 3E7
Queries regarding rights and permissions should be addressed to Carol Publishing Group, 600 Madison Avenue, New York, N.Y. 10022

Carol Publishing Group books are available at special discounts for bulk purchases, sales promotion, fund-raising, or educational purposes. Special editions can be created to specifications. For details, contact: Special Sales Department, Carol Publishing Group, 120 Enterprise Avenue, Secaucus, N.J. 07094

Manufactured in the United States of America
10 9 8 7 6 5 4 3 2 1

Library of Congress Cataloging-in-Publication Data

Laufer, Peter.
    Inside talk radio : America's voice or just hot air? / by Peter Laufer.
        p.   cm.
    "A Birch Lane Press book."
    ISBN 1-55972-278-9 (hardcover)
    1. Talk shows—United States. I. Title.
PN1991.8.T35L38 1995
791.44´6—dc20 94-44306                                           CIP

*Again, with love to*
*Sheila*
*for helping me listen carefully*

# Contents

# Preface

"Turn down your radio!" the talk show barkers demand. "Turn down your radio!" they tell the endless callers who jam the circuits and wait on hold for a Warholian moment on the air, a fleeting moment to engage the host.

The playing field is never level. "I'm running out of time" is the cavalier explanation from the host who cuts the caller off in mid-thought, mid-sentence. The nastier hosts just slam down the telephone receiver, reciting a litany of complaints about the caller.

Talk radio is pornographic. There is something absolutely perverse about lonely misfits and amateur information-distorters waiting on hold for an hour or more for the privilege of being verbally abused by a loudmouthed so-called host with no discernible credential other than an ability to make fast-paced patter. And this is what the millions of talk radio listeners who eavesdrop on these superficial, often mindless, conversations consider acceptable program material.

Talk radio is a carnival—an amusement show. Fancy parades as fact. Uninformed opinion is championed as thoughtful commentary. Groundless innuendo gets the same respect as investigative journalism. Hate is heralded as a valid response to problems. Too often, talk radio sounds like a noisy waste of time, like a bunch of malcontents yelling at each other or a bunch of blowhards impressing each other.

As much as I think I dislike it, I keep returning to it. It is seductive. It is a growing power in our society. It is fun and easy and lucrative to perform. It can be dangerous. I am part of it.

I was working at KSAN in San Francisco in the early seventies when, on one of the talk shows, oral sex was the subject under consideration. The subject was illustrated to the audience when the host and the guest engaged in the act being discussed, with the microphone—so goes the legend—adjusted to pick up the live sound effects. I was working at WRC in Washington when President Clinton dropped in on Larry King's show to explain his economic policies and press the flesh nationwide using the magic of radio imagery. In between, I've seen, heard, and experienced the gamut of what talk radio has to offer, on and off the air.

Its actors—both the stars and the journeymen (and women)—are my friends and colleagues.

This involvement provides me with unique access to behind-the-scenes material about the machinations of the industry, the motivations of the hosts, and the involvement of the audience. My files include letters from listeners dating back to the early seventies, private memoranda that circulated within the industry over the last two decades, unpublished research data commissioned by radio stations, and, probably most important, access to years of anecdotal information that explains how and why talk radio is outrageous, how insane the business is, and how such a bizarrely intimate relationship develops between the audience and the host, a voice who usually couldn't care less about those listeners even though they keep the host in business.

Talk radio is one of the fastest growing radio formats in America. A survey conducted in 1993 by the Times Mirror Center for the People and the Press concludes that "almost one half of Americans listen to talk radio on a relatively frequent basis." That is a huge audience. From just a handful of stations broadcasting talk shows only a few years before the study was commissioned, the format snowballed. By 1995 over a thousand radio stations were broadcasting some form of talk.

Talk radio is the latest example of the degeneration of American popular culture. At the same time it must be taken seriously, because it is such a powerful medium. Even Americans who listen

to talk radio cynically—the ones who call it base and uninformed—are subtly seduced by it. These are the listeners who
really want to understand the draw of the format, the inner workings of the industry, and the power (potential, real, and imagined)
of talk radio.

In addition to general interest talk shows hosted by experienced
radio performers, the airwaves are now flooded with a seemingly
endless supply of specialty talk shows, and it sometimes feels as
though everyone, from former California governor Jerry Brown to
disc jockeys frustrated with the limitations imposed on them by
most music stations, wants to be a talk show host. "We're going to
take apart the conventional wisdom, the dumb ideas that are
wrecking the country, the lies politicians tell, the greed of the corporate high and mighty, the phoniness of wannabe liberals," is
how Brown chose to open his daily broadcast offering—a talk
show carried on only a fraction of the number of radio stations
Rush Limbaugh claims for his own. "There are no sacred cows on
this show," insisted Brown as he tried to draw listeners.

I gleaned from my files this representative sampling of the
pitches that came to my office daily:

Disk jockey Mitch Beck wants to talk in a major market. From
KGLE in Carson City, Nevada, he sends a picture of himself atop
a step ladder, wearing a black fedora, sunglasses, a black leather
jacket, and a tough-guy look. He calls attention to a silly and arrogant quote in the Reno paper. "I'm going to be the biggest thing in
the radio business," he told reporters, forecasting that Howard
Stern will "eventually burn out" and that Rush Limbaugh "has
peaked."

Washington lawyer Ronald Karp wants to use a talk show to
analyze "hot legal topics." Sports attorney Andrew Brandt writes
that he wants his own weekly "cerebral sports program, using my
insight as an agent" to discuss "sports beyond the scores."

"Sparkle! Personality!" announces the publicity material for
Glenda Wright and her talk show. "It is parapsychology at its
informative best, mixed with entertaining humor that makes

America's airwaves hum with electricity!" She claims to have predicted the fall of the Berlin Wall, the 1993 Super Bowl results, and the Gulf War.

"Don't let the Ph.D. scare you," warns talk show host Robert Smith in a letter looking for a better opportunity than his role at WXXI in Rochester, New York. "I'm no fuzzy theoretician," he says to comfort prospective employers about his postgraduate work dealing with the legal history of the British colonies in North America before 1763.

Bosses looking at the résumé submitted by disc jockey Ruby Cheeks do not develop the concerns that Smith worries his Ph.D. causes. She lists no academic degrees, but under "achievements" notes with pride, "Guinness Book of World Records for longest kiss—132 hours."

Dick Summer's promotional material for "Relationship Radio" advertises his show as connecting with the "unconnected majority, the twenty-five percent of American adults who live alone, and the many millions more who are stuck in relationships that don't work." Smiling out from his slick literature from under a jauntily cocked, broad-brimmed hat, jacket casually thrown over his shoulder, Summer croons, "If you guys don't take care of your woman's emotional needs, I'd be delighted to do it."

Jack Kramer looks intense and thoughtful staring out of the press release for his show, "In a Man's Shoes." He calls it "two-way talk radio about gender politics from a male perspective." And Buck Harris hosts *The Gay Nineties* from his male perspective in Cleveland.

*Nutz and Boltz* is a car repair show; *Night Lite* is designed to be a comfortable companion, broadcast "live from the Blue Moon Hotel, a fictional setting in downtown Baltimore"; Lloyd Aruero wants to create a show about pet behavior problems; *The Super Foodies* deals with eating disorders. The list of radio shows and performers anxious to become—as Travus T. Hipp says about his radio show at KPTL in Carson City—"a fruitstand on the information superhighway" seems endless.

There is even a talk show on the air that deals with what is on talk shows. *The Talk Radio Countdown Show* is a weekly production featuring talk radio hosts talking about the "the ten most discussed topics on American talk radio."

As a talk show host in San Francisco, Los Angeles, and Washington, D.C.—and in whistlestops such as Carson City—and programmer of the talk station in the nation's capital, I have spent over a generation in talk radio. I have watched and participated as the format has developed from its infancy to its dominance—dominance not just of the radio industry, but of people's lives, people such as one of my favorite aunts and a cuckolded San Jose businessman who says I talked him out of committing murder when he called one of my shows.

*Inside Talk Radio* is an inspection of the talk radio business and its effect on late-twentieth-century American society. These pages tell the stories of the characters who make up talk radio. They explain the magic that makes the shows go on, offer readers who want to participate tricks for getting on and staying on the air, and suggest what the future holds for this influential and popular, lucrative and diverse form of radio.

Peter Laufer
Washington, D.C., and
Marin County, California

# Acknowledgments

My friend and colleague Markos Kounalakis assigned me the task of writing this book, informing me that my access to the inner workings of the trade required that I document the talk radio phenomenon. Another friend and colleague who came into my life through our common experiences in Germany, Ron Bee, was available at just the right time to offer research work, and I appreciate his expertise. Needed last-minute research help came from Tony Seton.

Just about all my fellow radio players deserve thanks, since we've learned so much from each other over the years, but a few must be singled out by name: Mike Powell, God rest his soul, for shanghaiing me into this business; Gil Haar for his years of mentoring; and the late Don Chamberlain for years of partnership.

My coconspirators at KSAN are a cabal that provided me with material and encouragement. Special thanks go to Milan Melvin for saving Susan Krieger's original doctoral dissertation; Willis Duff for his KLAC memos and assistance; Bonnie Simmons; Bob Simmons; Wes Nisker; C. Atcheson Laughlin III; Eugene Schoenfeld; Paul Krassner; and, of course, the late Tom Donahue.

Thanks also go to David Crane for hiring me at KGO and for his help as an agent. Jim Simon kept hiring me to talk on the radio despite the angry response he often faced from listeners and his bosses; his friendship and support is never forgotten. I'm grateful that Peter B. Collins saved so many documents and provided them to me. A tip of the hat to Jack Clements at Mutual is in order.

KXRX was another hotbed of talk radio experiences. I received great help for this book from radio pals there, including Sue Garfield, Mike Sugarman, and Stan Bunger. My boss at NBC News, Jim Farley, is always a fan, and I need that. Charles Jaco does what he does in his own inimitable manner, and I thank him for his support. At WRC, Evan Haning was a productive interviewer; George Papagiannis a most able friend and assistant; and Jeff Kamen an early reader of the work in progress and appropriately pushy friend. Thanks go out to Randall Bloomquist, Jeffrey Yorke, and Dick Rakovan, along with Jane Norris, Turi Ryder, Mark Davis, and all who provided access to their own material.

In fact, I must offer a blanket appreciation to all those in the talk radio business—and some would not want their names listed—who offered information, tapes, documentation, rumors, gossip, names, and dates to further this project. They know who they are. Of course, there is no talk radio without listeners, and I thank mine—especially Richard from Watsonville, who was always there when I needed a call in the middle of the night on KCBS.

My friend Michael Hassan helped by reading the manuscript with his professional eye. Bill Wellman provided a needed jaundiced look from his ivory tower.

Luckily for me, my editor, Jim Ellison, enjoys a periodic dose of talk radio, and his sharp pencil is appreciated as is the careful production editing of Carrie Cantor. My gratitude goes out to the Joan Shorenstein Barone Center on the Press, Politics and Public Policy of the John F. Kennedy School of Government at Harvard University for a Goldsmith Research Award, and to the Headlands Center for the Arts in Marin County for my idyllic studio.

As always, my family provided needed sustenance and support. Thank you, Ma, Michael, Talmage, Amber, and especially Sheila for all those years of listening and turning down your radios.

Despite all the aid I received for this study, any errors, of course, are my responsibility.

Finally, a toast to Steven Schragis, who saw the merit in this study and said, "Write it and I'll publish it."

# INSIDE
# TALK
# RADIO

The best part of all this is that my genius will be seen in so many more homes now. It's a dream come true. That's what's so wrong with America: that even a dope like me can realize his dreams.
—Howard Stern on signing a 1994 deal with E television network


If you preach hate you get a talk show. If you preach love you get a yawn.
—President Clinton at the opening of a memorial to Robert Kennedy and Martin Luther King Jr. in 1994


Is the storytelling and explaining industry in so much of a hurry that it can't be bothered to think about things and maybe even weigh them? The news is confusing enough. We are screaming our heads off for meaning, but everyone who's trying to give it to us is working way too fast to think.
—*Washington Post* editorial writer Amy Schwartz in the April 21, 1993, edition of the paper

# 1 | Are You Talking to Me?

 "*I blame talk radio hosts for the downfall of* America!" The voice on the other end of the line is strident and combines a sense of gross indignation with sadness. "There's a lot of hate coming through them."

I am sitting at my desk on the ninth floor of the World Building in Silver Spring, Maryland, at the studios of the radio station WRC. WRC belches out telephone talk shows twenty-four hours a day; I am the news and program director. One complete wall of my office is a window facing north, away from the District of Columbia and toward the suburbs of Montgomery County. When I look left and crane my neck, I can see the Silver Spring train station. Evenings, whistles find their way through my window, and I see the commuters line the platforms waiting for the trains that carry them out along the Potomac toward Point of Rocks, Harpers Ferry, and Martinsburg.

Farther out toward the horizon are the spires of the Mormon Temple. There is a fire station right next door. I watch the trucks and the ambulance speed up Georgia Avenue and eventually return minus the flashing lights and siren. I let my eyes drift directly north

where the suburbs dissolve into rural Maryland. I look to the right
at the hideous apartment building a few blocks away and its permanent FOR RENT sign. And I look down at the rooftops of downtown Silver Spring, the rooftops of the one- and two-story
buildings housing the Radio Shack, the Blue Nile Ethiopian restaurant, the art store, the Chinese restaurant, the out-of-business
tuxedo rental shop—trying and usually failing to make them
appear romantic. Downtown Silver Spring is an ugly sprawl, with
little feeling of community, like so much of modern America.

"I blame talk radio hosts for the downfall of America," the
WRC listener tells me yet again.

Periodically during my workday I handle complaint calls from
listeners. I push the speakerphone button, hoist my feet to my
desk, stare out at Silver Spring, and wait for the criticism from yet
another member of a new American subculture: talk radio junkies
connected to each other as listeners.

"They're getting away with telling people their own opinion" is
the frustration this woman expresses to me. She speaks well,
sounds educated. Her call comes to me the day Lawrence Walsh
formally ends his investigation into the Iran-Contra scandal. One
of my loudmouthed talk show hosts—a fellow in his mid-thirties
named Mark Davis—had met the final report from Walsh with
disgust, calling it a waste of taxpayer money and announcing that
presidents Reagan and Bush were innocent of any wrongdoing.
"That's not honest," argues my listener to me, "that's just giving
his own opinion. I think that if he's talking on the radio, he should
go down the middle. These talk shows are not fair and square.
Why should they be allowed to push out their own opinions?"

Her argument is coherent: She believes that it is unreasonable
for one man or woman to commandeer the power of the talk show
microphone and present opinion as if it were fact. She worries
about the effect of such a performance on the great unwashed who
listen in greater and greater numbers to talk shows.

"They don't know who they're speaking to," she insists about
the hosts. She talks fast, claiming to know who composes the audience. "They're speaking to ignorant people, they're speaking to

people who just watch television. They don't understand"—again she is describing her impression of the typical member of the talk show audience—"if people like a host, they'll follow him. If he says it's raining, they'll say, 'Oh, yeah, it's raining.' "

I ask her how she can be so sure that the audience is just a bunch of lemmings. "I listen to some of the calls," she answers right back with no hesitation, "and some of them really don't know what they're talking about."

She reiterates her concern about the power of the talk show as a social force out of control, and I ask her what the difference really is between some guy yammering on the radio and a loudmouth in a bar or café. "He doesn't have the public the way a talk show host has. He's sitting with his friends in a beer parlor and he's raising his voice—he's just talking to a few of his friends." She suggests that it is easy for the friends to simply ignore the fellow pontificating in the saloon, and then she adroitly makes another important distinction. "When you're listening to the radio, you're concentrating."

"Change the station," I suggest, growing tired of the call, looking without luck for some action to entertain me on the Silver Spring streets below me.

"I do a lot of times." Her answer is typical. "But this got me really angry."

———

Consider my aunt. She called me in late 1992 distraught—really upset. "Michael has been fired," she reported. "This is a disaster!" She was referring to Michael Krasney, the late-night talk show host on the West Coast powerhouse talk radio station out of San Francisco, KGO. Since Jimmy Carter was president, KGO has been the number-one radio station in San Francisco, churning talk programs out of its 50,000-watt transmitter from Canada to Mexico twenty-four hours a day.

"Michael has been fired," my aunt lamented again. Krasney is a colleague of mine. I knew he would land another job; he's a skillful radio performer.

"Don't worry about Michael," I told her.

But her voice was cracking on the other end of the line—she was almost crying—and then I realized that she wasn't worried about Krasney's career. My aunt was mourning her own loss. Although she had never met Krasney, he was her nighttime companion, her friend, her window on the world. In our anonymous society, his show was her town meeting, her barroom and coffee house, her backyard fence—her connection with her community.

My aunt felt as though she had lost a friend; in fact, she *had* lost a friend. And my aunt's attitude toward her radio companion is not unusual.

=====

No longer marginalized as trivial, talk radio as a news media genre played a significant role in the 1992 presidential election and the 1994 congressional races, and is fast developing into an important source of news and information for a growing number of Americans. Talk radio is now immortalized in the popular culture in the play and film *Talk Radio*; it plays an integral role in the movie *The Fisher King* and in the television shows *Midnight Caller* and *Frasier*. Radio commercials, airing on both talk and music stations, use the talk radio concept as the format for their messages, pretending that callers and hosts would be so insipid as to spend their time together discussing the benefits of the products being pitched.

"I am a hypocrite," acknowledges Barry Champlain, the fictional—but so accurately portrayed—talk radio host played by Eric Bogosian in *Talk Radio*. The movie, produced in 1988 and directed by Oliver Stone, was based on Bogosian's one-man stage show and the book *Talked to Death*, the story of the 1984 murder of Denver talk show host Alan Berg. "I denounce the system as I embrace it," Champlain assaults his audience in the soliloquy, a speech followed by his assassination. "I want money and power and prestige. I want ratings and success." As he continues to bare his tortured and frustrated ego-inflated soul, Bogosian plays a man losing control—reminiscent of the ranting anchorman in the movie *Network*.

"Who the hell are you anyway, you audience?" he asks. "Yes, the world is a terrible place!" he yells at them, charging that the talk radio audience feeds on the pain. "That's where I come in, isn't it? I'm here to lead you by the hand through the dark forest of your own hatred and anger and humiliation." Before talking with one last burst of callers, he defines his audience with a litany of rage. "You're a bunch of yellow-bellied, spineless, bigoted, quivering, drunken, insomniac, paranoid, disgusting, perverted, voyeuristic little obscene phone callers. That's what you are!"

Champlain's description does not fit my sweet aunt, who says, "Whenever I need to hear a voice, I turn on the radio. Especially at night." But Champlain's derisive litany surely reminds me of plenty of callers I've listened to and spoken with over my long years in the talk radio trenches. And the paranoia is on both sides of the microphone. Every night as I left the Culver City studios of KABC after hosting my often belligerent talk show there in the early seventies, walking past the security guard into the parking lot surrounded by barbed wire, I scanned adjacent rooftops and searched the blacktop, remembering the threatening letters mixed in with the fan mail. I never felt really comfortable until I was lost in the Santa Monica Freeway traffic, heading back to the beach.

The power of the talk show host to influence lives, to hurt feelings, to effect change, cannot be discounted—despite the lack of reasonable and established criteria for the job. I remember, with some pain, complaining fervently one night over KABC about the Los Angeles smog.

"It doesn't bother me!" responded a caller enthusiastically.

I acted horrified, asking him how he couldn't be bothered by the poison muddying the air. "Walk over to your window," I ordered. "Open the shade and look out at that filthy horizon!"

"I can't," answered my caller. "I'm blind and a double amputee."

Was he toying with me, or was he really blind and without legs? Who knows for sure? One of the bizarre beauties of talk radio is the anonymity of the callers. I believed him, believe him still.

The Jack Lucas character played by Jeff Bridges instructs a

lovesick caller in the 1991 movie *The Fisher King.* "Edwin, I told you about these people. They only mate with their own kind. It's called yuppie inbreeding. That's why so many of them are retarded and wear the same clothes. They're not human. They don't feel love, they only negotiate love moments." It's just radio theater for talk show host Jack, but the caller is paying rapt attention to the words, interpreting them as gospel. "They're evil, Edwin. They're repulsed by imperfection, horrified by the banality—everything that America stands for, everything that you and I fight for. They must be stopped before it's too late. It's us or them." Edwin proceeds to shoot up a yuppie eatery.

In the forgotten 1987 B movie *Choose Me,* actress Genevieve Bujold plays a radio advice-giver named Dr. Love who takes Dr. Ruth–type phone calls from a lovelorn audience. Dr. Love tells a new acquaintance about her radio alter ego, "She can help others, but not herself. Some people worship her. Can you imagine how hard that must be to live with, knowing that anything you ever say to anyone will count heavily, will be acted upon, whether you're right or wrong? There's tremendous responsibility in that, don't you think?"

"Do people really listen to that shit?" asks Dr. Love's friend.

A *Dave* Sunday comic by David Miller in 1993 shows the hero at a party. He's surrounded by other partygoers calling him "so profound" and "so enthralling."

"How do you keep so well informed?" he is asked.

"Shucks," is his reply. "I heard all that stuff on the radio!"

He's asked if it was on NPR or CNN, and when he says it was Rush Limbaugh or maybe Howard Stern, the crowd around him disappears in disgust.

"See," he philosophizes, "it just goes to show, it's not what you rave—it's who originally ranted it!"

≡≡≡

"I just came home a day early from a business trip. . . ." The caller to one of my talk shows was talking fast and crying, and it was clear to me that he wasn't making it up; his was a real crisis. "I walked into our bedroom and another man was in bed with my wife!"

Through his sobs he explained that he ran from the house to get his gun and then, before rushing back to shoot one or both of them, he decided to call for advice. We talked about his crisis and his options. The call came in the late seventies to KXRX in San Jose, just before four in the afternoon, when my show was scheduled to conclude for the day. I consulted with the news department and we delayed the start of the afternoon news while I continued our conversation, hoping to distract the poor fellow and keep him out of his house. Sure, I wanted to save lives, but it was also compelling radio. I doubt that any listener who tuned in during that call changed the station. Finally, when I viscerally concluded that he was no longer an immediate danger to his frolicking wife, I made a deal with him on the air. I broke my own rule to never meet with a caller and asked him to join me after the show at a bowling alley adjacent to the studios. We talked about his passion for violence, and he agreed to seek professional counseling. He called back several days later to announce that he no longer intended to shoot his wife and her lover.

Most talk radio hosts share similar experiences, some with less happy endings. From trivial consumer concerns to life-and-death crises, talk radio is often the most readily available institution that alienated citizens turn to for help.

Talk radio may be designed merely to produce revenue for broadcasters, it may be conducted by a coterie of questionably trained misfits, it may spew out misinformation, but from the 1994 elections to the murder of KOA host Alan Berg to companionship for my aunt, there can be no question that talk radio has developed into cultural force of consequence in America.

# 2 Live From the
# White House Lawn

*On the foggy, cool morning following President*
Clinton's 1993 speech calling for guaranteed national health care,
the White House lawn is littered with talk show hosts broadcasting
their shows live across America. Three rows of folding tables are
lined with starry-eyed radio announcers—talk show hosts from
around the country who scurried to Washington, lured by an invitation to originate their shows from the White House with spoon-
fed administration aides ready to perform as guests.

Smiley, blond Laura Schwartz, a twenty-year-old administration
intern, wanders through the rows of tables, hawking experts. "We
have some senior administration health care advisers available in
half an hour," she says, exuding fresh-scrubbed enthusiasm. "Do
you want to interview them?" she asks whoever is listening.

━━━━━━

Long considered a troubled stepchild of mainstream media—usually viewed with disdain by more traditional journalists—talk
radio finally demanded credibility and at least some limited respect
after claiming credit for defeating Congress's attempts to grant

itself a substantial pay raise. Although after the brouhaha generated by a loose network of talk radio hosts in late 1988 and early
1989 finally subsided, Congress proceeded to guarantee itself the
extra money it wanted anyway, the talk radio industry chalked up
the delay in the pay raise as a victory and convinced itself and
much of the listening audience that talk radio shows express the
ultimate *vox populi* of nineties America. "What's the third branch
of government?" asks a civics teacher in a recent political cartoon.
"Talk radio!" shoots back a confident student.

Ralph Nader launched the assault against Congress on December 16, 1988, the anniversary of the Boston Tea Party. At WXYT
in Detroit, talk show host Roy Fox recognized the pay raise issue
immediately as ideal talk show fodder and as material for productive self-promotion. "The idea came from a listener of mine," he
readily acknowledged.[1] "It was too good to pass up." Fox and his
producer started calling colleagues around the country, suggesting
they join the new tea party. Listeners needed little convincing to
send tea bags to their representatives and senators, adorned with
the message: "Read my tea bag. No 50% raise."

Congress was in an awkward position. Not only was such a substantial raise difficult for voters to accept in the middle of a deep
recession, but the talk radio campaign snowballed during the
Christmas congressional recess. While talk show hosts shouted
through the airwaves against Congress, there was no congressional
debate; the Capitol was closed down for the holidays. Even after
lawmakers returned to work and finally debated the issue, only a
handful of members of Congress spoke up against the popular
radio mouths. The House majority whip at the time, California
Democrat Tony Coelho, complained just before the February 7
vote was taken (he knew the raise was about to be defeated) that if
Congress conceded the issue, "We'll be hostage to this kind of
gamesmanship forever. The talk show hosts and Ralph Nader won
this round at the expense of the long-term interests of the country." A member of Coehlo's staff, David Drier, was unable to con-
tain his disgust for the talk radio assault on his boss. "I don't fault
the public," said Drier.[2] "I fault the talk show hosts for stirring up

the public. Compared with what most talk hosts make, the proposed salary increase for congressmen was a pittance." That statement was in fact wrong. Although some hosts earn munificent sums from their work, the bulk of talk radio journeymen do not.

In an attempt to minimize the public relations damage going out over the nation's airwaves, California Democratic Representative Vic Fazio complained on the House floor about the campaign against the raise, saying, "The media in general did a very poor job," lumping WXYT's Fox in with the *New York Times,* much to Fox's delight. "They provided, in some cases, biased coverage. We became cartoon cannon fodder for trash television and talk radio."

But Illinois Democrat Dan Rostenkowski refused to cave in to the pressure. "The bashing we have received in the press over this issue," he told Fazio and the rest of the House as the debate dragged on, "not only demeans us, it demeans all public servants. The criticism that has been heaped on us is bad enough," he complained. "Why are so many of us agreeing with it? It is high time we stopped whipping ourselves."

The talk show hosts involved were ecstatic about the vote. "When I heard," said Mike Siegel of KING in Seattle, who was considering parlaying his own new notoriety into a run for the Senate in 1994, "there was a real sense of euphoria. We'd made history."[3] It was not the first time. Three years earlier, at WRKO, Jerry Williams had managed to generate enough negative public reaction to the Massachusetts law that mandated the use of automobile seat belts to get the law repealed. In 1987, in Nevada, Travus T. Hipp used KPTL to lobby the legislature to change the automobile insurance law. Instead of requiring each registered car to be insured, Nevadans can now insure themselves and be covered no matter what they drive.

The actual and perceived power of the talk hosts and their callers made traditional politicos nervous; a new institution was playing their game and changing the rules. Even the antiestablishment *Nation* magazine cranked out an anti–talk radio editorial expressing its worry that talk radio posed a potential danger to the republic. The *Nation* credited to talk radio President Clinton's inability to nullify the military ban on homosexuals and the failure of the Senate to confirm his attorney-general nominees Zoë Baird and Kimba Wood. "Listeners were successfully mobilized to act on their blatant homophobia and only slightly displaced sexism," determined the *Nation's* editors on March 1, 1993. The magazine blamed the arrogance of a nonresponsive government and its corporate partners for creating the environment that led to the self-appointed saviors of talk radio. "But in instant referendums-by-radio there is always the capacity for bashing unpopular minorities," worried the *Nation,* before really lashing out at its broadcast competition. "The talk show demagogues are adept at manipulating anger and turning righteous resentment into fearful hatred of the oppressed. That, indeed, is a constant danger in any democratic system," the editors acknowledged, "but in more moderated forums—legislatures, town meetings, public hearings, op-ed pages—there is space and time for the development of coalitions, compromises and sometimes even common sense. Unmodulated majoritarianism can be as undemocratic as totalitarianism." The *Nation* did not call for censorship but blamed politicians for failing to engage the electorate in adequate dialogue on the issues of the day, thus creating the environment for allowing the "demagogues" of the airwaves to flourish and become empowered.

Following what they perceived to be a victory against Congress when the pay raise went down to initial defeat, some talk show hosts attempted to make permanent the loose affiliation they developed promoting opposition to the raise. The result was the National Association of Radio Talk Show Hosts. One of the organizers of the trade group was talk show host Michael Harrison, who is editor and publisher of *Talkers* magazine,[4] the only trade publication devoted entirely to the talk radio format. Between the two roles, Harrison managed to carve out a position for himself as a leading public spokesperson for an industry that traditionally has been peopled by iconoclastic gypsies. And it is Harrison who produces the weekly *Talk Radio Countdown Show.*

Harrison adorns the back page of *Talkers* with his picture and a column of observations based on the limited perspective of a life steeped in talk radio affairs. "As the days go by," he wrote in the October 1993 edition, "the initial infatuation with the health care plan is fading as a majority of those who choose to express themselves don't trust Clinton, don't trust government, and don't trust anything that smacks of socialism." The primary trouble with Harrison's assessment is a lack of perspective—a lack of perspective suffered by many talk show hosts who easily can be deceived to believe that a few telephone calls to a radio station are necessarily representative of American society. As anyone who has spent any length of time behind the scenes at a talk radio operation knows without a doubt, callers to a radio station—let alone callers who manage to get on the air—can in no way be considered, by any stretch of imagination or social science, necessarily part of "a majority of those who choose to express themselves."

Not all talk show hosts are ready to believe that the noise they generate amounts to real and long-term political power. Longtime Washington, D.C., talk show host and congressional staffer Ron Aaron rejects the idea of what he calls "talkocracy" as a new force in representative democracy. From his chair behind the talk radio microphone at KTSA in San Antonio, Texas, Aaron challenged the role that seemed to be emerging for talk radio hosts as another branch of government.

"As a talk show host, I don't want the power to change the government," he wrote.[5] "I don't want to shape public opinion. And frankly, I don't want the responsibility that comes with phone-in democracy." Few talk show hosts' egos would agree with Aaron's decision to abdicate what seemed to be a growing opportunity to assume a powerful role in governing the nation and forging public opinion. But Aaron was adamant. "We're entertainers. Talk show hosts are not paid to formulate domestic and international policy. We don't have a seat in the United Nations."

Aaron cited the tiny percentage of the talk show audience that ever gets on the air as abundant evidence that talk show conclusions should never be presumed to be representative of public opinion.

==========

Typically, callers to talk shows are seeking companionship. They are lonely, stuck at home, or stuck in traffic. They feel disenfranchised from society and desire an opportunity to be heard; they are convinced they have something to say. Groups throughout the spectrum of ideas are fast learning how to manipulate talk radio. A steady and growing number of the callers who wait interminably on hold for the chance to gain some free radio air time are members of some activist political organization. Some callers seem quite average and normal and are successfully spurred to participate in a show by skillful hosts. Most are subject to restrictive screening by producers before they can get a chance to get on the air. And when they get on the air, they risk being cut off at any moment. Luckily there are plenty of other avenues of expression left for society and, despite the seriousness with which many talk show hosts insist on taking themselves, the medium usually remains one primarily of entertainment, not journalism. At times, talk show hosts do practice journalism. Too often, though, the audience is confused and interprets the entertainment as journalism. Worse, skillful manipulators hide behind the guise of entertainment to spread hate and lies—intentionally confusing the audience.

"If we keep blurring the distinctions and standards between news and entertainment," wrote Dan Rather in a thoughtful and concerned letter to the *New York Times,* "we're all going to have to pay. And I respectfully submit the price is too high."[6]

Witness Roger Ailes on national radio on March 10, 1994. Ailes knows what he is doing when he speaks over the airwaves. He is one of the driving corporate forces behind the Limbaugh phenomenon, one of the owners of the Limbaugh property. He was a senior adviser to presidents Reagan and Bush. In 1994 he was president of CNBC, the cable network owned by NBC, which is owned by General Electric. Ailes joined Don Imus on the air for a chat and went after the Clinton administration with a vengeance and with lies. Referring to the death of Vincent Foster, Ailes accused the administration of "moving bodies." He charged the Clintons with destroying evidence and an overall cover-up in regard to the Whitewater investigation. Whitewater, he described to Imus, is "land fraud, illegal contributions, abuse of power, suicide cover-up, possible murder." Ailes went after President Clinton personally, too. "He's coming up to New York today and he's here because he heard Nancy Kerrigan's on *Saturday Night Live*. She's the only one he hasn't hit on."[7]

"It was a joke. It's Don Imus. Don't take it out of context," was the reaction from Brian Lewis at CNBC corporate headquarters to complaints about Ailes's assertions. "It was said in the context of a comedy radio show, and that's the way it should be treated," he insisted and then went on the offensive in reaction to questions from the *Washington Post*'s Mary Alma Welch. "You know freedom of speech? Two hundred and fifty million Americans have that right."

The excuse, "It's Don Imus," bears some attention. It may be a First Amendment right, but is it right in the moral sense to lie on the air, make false unsubstantiated accusations, or pass undocumented theory along as fact just because Ailes is broadcasting on a radio show that is primarily known as a comedy outlet? And is the radio audience in general equipped to distinguish between attempts at reporting the news and attempts at promulgating propaganda? White House Chief of Staff Thomas "Mack" McLarty reacted with a telephone call to NBC president Robert Wright—the contents released to the public by the White House—calling Ailes's words "just simply inappropriate." Even Imus—known for his outrageous behavior and radio rule breaking—seemed uncomfortable with his role in the affair, perhaps because he is a supporter of the Clinton administration. Welch quoted him as saying he tried—while Ailes was on the air—"to make it plain that this wasn't someone you can take seriously."

Since Imus regularly engages newsmakers as guests, including President Clinton, it is especially difficult to expect the radio audience to understand Ailes's comments are jokes in the context of the Imus show. In fact, it was then-Governor Clinton's appearance with Imus on the radio that marked both the enthusiasm of the Clinton campaign for nontraditional media outlets for their candidate and the beginnings of the seriously blurred line between news-talk and entertainment-talk broadcasts on radio.

"Well, here now on a phone with us, the governor of Arkansas," Imus announced to his audience on April 2, 1992, "who, as you probably know, is running for the presidency of the United States. Good morning, Governor Clinton."

Clinton was comfortable with the genre. "Good morning, Don," he said.

"How are you?" asked Imus.

"Well, I'm all right." Clinton played to the audience, knowing he would be spared tough political questions. "I'm disappointed," he told Imus, "you didn't call me Bubba."

"Well . . ." Imus was caught off guard.

"It's just such an honorable term where I come from. It's southern for mensch."

Imus brought up some of the dirt following Clinton around the campaign, but in a manner that allowed Clinton to laugh at himself and his potential problems.

"At least you haven't been accused of having any sort of relationship with unattractive women," Imus lauded Clinton. "I mean, what if Roseanne Arnold were calling Ted Koppel, saying, 'Yeah, I been sleeping with Governor Clinton?' I mean, that would be a problem."

Clinton came back with, "Listen, if she did that I'd file a palimony suit against her. She's got the number-one show in America, and I could finance the rest of this presidential campaign. It would be better than Jerry Brown's 800 number!"

The questions and the answers were different from what they would have been in an interview with the *New York Times* or National Public Radio, but the Imus-Clinton exchange was journalism—the gathering and disseminating of news.

Some of the hosts making the noise that constitutes talk radio strive for credibility based on thorough research. They seek to transmit accurate information while they entertain. Others make no attempt to achieve fairness; they don't worry about broadcasting misinformation and misrepresentations. Still another group of talk show hosts actively use the medium for propagandistic purposes—distorting facts to mislead the audience and further a specific cause.

"With the help of clever persistent propaganda," Adolf Hitler wrote in *Mein Kampf,* "even heaven can be represented to the people as hell, and the most wretched life as paradise."[8] Whether or not through study of the use Hitler made of radio, successful talk show hosts such as Rush Limbaugh have been able to convince huge segments of the population to believe as they themselves believe about politics and culture. "The masses are slow moving," wrote Hitler, "and they always require a certain time before they are ready to notice a thing, and only after the simplest of ideas are repeated thousands of times will the masses finally remember them." Excerpts from *Mein Kampf* read as if they were written as a talk radio textbook. "Propaganda must not engage in an objective search for the truth (which might equally serve the other side) and then submit it to the people with doctrinaire honesty. Rather, it must unceasingly serve its own truth."[9]

Rush Limbaugh and his peers are not Hitler, but the techniques being used by the strident, politically motivated talk show hosts mirror the skill Hitler and Goebbels used to build national socialism: merciless clever repetition of misinformation and disinformation to a captive audience. American talk show hosts keep the audience captive by successfully combining entertainment with the delivery of information. Examples of misinformation and disinformation and downright false statements spew out of the Limbaugh shows. They range from the ridiculous to the potentially dangerous, the latter because so many Limbaugh listeners take his words as gospel. In March 1991, Limbaugh was using Judi Barri and Darryl Cherney as foils for his anti-environmental-movement histrionics. Barri and Cherney were the two Earth First! activists whose car was blown up with them in it in a crime poorly investigated by both the FBI and the Oakland Police. The law enforcement agencies initially suggested the crime, which remains unsolved, was the fault of the victims, who were transporting the explosive to perpetrate a terrorist attack. Limbaugh announced, as if it were fact, his musings that Barri and Cherney were in hiding in rural northern California guarding the illegal marijuana plantation that they used both as a source of income to finance Earth First! activities and to keep themselves intoxicated. Limbaugh cited no sources, he broadcast no documentation. He merely announced the charges as "facts."[10]

As the Whitewater affair escalated as a news story in late winter 1994, Limbaugh, who uses Clinton-hating as a mainstay stock-in-trade on his program, escalated the dispersal of erroneous information with carefree abandon. On March 9 of that year a newsletter—with no documentation—published a story claiming that Clinton's lawyer Vincent Foster killed himself not at the Virginia park where his body was found but at a secret apartment in Washington maintained and used by Clinton administration officials. The newsletter, a creation of the consulting company Johnson, Smick International, said the body was then moved to the park. When Limbaugh got his hands on the story, he used it—still with no documentation—as the basis for his own fabrication. He broadcast that the Johnson, Smick newsletter "claims that Vince Foster was murdered in an apartment owned by Hillary Clinton."[11] From Limbaugh's mouth suicide became murder. The newsletter and Limbaugh attention led to other stories such as the New York Post's "Foster's Secret Apartment Hideaway Revealed," and forced White House press secretary Dee Dee Myers to dismiss the story as "a complete fabrication."

Limbaugh and his colleagues' defense against such charges is pat. We're just entertainers, they say. Don't take us so seriously, they say, we're just talk show hosts. It's not our fault if the public believes everything we say, misinterprets our intent, and doesn't seek alternative sources of news and information.

When the Clinton administration launched its campaign to reform the nation's health care system, it saw an opportunity to use the trappings of the presidency to influence talk show hosts. In what *Talkers* proudly referred to as "a historymaking, unprecedented action," more than 200 talk show hosts from all around America were invited to a briefing on the health care proposals on September 21, 1993, followed by the opportunity two days later to broadcast their shows from the White House lawn.

"At least a dozen of us were standing outside the southwest gate of the White House," remembers Washington talk show host Mark Davis[12] about his experiences the day of the briefing, "tapping our toes as the excruciatingly slow clearance process continued." One of his favorite stories from the talk show host invasion of the White House deals with ego.

"One by one at a slow trickle," Davis said, "names were called by a guard, indicating that our security checks were free of highgrade felonies." At ten minutes past noon, many of the hosts were still outside waiting, although the first briefing for them was scheduled to begin at noon. "We were not burning with impatience," Davis said about the delay. "It would happen when it would happen. We shrugged and joked. 'Welcome to Washington,' I said to a number of hosts from the hinterlands."

Not taking the showdown in stride was Lisa Sliwa. At the time, the wife of the founder of the Guardian Angels held down a morning show with her husband on the dominant New York talk station WABC. (A few months later they were relieved of their duties; talk radio is rarely secure work.) "Her name came up and she bolted for the gate," Davis reported with evident enjoyment, "only to realize that her producer had not been similarly smiled upon. 'We need to get him in,' insisted Lisa to a guard carrying five clipboards. 'We need to get him in *now*.' "

As Davis recounts the developing conflict, Lisa Sliwa kept badgering the guards, demanding speedy access for her producer. A few more people were cleared ahead of the producer. "Lisa was pacing like a caged jaguar," said Davis. Finally she snapped.

"Hey," Davis says she barked at the guard with the clipboards, "we are from W-A-B-C." She spelled out the call letters carefully before adding the all-important "in New York!" Sliwa wasn't finished. "The number one market in the country!" And then, for her finale, "We're the only show on the station that supports the president!" The guard, more accustomed to the usual dignified visitors or anxious tourists who come visiting the White House, looked at her, bemused. The telephone finally rang again in the guard shack and the producer was waved through.

"Lisa," recalls Davis, laughing, "walked quickly, checking her makeup."

Lisa Sliwa would not be alone in making a fool of herself that day. The motley collection of broadcasters gathered in an Old Executive Office Building briefing room. "WCBM host-psychotic Les Kinsolving was in one of the first few rows," Davis reported, "where he had made sure he could be heard in loud conversation blasting the president, the First Lady, and their health care plan for the minutes prior to the official program." Mrs. Clinton spoke first, but engaged in no repartee with her audience, nor did she take questions. Then the administration's health care expert, Ira Magaziner, spent an hour with the talk radio hosts, answering their questions.

Kinsolving was out with the first question, which was actually a typical talk-show-host-as-pit-bull attack on Magaziner for Mrs. Clinton's failure to suffer questions. "Every sixth question or so from the crowd was from Les," said Davis. "He unleashed his invidious arsenal of trap-door questions, designed not to shed light, but to add more notches to his ever-lengthening belt. Groans from his colleagues had no effect."

As the afternoon of detailed briefings continued, David Gergen took the podium. He was followed by Health and Human Services Secretary Donna Shalala. Les Kinsolving stood up again and demanded that Shalala release President Clinton's complete medical records. "This was such a display of boneheaded grandstanding that even a room full of talk show hosts fell briefly silent," said Davis.

Mark Davis took advantage of the silence to press his own question, one about health care for senior citizens as envisioned by the administration.

"Madam Secretary," he prefaced his remarks, "I can't purport to speak for the whole room, but I am truly sorry for the impertinence of my colleague"—he looked over at Kinsolving—"and I'd like to ask a question that is actually on the subject."

As he began to query her, Kinsolving leapt out of his chair, screaming, "You don't apologize for me! I'll apologize for you! I don't need your approval for the questions I ask!"

"Sit down, Les," said Davis, who again started to ask his question.

But Kinsolving was still yelling. "How dare you! Who are you to apologize for me?" Other talk show hosts spoke up, encouraging the "host-psychotic" from Baltimore to sit down. "Drop dead!" he told the room over and over again. "Drop dead! Drop dead!"

"Excuse me! Excuse me!" interjected Secretary Shalala, trying to refocus the attention on herself and national health care.

"Sit down, Les," Davis instructed yet again, and this time Kinsolving took his seat.

Kinsolving shouted back at Davis, "You're just rude because your ratings are sagging!" At the time, Davis's show and the station he talked for were in twenty-first place overall in a field of twenty-four Washington commercial radio stations.[13]

When I asked Davis later if the public encounter was one he would repeat, it was a question that he had already thought through for himself. "I care deeply about the image of people in my profession. Talk show hosts are perceived as blowhards and buffoons, and there are just enough who are to keep the perception alive for a good while. If I could stand up for civility and give Les the back of my hand at the same time, that struck me as two noble goals. To this day, I hear ripples of recollection of me as 'the guy who got into a shouting match with Kinsolving at the White

House.' That's fine, just so they remember who was sane and who was not."

"They got into a shouting match," is how Tom Leykis—then a host for WRKO in Boston—remembers the encounter, a shouting match that reinforced the image of talk show hosts as just a bunch of carnival act louts. "Everything that people think about talk show hosts was all coming out there—that we are a bunch of people at the low rung of the show-business totem pole, just dying to get some attention, and to a certain extent, we are."

WABC New York talk show host Barry Farber told the *New York Times,* "There was a lot of classless behavior. We were like the nouveau riches who don't know what salad fork to use."

After the White House health care show, in a special edition of the National Association of Radio Talk Hosts newsletter *Open Line,*[14] WOR host Gene Burns, whose New York–based show was syndicated nationwide at the time, recounted with pride the call from Richard Strauss, the Clinton administration's radio coordinator, to the association for help in orchestrating the health care briefing for the hosts. "Clearly one of the most effective routes to the people of the United States was talk radio, the most efficient reconnect mechanism between the governed and those who govern," wrote Burns. "It gave me great satisfaction to hear First Lady Hillary Rodham Clinton, health czar Ira Magaziner, Secretary of Health and Human Services Donna Shalala, presidential adviser David Gergen, Vice President Al Gore's wife Tipper and even the President himself attest in their remarks to the vital role played by talk radio in the orderly exchange of ideas so central to the concept of self government which is the genius of the American political system."

The words from Burns were obviously picked to connote enthusiastic passion, but with talk show hosts such as Kinsolving acting as sieves between the governed and those who govern, talk radio is at best a marginal medium for crucial information transfer.

Two days after the briefing, KFMB of San Diego is one of the radio stations taking advantage of the invitation to broadcast live from the White House. The *Hudson and Bauer* morning show is on the air, along with the show's news reporter, Pat Gaffey—starstruck at being transported from the confines of provincial radio to a perceived taste of power in the nation's capital. CNN White House correspondent Wolf Blitzer wanders past the tables of radio announcers, headed for his office in the White House outbuilding set aside for reporters. Gaffey feels the lure of Blitzer's notoriety and intercepts him for an interview. The lawn is crawling with such incest: Newspaper reporters are interviewing talk show hosts while talk show hosts are interviewing celebrity television journalists such as Blitzer. Meanwhile, media-conscious White House advisers are answering questions about health care policy from talk show hosts who cannot possibly have had time to adequately digest President Clinton's initial speech on the matter, and yet they are already on the air analyzing it—trying to influence opinions and raise ratings.

The magic of the White House venue is at work, influencing the content of the day's radio broadcasts just because the regional news reporters and the talk show hosts are on the White House grounds—enjoying unique and unprecedented invitations and seeming access to political power. Just a few days before, few of them would have dreamed that they would be here.

KFMB's Gaffey is on the telephone with his producer back in San Diego, organizing the next live newscast; minutes later he is on the air in southern California. "The administration likes the response so far to the health care proposal," he announces in the middle of the *Hudson and Bauer* show putting a positive spin on the president's speech that comes not from an independent analysis he conducted, but from the mood he felt inside the cocoon of the White House grounds—grounds alive with administration aides instructing and propagandizing radio men and women like Gaffey. "At the White House this morning, I asked Vice President Al Gore . . ." and Gaffey cues his engineer to broadcast an excerpt from a conversation between the vice president and the reporter recorded earlier. The excerpt ends and Gaffey finishes his report with a flourish: "After that KFMB radio exclusive, the vice president was hustled away. From the White House, Pat Gaffey, 760 KFMB." Gaffey is off the air.

Do any of his listeners really believe that there was some breaking news in his interview with the vice president? Probably. Don't most of his listeners know that what Gaffey promoted as an "exclusive interview" was just one of many such orchestrations performed by Gore that morning to advance the administration's point of view? Maybe. Maybe not.

Gaffey is back on the line, off the air, with his colleagues in the radio station's San Diego studios. "Now the six o'clock tease," he tells the studio engineer; he's full of excitement. Gaffey is thirty-four years old. He's smiling, looking dapper in his camel-hair sports coat, his flowered tie, his two-tone brown-on-tan wingtips. Gaffey records his tease. "This is Pat Gaffey at the White House. I had an exclusive interview with Vice President Al Gore and that's coming up after the CBS news at six!" Score another point for the Clinton administration and its radio specialist Richard Strauss.

It was Pat Gaffey's first trip to the capital, and after he recorded his six o'clock tease, we talked. (I was broadcasting from the White House lawn that day too, airing a talk show about the role of talk shows in modern America.)

"Nobody turns down an invitation to the White House, to get to talk with the president and the first lady," Gaffey readily acknowledges. "There were exclusive opportunities." He is understandably quite taken with his one-on-one chat with Gore. He agrees that it is fun to be at the White House, it is fun to say "exclusive interview with the vice president." Although he acknowledges that he has been used by the administration, he is convinced it has been a fair swap. "It plays into ratings and competition, and to be able to say 'an exclusive' is something the station will then sell in playing itself as the best station in San Diego. They recognize," he says about the Clinton administration, "the power of talk shows and talk radio as the forum—it's the town hall thing every single day—where people are expressing ideas and there's an exchange."

=====

Paul Lyle was in the mood to be impressed that day, too. He came to Washington from Long Island, expecting not only to broadcast his WGSM talk show from the White House but also to jog with President Clinton, picked because he was 1993 president of the National Association of Radio Talk Show Hosts. "The egomaniacs club," Lyle says by way of identification.

There was no morning jog. "He did not go this morning," Lyle reports to me. "Had he gone, I would have been able to go jogging with him, yes." I ask if he's disappointed, and Lyle is ready with a clever answer, "Yeah, because I need the exercise." But he says he really feels a bond would have developed between the talk show host and the president, stimulated by the shared love of sport. "It would have been a lot of fun. I think that if we were out there jogging together," he says dreamily, "perhaps we could have a little more open conversation with one another."

A few months later, Paul Lyle would be looking for another job, his radio station sold out from under him by its absentee owners, the new operation interested in music, not talk. But at the White House that morning, Lyle was in his glory, happy to explain his theory of talk radio. "We're all about entertainment, because we have to entertain people to hold their interest." He's correct. "At the same time, we need to give to them a certain amount of information." Okay again, but then he gets lost—as do so many in his business—in his own sense of self-importance when he defines that need further as "the information that they need to know to carry on their daily lives. They have to get the weather, the traffic, the sports, et cetera. Then I think it's incumbent upon us to give them the information that they will need so that they can decide on issues. If I can give any citizen one modicum of information which will make him or her that much better informed, so they can arrive at a decision with which they feel more comfortable, I've done a great job."

I ask him if he really feels talk show hosts are in general in a position to be in the business of such high-minded information transfer as he just described. We look out at the rows of tables of broadcasters, gleefully screaming their call letters and the constant refrain, "Live from the White House!" We're watching their instant analysis of a health care initiative that few if any could possibly have studied in any detail prior to their air time. "Be realistic," I suggest to Lyle. "Aren't talk show hosts much more clowns and entertainers transmitting misinformation than a serious element of the national and social debate?"

He rejects the criticism, insisting talk show hosts are qualified to carve out a niche as legitimate leaders. "I entertain. I sometimes inform. I sometimes become a facilitator. Oftentimes I become a very strong advocate." I describe the talk show genre from my point of view to Lyle, telling him we are the midway on the carnival of journalism, and he disagrees with me again. "I think there are any number of very serious and cerebral talk show hosts around the country who firmly believe that they have a mission." That they believe they have a mission, I do not doubt. Lack of zeal rarely troubles a talk show host; a commitment to feeling a valid and valuable membership in the fraternity of intellectual journalists exists among a growing number of hosts. The White House frolic fed on that sense of mission.

Lyle continues to define what those serious and cerebral radio men and women consider their challenge. "They have a mission to help educate the American public and to help that dialogue continue. Then there are the rest of us," he confesses with a self-effacing smile, "myself included, who do a bit of entertaining, who have a lot of fun, but at the same time take their job very, very seriously. I don't want to mislead or misinform my listening audience because that could be very harmful and damaging."

He jumps at the chance to compare a talk show to an old-time New England–style town meeting. It is a reference often dragged up for an intellectual rationalization of the talk show. But the differences are extreme. The talk show host is in control of the medium in a manner never dreamed of by any town council lead-

ers. The talk show host decides who speaks, can arbitrarily interrupt, can use electronic means to win an argument by default. And,
perhaps most important, the talk show host can simply hang up
on the caller with a virtual guarantee of no recrimination. Imagine the problems caused at town meetings if speakers from the
audience were tossed out of the town hall with the frequency that
talk show hosts blithely tell callers, "Sorry, we're running out of
time, thanks for the call. Good-bye!"

═══════

"Fuckin' Howard, radio God!" Howard Stern quotes one of his
listeners as saying after enjoying one of Stern's lascivious fantasies.
The "radio God" reference is in Stern's book *Private Parts,* attributed to a listener who claims he masturbates to the accompaniment of Stern's show while commuting to work. And radio god is
often the role most talk show hosts place themselves in on the air.
It is bizarre that so many listeners and callers bow and pray to that
self-proclaimed deity. "Thank you for taking my call!" they say,
setting up their encounter with subservience. "I'm a first-time
caller, longtime listener," comes out like a chant to an almighty.
While the talk show host uses the callers as free actors in the ongoing and extemporaneous radio play that constitutes a talk show, a
dynamic is successfully created to convince the callers that the
radio god is actually indulging the callers by allowing them the
opportunity to fill some air time between the advertisements that
the radio station needs to pay its bills. What the callers rarely realize is that most talk show hosts exist in abject fear that there will
be no calls, a sign most feel means the show is a failure. While the
callers wait for communion with the radio god, the host is praying
for calls so that he or she is not forced into an hours-long monologue and an uncomfortable after-the-show meeting with the boss.

The town meeting analogy further breaks down because of the
anonymity of talk radio. In a cross-roads New England town, the
citizens all know one another. Their kids go to school together.
What they say and do at the town meeting will follow and haunt
them throughout the rest of their local lives—at work and play.

Screaming and yelling insults and accusations rarely goes unchallenged. Speeches with inadequate documentation rarely find acceptance. Follow-up conversations are easy to conduct and frequently occur. The people are really interconnected; they must face the consequences of their town meeting actions. In the cyberspace of talk radio, there is no worry about responsibility for speeches; there rarely are consequences.

Lyle interrupts me. "I think we are a town meeting," he says, "a new town meeting. As Ross Perot was saying, an electronic town hall. We are shaking hands electronically."

But again I remind him of the crucial differences, best epitomized by the fact that talk show hosts can and do arbitrarily hang up on citizens.

"It is," he says predictably, "our show. And it is only okay," he says about the manipulation conducted by the radio gods, "if we produce a profit and continue to have reasonable ratings. If enough people think we are mishandling the public, they will click. They will edit us out with their fingers. They'll switch to someone else." And those ratings, says Lyle, are more than enough of a check on the power of the talk show host.

"Remember," he cautions, "our revenue is based on our ability to attract advertisers. If we're not doing the job for them, if we're not doing the job for our listeners, we'll be tuned out."

I once lived in a tiny mining town in Nevada. Public business was conducted at regular town meetings. As I listened to Paul Lyle insist that ratings provide talk show hosts with the credibility to claim the role of modern town meetings for their shows and that advertiser support is further proof of success, I imagined breaks in town meetings for sponsor messages, big banners advertising Coke, Hooked on Phonics, and used-car lots strung behind the podium up on the town-hall stage. I imagined town council chairmen and women telling the gathered townsfolk that debate would continue in a moment, but first he or she would interrupt to read several messages promoting the services and products offered for sale by town merchants.

There might be some similarities, but talk radio, especially commercial talk radio, is no replacement for the town meeting.

"Maybe we're the gathering at the street corner," suggests Lyle as an alternative, as I continued to complain about his comparison. That sounds better. "Maybe we're the poet in Poet's Square in New York City. We're standing on our soapbox. But," he says, getting down to selfish reality, "it is our show. We do have the right to control it."

Later, in a special issue of *Open Line,* Lyle concluded to his peers that the result of the White House experience for talk radio was "an elevation of our industry from gadfly to peer status with this country's policymakers."

Along with the continuing attempts to equate talk radio with the traditional town meeting comes suggestions that listening to talk radio offers a glimpse into the American psyche. Alexis de Tocqueville's name and work is cited regularly by talk radio observers. "A contemporary Tocqueville trying to understand 1990's America could do worse than to go to its major cities and listen to its successful talk radio shows," wrote Michael Barone and Joannie Schrof in *U.S. News and World Report.*[15] "If some present-day Tocqueville were planning a sequel to *Democracy in America,*" wrote Geoffrey Morris in the *National Review,* "he would be well advised to tune in to talk radio. He would find there the lively interchange of ideas that the learned Frenchman found so pervasive in nineteenth-century America."[16]

The manipulation of the callers who manage to make the airwaves on a talk radio show precludes any credible comparison between Tocqueville's study and the banter that cascades from radio speakers.

# 3

## The Stretch
## Toward Credibility

*"We've discovered another means of communica-*tions," says Cliff Zukin, who has just completed an exhaustive, comprehensive, and independent study of talk radio. Titled "The Vocal Minority in American Politics," the study was conducted by the Times Mirror Center for the People and the Press in the summer of 1993.[1] Zukin and his associates quickly learned that talk radio is cheap and easy to produce and makes plenty of money. "The other thing we learned is that it's popular. People like it. This is something that is genuinely filling a need for people—they like listening to other people, they like discussing ideas, and it's a neat forum for them."

I ask Zukin if he has been able to discover why talk radio is so appealing, why people find it attractive to listen to other people and discuss ideas in an anonymous environment. "Yeah, and it was a surprising finding," he replies. "We asked people to tell us the most important reason why they listened and we expected it to come back to the host, 'I like the host of a show or Rush Limbaugh or Larry King or whatever.' " The surveyors then read their sample lists of potential reasons for listening to talk radio.

The host of the show came out last. "What came out first," Zukin tells me, "was to learn information. What's sort of secondary is to listen to opposing views." This is an unnerving result when one realizes just how much misinformation is spread intentionally and unintentionally by talk radio hosts and when one further takes into account just how thoroughly manipulated callers and their opinions are by individual hosts and the talk radio system. Survey respondents—by a slight plurality—indicated that they wanted to listen to viewpoints different from their own. "In that sense," Zukin interprets the results, "it's a good medium for democracy. What citizens are listening to are the opinions of other citizens."

The listeners that Zukin and his colleagues checked with expressed a remarkable lack of concern about the credibility of the information they glean from talk radio. "People sort of like the entertainment value. Let's be honest, people like listening to some more wacko calls, they like entertaining hosts," and he adds, "they adjust for credibility." I ask him to explain his last remark. "I think people adjust for credibility on talk radio the same way they do in their daily lives," is his conclusion. "They listen and see if an argument makes sense, if the person seems to be rational, if the person seems to have some facts."

The survey revealed to Zukin that listeners don't turn to talk radio just for information and entertainment; they're often looking for another component that's lacking in their lives. "It's not only an informational medium," he says, "it's a medium people like to get emotionally invested in. They like to get angry at the callers, they like to react to things."

The enormous stack of listener letters that litter my files—and the files of most talk radio hosts—are testimonials to the fact that the audience reacts.

———

Most talk radio performers keep a representative sample of the avalanche of listener letters that pile up at radio stations. Love letters, hate mail, incoherent ramblings, newspaper clippings, political diatribes, requests for photographs—the response reflects the intimate, one-to-one relationship that develops between host and listener. Unlike television, radio is usually used by a lone consumer. The listener experiences the successful talk radio program as a conversation conducted with or for the individual listener. The magic of the medium forces the imagination to create an image of the host, especially when listening habits include tuning in a particular host regularly over a relatively long period of time. The host's personality takes shape in the listener's mind. A cyber friendship—albeit usually one way—develops with this new companion.

Periodically, some listeners attempt to develop the relationship further. They may call the program to make telephonic contact with their radio friend (or enemy). Talk radio lore—there are no reliable data in this regard—suggests only about 1 percent of the audience ever calls in to a show. The Times Mirror survey concludes that 11 percent of Americans in general, not just talk show listeners, have ever tried to call in to a show and that only 6 percent have managed to spend any time talking on the air.

Some listeners take advantage of opportunities to meet talk show hosts during public appearances. Hosts show up at events ranging from lectures at universities to glorified advertising exercises at car dealerships. Rush Limbaugh developed this act into what he dubbed "Rush to Excellence" and filled halls around the country with his followers. He videotaped the events and sold the tapes to members of his audience looking for a further connection with their hero.

Correspondence is another device used by the audience to establish a connection with the host that extends beyond passive listening. Much of the mail I've saved over the years dates from my days in the early seventies at KGO. When I was fired, the program director called me into his office. He had two stacks of letters on his desk, one short and the other looming up toward the ceiling. "This stack is the hate mail," he told me as the reason for canceling my show—controversial at the time because of its left-leaning counterculture nature.

At KGO in the early seventies we broadcast from San Francisco's tough Tenderloin district. Our studios were on Golden Gate Avenue and were equipped with a window facing the sidewalk so the audience could come and gawk and wave as they listened to the show over loudspeakers. One day a crazy man showed up with a gun and began blasting at the host. The glass was bulletproof and the bullets bounced off, causing no harm. The frustrated maniac made for the entrance and managed to get into the radio station's offices. He killed a KGO salesman before killing himself. The sidewalk window was replaced with a wall.

"Ms? Laufer," reads a letter I received while the window was still in place. "My mother, sister and I saw you in the KGO Cage. My sister who is 18 turned away. She said your appearance nauseated her but I (aged 19) burst out laughing. Mother said I shouldn't make fun of you or any of you neuters (a *thing* which you may know is *sexless*) I should feel pity for you. I cannot understand why you want to make yourself uglier than you are. Take a slow boat to China." It was signed, "Ha! Ha!"

Another, dated November 12, 1972, reads, "You are a menace to society. Why haven't you done something for your country you *Rat* with the *braid* down your back and now I wonder if you are a *Real He Man* you good for nothing 'Red'—Go to some other country and broadcast your horrible Communist remarks." This letter followed a show during which I expressed my opposition to the Vietnam War. "You should be shot at sunrise," McFadden continued, "and you would be if you were in another country. This country is too *good* for *you*. I am sending your tapes to the President and also to the F.B.I. and I hope they get you and all your kind." She finished with a flourish: "Get out of this country you Dirty Rat," and then signed her message with a sweet "Sincerely, Esther McFadden."

Not all the mail is filled with attacks or praise. Virginia Hanscom wrote, "Listening to talk shows I have come to the conclusion that people only *think* they are free to choose their topic. The choice is really made in general by the position of the moon. Next Saturday and Sunday the moon will be in Taurus. See if they don't get hung up on sex or money. When the moon is in Pisces," she informed me about the current moon position, "they get off on mysticism, conspiracies, plumbing, sewage disposal, nuclear waste, anything having to do with the dissolution of matter." Her letter came in response to my wondering on the air why so many callers were being exceptionally nice and charitable and benevolent a particular Sunday. "The answer is simple," said Virginia. "The moon was in Aquarius."

===

The Times Mirror survey identifies talk radio callers as the "vocal minority." For the survey, 112 talk show hosts nationwide were interviewed, all working in the top 100 metropolitan American markets. Samplers chose hosts who conduct shows dealing with news and politics.[2] Despite the fact that the hosts overwhelmingly expressed disapproval of President Clinton and despite the dominance of the medium by Rush Limbaugh nationwide, the survey interpreters found the hosts overall to be politically independent and basically middle-of-the-road. It is the audience that is overwhelmingly right wing; conservative callers and listeners outnumber liberals two to one. The researchers polled a nationwide sample of 1,507 adults, randomly selected to be representative of the nation's population.[3]

Although hosts overall, according to the survey, were not predominantly espousing a right-wing viewpoint, it is important to note that the dominant hosts do veer right. From Limbaugh, Pat Buchanan, and G. Gordon Liddy nationwide, to Gene Burns in New York, Ken Hamblin in Denver, and Ronn Owens in San Francisco, the examples of local and syndicated right-wing hosts are everywhere, filling prominent time periods and generating high ratings.

Talk show listeners and callers surveyed were not only much

more critical of President Clinton than is the general population, the figures were similarly distorted in regard to appraisals of Congress. Other societal institutions suffered similarly from talk show aficionados: newspapers, network television newscasts, the United Nations, and the United States Supreme Court all take a shellacking from the know-it-alls who populate the talk radio universe, criticism that is disproportionate to the assessment offered by the rest of America.

Talk show hosts supported the conclusions of the survey, characterizing their callers overall as angry, antigovernment, critical of the president and Congress, and conservative. The bulk of the 112 surveyed are a pretty self-satisfied bunch, believing, according to the survey, that "they play a significant role in shaping public opinion and have an impact on public policy and politics. While a significant number acknowledge the entertainment value of their programs, more see their job as informing the public."

After interpreting the results of the survey, Cliff Zukin and his staff concluded that "American public opinion is being distorted and exaggerated by the voices that dominate the airwaves of talk radio." They determined that "these new voices of public opinion can caricature discontent with American political institutions, rather than genuinely reflect public disquiet."

Such a conclusion from a credible study mandates that talk radio practitioners, and our vulnerable society, understand the nature of the noise emanating from our millions of radios. We must pause and consider the source before we allow ourselves knee-jerk reactions to the "vocal minority" yammering for attention over a medium that solicits audience participation as a device to create entertainment programming.

Few if any commercial talk radio shows are being produced for the purpose of educating and informing the listening public. Few if any commercial talk radio shows are being produced to further public debate on issues of importance to the republic. Those lofty goals may be productive by-products of talk radio enterprise. However, the shows are being produced to generate revenue for radio stations. The callers are used to separate commercials and generate interest in the programs. There is an ideal symbiotic relationship between a radio producer looking for an entertaining and rabble-rousing call to put on the air and a member of the "vocal minority" looking for an outlet for his or her discontent. But talk radio should never be mistaken for the voice of democracy.

# 4 The Genesis of Talk Radio

*The beginnings of interactive talk on the radio* between the audience and the host are vague. Broadcasting consultant and researcher Willis Duff traces it to the thirties and John J. Anthony's *The Goodwill Hour* advice show, aired over the Mutual Broadcasting System. "You have a friend and adviser in John J. Anthony," his announcer started each program, "and thousands are happier and more successful today because of John J. Anthony!" Anthony would simply paraphrase over the air his listeners' letters and telephone calls. Other listeners were in the studio, and part of Anthony's trademark was to remind them not to touch the microphone and to use "no names, please" as they told him their deepest troubles. Eventually he joined the staff of what Duff identifies as the first twenty-four-hour talk station in America, KLAC in Los Angeles.[1]

Alexander Woollcott started talking on the radio over New York's WOR in 1929, although without the interaction with the audience that characterized *The Goodwill Hour*. Woollcott announced that on his show he would "talk of people I've seen, plays I've attended, books I've just read, jokes I've just heard." He switched to the CBS network the next year, naming his show *The Town Crier*. He launched into each edition with the call, "Hear ye, hear ye. This is Woollcott speaking." As became the case with the telephone talk format, Woollcott's approach to broadcasting was to offer himself to the audience in a conversational manner. He was a radio acquaintance, not an authoritative voice talking at listeners.

Other radio historians trace the talk format back to the twenties. Kenneth S. Stern is program specialist on anti-Semitism and extremism for the American Jewish Committee in New York. For a study on hate in talk radio, he concluded that the first talk show was about farming, broadcast in 1921 over WBZ, then headquartered in Springfield, Massachusetts.[2]

Wayne Munson, an assistant professor of communications at Fitchburg State College in Massachusetts and a talk show scholar, believes that talk radio and the first radio broadcasting developed concurrently. He studied the 1928–29 schedules of the American radio networks for an example and found twenty-one programs he defines as talk radio. "Most of these programs were monologues," Munson learned,[3] "experts talking at the audience rather than dialogue or audience participation shows." A later exception Munson found was *The Voice of Experience,* an offering that ran from 1933 until 1940 on CBS drawing attention to people in need of help. Audience participation took the form of listener contributions to host Dr. Marion Sayle Taylor's fund for whom he called the "less fortunate."

The same type of do-gooder device became a mainstay of talk radio involvement with the audience. "Any kind of programming can lead a crusade," wrote Duff in *The Talk Radio Handbook,* "but none so powerfully as talk." He cites Joe Pyne's "Soap for Vietnam" project; in the sixties over half a million bars of soap were collected for South Vietnamese civilians from the KLAC audience. The same Los Angelenes filled three cargo planes with food and clothing for the Alaska earthquake victims. In the early seventies at KSAN, although it was predominantly a music station, we used the techniques of talk radio to organize volunteers for emergency cleanup efforts after a massive oil spill in the San Francisco Bay. And in the nineties at WRC, we mobilized the audience to equip a needy inner-city school in the District of Columbia with musical instruments.

Munson lists variety shows that took listener requests into consideration, game and quiz shows, and amateur shows all as progenitors of today's telephone talk show—along with interview and debate programs dealing with current affairs and offering opportunities for participation from an audience listening in the radio studio. One of those early shows, *Vox Pop,* ran from 1938 until 1947, jumping from NBC to CBS to ABC. It first aired in 1935 under the title *Sidewalk Interviews,* and featured street reporters interviewing passersby in encounters that sounded remarkably like a current radio talk show.

On a January 1936 edition that I listened to from the NBC archives, the questioners hailed what sounded like impromptu guests and engaged them with questions such as "What is the difference between lingering and loitering?" and "How wide is a half dollar?" and "Would you feel better if you knew nobody was listening to you right now?" Not all of the conversation was based on silly questions; political matters were mixed in with the funny responses and the resulting laughter from the studio audience. *Sidewalk Interviews* was captivating because of its spontaneity and because the interviewees really sounded as if they were average men and women on the street—especially in the face of the polished questioning coming from the professional announcers (Parks Johnson and Jerry Belcher were the original interviewers; Wally Butterworth eventually replaced Belcher, and Warren Hull took over from Butterworth before the show finally went off the air.)

"Contrast and incongruity are at the root of the humor," is Munson's review of *Vox Pop.* "The common folk become the slick interviewers' foils. Arcane or absurd questions surprise the people, thus magnifying their performance awkwardness and prompting their honest, emotional reactions. Sometimes their laughter breaks the formal frame of the interview situation; more often, the interviewee plays along, heightening the listener's sense of the absurd."

Not only do modern talk shows use the telephoning audience as foils, live inserts from street reporters interacting with the public—in the *Vox Pop* style—are an element of many current talk shows. At WRC in 1994, reporter Jeff Kamen wandered the streets of Washington, D.C., in the early mornings, carrying his cellular telephone and using it to integrate the city into the morning talk show. His act included bursting into coffee shops, asking questions of unsuspecting patrons, and thrusting the phone in their faces for a live on-the-air answer. Kamen took his phone jogging, panting reports and interviews with fellow runners onto the morning show. He carried it onto city buses and talked with passengers; during a particularly fierce ice storm he sidled up to pedestrians and offered on-the-air instructions for avoiding spills on the slippery pavement.

Programs all over the country contained precursors of telephone talk radio. Fueled by the Depression, Father Charles E. Coughlin harnessed millions of radio listeners who were captivated by his oral response to their needs. As his following grew, he strayed far from Catholic teachings to promote fascism; as World War II began, he was prevented from buying the radio air time he needed to maintain his popularity.

Just after the war, Barry Gray hosted his WMCA show from a New York bar called Chandler's. Interviews with celebrities were a primary element of that program. From the mid-fifties into the sixties, Kenny Mayer talked on WBOS in Boston. A columnist for the *Boston Herald,* Mayer broadcast from his Brookline home and would pick up the telephone if it rang, talk with the caller, and then relay the conversation to his radio audience. Larry Glick was an early practitioner of talk on the radio, using the telephone on his WBZ show in Boston as a device to connect with the audience by calling out to the city and talking with on-duty policemen, customers at truck stops, and waitresses in doughnut shops.

Wolfman Jack mixed talk radio techniques with music to hawk an endless array of products over the Mexican-border-blasters XERF and XERB and become a legend for American radio listeners growing up in the sixties. "Who is dis onna Wolfman telephone?" he would howl at callers.[4] "Speak up! You gotta mind tumor? How sweet are your little peaches? Stand on your head and howl! 'Bye!" is typical of the Wolfman's popular one-way exchanges with listeners.

Pacifica stations in New York and Berkeley broadcast variety shows in the sixties that included what is now identified as talk radio. In New York, the Pacifica outlet WBAI showcased Bob Fass's Saturday night program *Radio Unnameable*. Aficionados of the program remember it fondly and in detail thirty years later as a counterculture radio oasis.

"Fass used to say that what he was doing was running a giant switchboard," said one of his WBAI colleagues, Steve Post.[5] "Fass would use his program and the telephone lines to put people in touch with one another. As was the case a few years later at KSAN, WBAI—and several other so-called underground stations around America—did not simply report the news or observe the parade, the stations and their personnel participated in the breaking news. KSAN's first news director, Scoop Nisker, became famous for ending his newscasts with the stock line, "If you don't like the news, go out and make some of your own." Such interaction made for exciting talk radio.

Joel A. Spivak was at KLAC in the early sixties, as a disc jockey playing recorded music. Soon after he was hired, the station added Joe Pyne. Pyne's aggressive and offensive form of telephone talk was a huge hit with the Los Angeles listeners and the station adjusted its format to all talk in 1963. "Nobody knew a damn thing about it," Spivak said of the format.[6] "Because of Pyne's success, we presumed the way to get audience response was to say the most outrageous things you could on-air to make people angry, shock them, or startle them. Whether or not your remarks made any sense was irrelevant."

Spivak remembered Pyne as a mentor to learn from but not copy. "Pyne was a great showman, and we all tried to emulate him. After a while, things calmed down a little bit. Pyne didn't, but the rest of us did because we suddenly realized when you're talking about issues that are important to people, you have a public trust to be responsible about it. So it evolved from what was shock radio in 1963 into something a little bit more responsible—but still a heck of a lot of fun."

Spivak and I met at the Carnegie Deli's Washington outpost to discuss radio,[7] and those old days at KLAC brought a dreamy look to his eyes. "We owned that town," he said about Los Angeles in the early sixties before I changed the subject to Joe Pyne.

"He was a master showman," he said about Pyne. "He created a sensation. Forget about his right-wing politics. Forget about the fact that Joe wasn't a great intellect. He talked a language people understand." With fondness, Spivak recalled, "He could be devastating. Limbaugh is bright," he said about the man many radio students believe is the direct descendant of Pyne. "I would rather listen to Pyne. Limbaugh does the same show every day. You could never fully predict what position Pyne would take on anything." As an example, Spivak cites Pyne's decision to come out against the death penalty after he witnessed an execution.

"He didn't scream all that often," said Spivak about his teacher, "but he was very animated. It was like professional wrestling. People just loved to hear Pyne do battle. He would lacerate people, but he was funny. Pyne was really a phenomenon. One of those comes along once or twice in a lifetime. He was way ahead of his time."

As for Pyne, one of his own memorable lines long outlived him: "I have no respect for anyone who would come on my show."[8]

By the late sixties talk radio matured into a money-making and audience-building institution. Stephen Singular characterized its niche well in *Talked to Death*. "A hundred years earlier," he wrote, "Walt Whitman had listened to his countrymen speak and written that he could hear America singing. Talk radio became the sound of America singing, arguing, whining, bitching, confessing, and letting raw feelings, private problems, and political or social opinions hang in the air for everyone with a radio to absorb."

===

My first radio job was at one of the first radio stations to program interactive telephone talk shows twenty-four hours a day. It was

1966 and Metromedia had just bought the old top-forty station KEWB, licensed to Oakland. "KEWB, channel 91, color radio!" was a jingle pounded into San Francisco Bay–area teenage brains throughout the sixties; most of us who heard it then can still sing it. The call letters were changed to KNEW and the station was converted to talk, with a massive billboard campaign advertising it as "Radio Free Oakland." It was the sister station of Duff's Los Angeles talker KLAC, also owned by Metromedia. Both stations, along with several CBS-owned stations, talked through the late sixties and into the seventies before changing their formats. KLAC and KNEW went to country music. Most of the CBS stations slid toward an all-news presentation.

In its prime, KNEW broadcast energy and excitement. Opinionated hosts challenged a nonstop assault of opinionated callers— and each other. Two of the KNEW stars fostered their disagreements with each other. Pat Michaels played the right-winger, Joe Dolan the liberal. Their on-the-air conflicts were developed by the station's promotion department, escalating at one dramatic (and well-attended) point into a staged duel between the two, set in a Golden Gate Park meadow. It was talk radio that refused to take itself too seriously.

# 5 The Mechanics of a Talk Show

*The formula is deceptively simple. To brew up a* talk show—in addition to a host—only a telephone, a microphone, and a radio transmitter are needed. No matter how elaborately a radio station or radio network chooses to develop a talk show operation, the basic formula never changes: just a host with some wit, confidence, and a microphone, at least a couple of incoming telephone lines, and a radio station to transmit the conversations.

The skill of the host to tell a story and generate excitement, combined with the luck of the draw from the pool of callers, works its magic to create the aura of something more than simply an announcer sitting in a cluttered little room. The listener conjures up a mental picture of the host, a picture that is usually romantic and wrong. "Oh, you don't look like you sound!" is a common greeting when listeners meet a host. A physical meeting can destroy the spell. The host degenerates from a soothsayer to a commoner. The voice over the radio, emboldened by the actual control the host maintains over the callers, is a voice of authority.

The talk show host is in charge of the aural stage until the listener chooses to take the one and only step available to change that dynamic—and that is to switch the station or turn off the radio. Even after that decision is made, the listener is left with a lingering concern. He or she knows that the talk show is still on the air, the host is still broadcasting. The listener who tunes out does not affect the ongoing program but merely eliminates his or her participation. The host is always the radio god, and the radio god is in control, the final arbiter of what is transmitted.

Few stations operate talk shows at the minimal level. One of the rare examples is KPTL in Carson City. There Travus T. Hipp promulgates his show equipped with just those basics. He operates the sound-mixing equipment that allows him to adjust the volume of his voice and the voices of the callers. He starts the tape machines that play the commercials that are pre-recorded. He switches to the satellite once an hour to receive the ABC network news. He watches the old Western Electric desk set for the telltale blinking lights on the buttons of the two incoming telephone lines, lights that signal to him a listener is calling. He answers the telephone on the air. There is no call screener; there is no device to delay the broadcast a few seconds to allow for censorship.

A show run in such a fashion is probably the closest talk radio gets to a form of direct democracy in programming. But it still falls short of such an ideal. Hipp decides when to stop talking himself and select a telephone call. He decides how long to engage the caller in a discussion, when to hang up and choose another call. If he and the caller argue, he can win by default simply by dismissing the caller. And, as is the case with all commercial talk shows, he must defer to the commercial commitment foisted on his forum by the sales staff of the radio station; he must interrupt the conversations and his own soliloquies to transmit the commercials.

At the Mutual Broadcasting System, Jim Bohannon practices nationwide talk radio, taking calls without the benefit of a call screener. His phones ring until just before he is ready to take a call, and then his producer asks only one question: from where is the call coming? "I don't want to know in advance that Peoria is going to talk about abortion and Pensacola is going to talk about gun control," Bohannon told *Crystal City Etc.,* a magazine published in the Virginia suburb where Mutual's studios are located. "That would make the show leaden, dull. Open phones is like playing shortstop—I never know if the next guy up is going to hit a line drive, a little dribbler, a high hopper, or a pop-up. That's what gives me my adrenaline rush. When I sound surprised on the air, it's because I am surprised."

Most talk shows are operated under much more sophisticated conditions that KPTL provides its hosts or Jim Bohannon uses to produce his show. Typically, in a major market commercial station, the host is assisted by at least a call screener and a board operator; at many talk radio outlets the staff includes producers and news departments.

The board operator takes on the technical responsibilities—maintaining the appropriate sound levels for the incoming telephone calls and the host's microphone, ensuring that the commercials are aired and recorded on the legal log of station activities. As a salary saver, the hosts are being forced to fulfill these functions for more and more shows, even at the most prominent stations.

The call screener sits in a room adjacent to the host. The two are visually connected via a soundproof window and they are able to speak with one another over an intercom. The incoming telephone lines are answered first by the screener. Most stations offer their hosts more than the two lines that exist at KPTL—as many as a dozen is not uncommon when the special lines set aside for news reporters and guests are included.

Larry King often boasted that his calls were not screened. But he did not operate with the randomness of simply picking up the ringing telephone. A screener ensured that there was a coherent connection and informed King of the city from which the next listener in the rotation was calling. Usually the screeners are much more active participants in the development of a talk show.

A skillful screener is a warm-up artist. He or she engages the caller quickly to determine what the listener can add to the program. First the process eliminates the deadbeats. Is the caller drunk or medicated to the point of slurred speech? If so, the screener wastes no time in saying something such as, "Thanks for the call, but I don't think we'll have time to get to you today. Good-bye." If the caller is insistent and calls back repeatedly, the screener simply parks the call on hold and neglects it until the end of the show. With a dozen incoming lines, there are always a few to spare.

Similarly, the screener checks for accents. A slight accent that does not interfere with the intelligibility of the caller's speech adds a cosmopolitan texture to the overall sound of the program and is encouraged. But a thick accent translates poorly for an American radio audience. Such callers are abandoned quickly.

Next the screener engages the caller in a fast series of questions: "What do you want to talk about? Why do you want to talk with the host?" With these questions the screener is trying to determine a few things. Is the caller glib? Has the caller organized his or her thoughts? Might he or she be funny? Working like a picador, the screener will try to flesh out the caller, focus the theme of the call, maybe even antagonize the caller a bit to increase the flow of adrenaline and make the ultimate encounter on the air more intriguing for the audience. The screener is concerned about the caller only as an element of the program; the challenge is to find the best callers and prime them as thoroughly as possible in order that the host need waste no air time developing the caller's smooth interjection into the show.

The screener walks a fine line between preparing the caller for the host and not allowing the enthusiasm and excitement of the call to be used up in advance. "Evaluate the caller and the content of the call pleasantly but briskly and get off the line," is the advice from Willis Duff from one of the KLAC memoranda collected in the *Talk Radio Handbook*. "If the caller has given his all to you," he instructs producers, "he has nothing left for the Communicaster when he gets on the air." Another admonition from Duff to his staff: "Cherish and expedite the call that is in vehement, rational (or sometimes even irrational) disagreement with the Communicaster. An abrasive conversation is like a shot of adrenaline to the program. Would you be likely to fall asleep if you could hear a couple of your neighbors carrying on an argument quite clearly? Neither would your audience."

During this process, when all the phone lines are flashing, the screener is bouncing from call to call, trying to find the hottest properties, rejecting the losers. A question or two is asked and then the caller is back on hold, listening to the live program over the telephone line. The show is piped into the line so that whenever a caller is on hold the program is heard through the telephone earpiece. This is not only to keep the caller current with the pace of the show, but also to discourage the callers from leaving on their home radios. Most talk shows take advantage of digital devices that delay the air product about seven seconds, time enough for the board operators to censor foul language or slanderous comments. In reality the dump buttons are rarely used. But if callers go on the air with their home radios playing, they hear their conversation with the host about seven seconds later. Few people are able to carry on a coherent conversation under such circumstances and the double audio is confusing to the audience. "Turn down your radio!" exasperated hosts demand with disgust when callers fail to switch off their sets.

The next series of questions the screener asks relate to the personal life of the caller. "Where are you calling from? How old are you?" Maybe even questions about professions are tossed in at this juncture. The purpose is to give the show host the most ammunition possible for selecting not only the best call, but also for creating a mix of calls that allow the show to flow with some seeming sense of purpose and style.

The live telephone talk show is largely improvisational. The host usually comes to the microphone with a sense of where the show is going and what makes a complete-sounding hour. But the incoming calls can change all that and can be used to bolster the host's plans. The host picks and chooses from the menu, hoping that the next call is ready game, pliable as material to enliven the program and showcase the perceived virility of the host. It is this real spontaneity that creates much of the allure of talk radio. In an era of lives dominated by routine, of radio plagued with formats trapped in repetitious and predictable programming, talk radio is a bastion of relief, and the clever host plays to that by seeking calls that deviate from the norm. It is the screeners' job to locate and identify those calls.

Most screeners and hosts are connected with a computer link. The screener enters the callers' first names, the number of the phone line where they are waiting, and some basic background. This information appears on the host's screen. The form it takes is usually something along the lines of, "Line 4. Bill from Yonkers. Hates his boss. Wants advice. Sounds sincere and mad." The screener also uses the computer to send other messages to the host. Information from various data bases is flashed on the monitor to make it sound as if the host knows an incredible amount off the top of his or her head. The host can also draw on breaking stories from news agencies with the computer. The screener taps in advice, too, such as, "Dump this jerk," or information that the screener gleaned during the warm-up process, "Make him tell you what his wife did last night!"

The best screeners are animated, jumping up and down, making hand signals through the glass, writing notes and holding them up to the window, running into the studio with clippings and messages, maybe even calling pay telephone numbers for additional voices for the show when there is a dearth of calls from the audience—acting as a producer of the show. In an ideal situation there are almost two talk shows in progress—one off the air between the caller and the screener, the other being broadcast with the host. In fact, callers often refer on the air to their encounters with the screeners, and the screeners develop an on-the-air persona without ever saying a word on the radio.

This process is show business, not some form of democracy. It makes for engaging radio programming, but hardly can be construed as representing a cross section of American opinion.

The host is often jumping up and down, too. Typically his or her desktop will be cluttered with clippings and notes, perhaps a few books pertinent to the expected direction of the day's show, a few magazines. The host is looking for a rhythm for the show, a manner of juggling the mandatory commercial breaks, the newscasts, and the callers to create the whole show and units within it that usually can be divided, chapterlike, into hour-long increments.

While it usually sounds as if the host is deeply involved in the nuances of each conversation with each caller, more likely he or she is carrying on several other conversations at the same time, keeping just enough attention directed to the content of the call so that when there is a pause the host can turn on the microphone in time to say, "Right, I understand. Tell me more," or dismiss the call with a quick "Thanks for calling, keep listening," or, if the caller seems to offer potential for more valuable material, perhaps something combative to whip up some passion: "Just where did you get such an idiot idea?"

Although certainly the hosts are sometimes intently digesting the contents of a call in order to be ready with a deft comeback—especially if the caller is an expert guest—they usually use the air time consumed by the callers to consult with the screeners about which calls waiting are the most intriguing. They work out times for commercial breaks with the board operators or plan for the dismissal of the caller. I sometimes spent the time while callers were on the air chatting with my wife on another telephone line—careful to check that my microphone was off.

═══════

The host always has the electronic power to be victorious in any conflict with a caller. Obviously the host can simply hang up the phone. But there are more sophisticated tools available for stacking the deck against the audience.

Some stations equip their hosts with a device that automatically gives the benefit of the doubt to the host's voice. If both the host and the caller speak at the same time, the caller is overridden by the host, forced by the design of the apparatus that produces the signal being broadcast to succumb to the overriding authority of the host without realizing the loss of influence.

At other stations, the volume of the host and the caller are controlled with separate sliding switches or knobs—just like the volume knob on the radio at home. If a call becomes a shouting match and the host wants to win by default, he or she simply signals the board operator, and the capacity of the caller to maintain an equal footing in the debate just disappears. The caller can yell and scream, and no one listening on the radio hears a thing. Or the yells and screams are vague and muffled as the host takes all the time needed to sound clever and smart, finally nodding again to the board operator to allow the exhausted and frustrated caller to speak to the audience. When the host engages in this type of verbal combat, the caller is unaware that he or she has been electronically erased during the conversation. Because of the seconds-long delay in most talk show broadcasts, it is virtually impossible to maintain a clear train of thought with the radio on at home, even if it is on low enough so that the host cannot hear it to admonish the caller to turn it down. Consequently, at the caller's end of the telephone line, there is no opportunity to detect this editing process; there is no way for the caller to realize that his or her impassioned arguments went unheard.

Some hosts at times make use of this power to reinforce to the audience at large just who is in charge. A host can pull back the theatrical curtain and say things to the general audience about a recalcitrant caller such as, "Listen now, this guy thinks he knows it all, but he won't listen to me. I'm shutting him down so he'll be forced to hear what I have to say." Then the host instructs the board operator—over the air—to keep the caller from speaking on the radio while the host finishes an argument. In conditions of dictatorial control like this scenario, the host is conspiring with the rest of the audience to marginalize a bothersome caller. It is a device that must be used with care, so that the audience does not end up identifying with ridiculed callers and eventually reject the host. Finally the host can return the caller to the air with a sense of gracious charity and words such as, "Okay, if you've calmed down enough, go ahead and make your point."

The medium is ideally designed for creating and perpetuating the radio god.

---

It is just this unbalanced dynamic between host and audience that the character Barry Champlain addresses as he breaks down emotionally in the movie *Talk Radio*, saying over the air, "I am a hypocrite." That movie speech was based on a real exchange between Denver talk show host Alan Berg and an elderly woman caller.[1] The Hollywood version of the encounter lacks the raw intensity of the real exchange, a poignant display of talk show arrogance feeding off of a sychophantic caller.

"I expect you to hang up on me," the woman says to Berg. "You are the great humanitarian who makes people miserable 365 days a year."

She knows he has the ultimate power in their relationship and he reminds her even as she just finished acknowledging it.

"It shows what masochists people are," Berg tells her, "when you look at what I've done in talk radio. If people have such a need to listen all the time, they must have an enormous need to be masochistic." Then he abuses her directly. "Why are you listening now?" he challenges her.

"I'm listening—" she begins, but he interrupts.

"Why?" he demands again. "If I make people miserable 365 days a year, you must have a need to be miserable." Then he ridicules her. "Also, considering that I'm not on the air 365 days a year, you don't count well."

"That's right," is all she can manage to respond.

But Berg refuses to leave her alone. She is just one listener. He can afford to alienate her. She probably will not stop listening even after the abuse he unleashes against her because she is lonely and needs her radio companions. She just wants to talk; he is a professional speaker. There are some talk show callers who have honed their own skills to make use of talk shows to vent their egos or promulgate their causes. But much more typical is this little old lady.

"Unless you play tapes of my show on the weekend to make yourself further miserable," Berg continues. "If you really think I am such a terrible broadcaster, you really are a masochist. I don't stay tuned to anything I don't like. You really have a problem."

"I do, I do," she whimpers. "I agree with that."

"Now, maybe we can find a cure for you." Berg is relentless. "Would you like the name of a doctor? Would you like to come to my Common Sense Counseling Program?"

"No, I don't think so," she says.

"Perhaps I could help you through this grief you're experiencing."

"I'm not experiencing grief."

"What is the point you're making—that I bring grief to people?" Again he asks, "Why do you listen to me?"

"I don't, Alan," she says, "I don't." The intimacy remains even in the face of his tirade. To her, he is her radio friend Alan. To him, she is simply show product to be manipulated.

"Oh, darling," he crows, "I don't think you've missed a show I've done for the last seven years I've been in the business. You're always there and you always know what I've done. It's an amazing thing for a lady who says, 'God, you make me miserable.' "

"I'm waiting for a certain program to come on," she protests.

"Well, why turn here?" The radio god rejects her. "There are thirty-four other radio stations in this town. Why turn here if I make you miserable?"

"You don't make me miserable."

"You realize what a hypocrite you're making of yourself?"

"I feel sorry for you," is her counterattack.

"You made an utter fool of yourself." He goes in for the kill. "You have no credibility. You dig what I do. You have a need. Unfortunately, you have no sense of humor. And that's why you can't ever enjoy this show. And that's why you're a loser, as are all people who have no sense of humor. And you are categorically one of them. 'Bye!" Berg hangs up the telephone.

Only the elderly woman, the disposable pawn, loses in such an encounter. The voyeuristic audience enjoys the thrill of eavesdropping on a nasty fight, and the host feels a sense of perverse power, a rush of adrenaline, the rewards of being a bully.

# 6

## Stern and Limbaugh: Household Names

*Credit for the universal acceptance by the audience* of the term *host* to describe a radio talk jockey can be given to Rush Limbaugh. Early in the development of the talk radio format, terms such as "air personality" and "communicaster" were used. As Limbaugh's national show was gaining acceptance, he repeatedly bombarded his acquiescing listeners with the moniker "host." He used it to impart a sense of value and prestige to his position. The fatuous announcements during debate with a caller would come out something like, "I am right. You know why I am right? Because I am the host." Or he would construct a reference to the title based on a listener complimenting him for seeming to know some fact or for expressing a seemingly correct opinion. "That," he would say, "is why I am the host.

Without belaboring its importance, the choice of the word *host* to identify the talk radio broadcaster is intriguing. The word means someone who entertains a guest—the guest in this context being the caller or the subject of an interview. Its biological meaning is amusing to consider as regards a talk show personality. A host organism entertains a parasite living in or upon it—a definition that fits the relationship between plenty of talk show callers and talk show announcers. And there is the religious meaning of the word. A host—such as Christ—is a victim for sacrifice, and the bread consecrated in the Christian Eucharist service is the host.

When one of Stern's listeners called his favorite host "Fuckin' Howard, radio God," at least the first two uses of the word *host* worked.

---

The stars of talk radio dominate the airwaves from coast to coast and border to border, filling offices, taxicabs, all-night gas stations, and insomniacs' homes. Their voices come careening out of millions of car radio speakers day and night.

"Hello, you're on the air!" is the familiar cry of talk show hosts as they hook still another anonymous caller to play a cameo role on their shows. Many of these hosts are now household names in America, especially those whose shows are nationally syndicated. Larry King's name means "talk show host" to most Americans, Howard Stern means "shock jock." Some of the talk radio hosts are already celebrities, such as presidential candidate Pat Buchanan. "I saw you at the Alamo," gushes a typical caller to Buchanan's show, "when you were running for president!" Just as Limbaugh fans love to show their solidarity with their radio god by announcing "dittos" as they begin to commune with him, so do Buchanan followers frequently start their conversations with their presidential favorite by citing his failed candidacy. Callers, such as the one I heard in 1993 refer to the Texas campaign stop, often tell Buchanan that they voted for him and hope he runs again.

Watergate burglar G. Gordon Liddy elicits similar fan calls. "Mr. Liddy," asks an anxious caller to his program, "how many techniques do you have to kill a person with your bare hands?" The line was collected by Randall Bloomquist for a 1992 *Washington Post* magazine article on Liddy. Bloomquist describes Liddy: "While the macho muscularity and intense stare remain, Liddy's fearsome appearance has softened with age. The once ominous mustache has grayed, and most of his hair is gone, victim of a preemptive shearing. Dressed as he is in a brown tweed jacket, striped shirt and tie and brown wool pants, Liddy somehow reminded me of a high school Latin teacher. The one who ruled his classroom with an iron fist."

Still other nationally syndicated hosts are local heroes in major and minor radio markets across the country, and manage to catapult to stardom—none higher, so far, than Rush Limbaugh.

When Limbaugh considers his role in American culture he smirks and describes his goal: to "capture the largest possible audience for the longest possible time, so we can charge confiscatory advertising rates." He is famous for his simplistic one-liners: "When a gay person turns his back on you, it is anything but an insult, it is an invitation." "The most beautiful thing about a tree is what you do with it when you kill it." "Feminism was established to allow unattractive women easier access to the mainstream."[1]

Wielding phenomenal skills of self-promotion, Limbaugh and his handlers in just a few years in the late eighties and early nineties, managed to foist him on American popular culture. His two books, collections of his simplistic political and social analyses, dominated bestseller lists. He found podiums as varied as his late-night television show, the speaking circuit, a newsletter, the *New York Times* op-ed page, a *Playboy* interview, the cover of *Time* (twice, once shared with Howard Stern), a guest labeled "conservative commentator" on *Nightline* and *The Mac-Neil/Lehrer Newshour,* and a seemingly endless array of radio stations from coast to coast.

The message is always the same: a clever production of the world according to Limbaugh. That world is a fantasy based on a television sitcom memory of the American dream. The world according to Limbaugh is the world of *Leave It to Beaver.*

Limbaugh commands attention from his audience as it follows his political lectures. Listeners otherwise unfamiliar with world events hear Limbaugh's manipulation of the news and consider themselves informed and armed with a valid opinion: The callers have been instructed to use the word *ditto* as shorthand for "I agree with everything you say." WABC program director John Mainelli identifies Limbaugh as a news reporter. "I'm convinced these people want to learn," Mainelli said about Limbaugh's New York audience,[2] "but they don't want to wade through the *New York Times* to do it."

When Limbaugh was signed to air on KNBR in San Francisco, his show was followed by Peter B. Collins, a local broadcaster with a definite liberal slant to his talk show. "My first encounter with ditto power," Collins wrote,[3] "came immediately. Right at the end of Limbaugh's first broadcast on my station, I said, 'and that's our preacher feature for today,' reacting to his sermon-style mono-logues." Hours later Collins was in the KNBR program director's office; Limbaugh was on the telephone, complaining about the ref-erence. A KNBR listener had faxed Limbaugh a report on the Collins reaction to the debut Limbaugh show. "The dittoheads had turned me in," wrote Collins about the incident, "the first of many times."

In September 1991, Limbaugh came to San Francisco for the National Association of Broadcasters convention and originated his show from the KNBR studios. Collins took advantage of the opportunity to interview the station's new star performer. "While I was given no instructions," Collins wrote later, "it was clear to me that I could spar with him but I shouldn't pull back the cur-tain on the Wizard. My boss [Bob Agnew] and the station man-ager led a peanut gallery watching our exchange through the fishbowl window. It was one of the stranger interviews I've done, as I was conscious of unstated orders not to shoot to kill."

Despite being identified as a news reporter by the program direc-tor of his flagship station, Limbaugh hid behind the guise of enter-tainer as he explained his act to Collins. "This is show biz," Limbaugh hollered enthusiastically. "I really believe that radio is turned on for three reasons: People turn it on to be entertained, to be entertained, and to be entertained. Some people say what I do is shtick and other people say it's an act. It's just my sense of humor. Sometimes I self-deprecate, other times I go into this pompous arrogance. But it's all intended lightheartedly." Such a glib response plays well to the audience. But those taking his defensive words seriously are beguiled by Limbaugh, whose ultimate goal—anchored by his radio show—is to influence the social and political orientation of America. Not that there is anything wrong with his desire to influence society, but the deceptions he fosters are only made more offensive when he hides behind the protection of calling his show just entertainment.

Limbaugh argued with Collins about whether his show is mere entertainment. To help make his own case, Limbaugh drew attention to the role of callers on his program. "I look at my show as an entertainment forum for people and I screen calls to find the best call. "You know what the main purpose of a good call is on my show? It's to make me look good. I'll tell you flat out, this show is not about what anybody else but me thinks. Calls are there to make me look good, to bring up interesting things, but there's no First Amendment aspect involved." Again, there is nothing wrong with Limbaugh using all the techniques of show business he can muster to further his act. What is confounding is that the audience does not just listen for a chuckle; many listen for news analysis and to be instructed how to think about social issues and world affairs without questioning their teacher's credentials and motivations.

Obviously the entire audience is not amused and converted. From the casual listener to the professional critic, complaints began being registered as Limbaugh's success developed.

"Dear Peter," one of Collins's listeners, Paul Schneider, wrote him from San Mateo County in the late summer of 1991. "As a manufacturer's representative I travel throughout the Bay Area and as many radio listeners do, I flip the radio dial. Several months ago I found Rush Limbaugh on KNBR. I still cannot believe that this man is authentic. He has to be a throwback to the McCarthy era. Furthermore, he demeans the integrity of KNBR, which has always had a fine reputation in broadcasting circles. I wrote of my amazement and displeasure to the general manager of the station, but never received an acknowledgment from him."

It is not surprising that the station management never bothered to respond to listener Schneider's letter. Limbaugh's arrival at the station was orchestrated for one reason: to raise the ratings. "This move is being made to strengthen KNBR's position in the market," program director Bob Agnew wrote in his October 29, 1990, memo to his staff announcing the arrival of the Limbaugh show on the station. He was even more forthright in his remarks to *San Francisco Examiner* media critic David Armstrong. "You can go on the air and say, 'Let's talk about famine, let's talk about abortion,' but after a while it gets to be the same old thing. It goes in one ear and out the other. It doesn't solve anything." So he sought sensational screamers in the Limbaugh mold. "You know," he rationalized with disarming honesty, "some people say, 'You guys in broadcasting have a public trust.' Bullshit. We are a business. We are in the entertainment business. Radio is an emotional medium. If we get you pounding on the dashboard, we've done our job."[4]

In fact, according to the restrictions of KNBR's (and all American radio stations') Federal Communications Commission license, guys in broadcasting do have a public trust, and Schneider continued in his letter to outline why he felt Limbaugh violated it. "This man calls himself a conservative," he wrote. "A true conservative is cautious, moderate, [and has] a tendency to oppose change in prevailing institutions. [Limbaugh] does not subscribe to these principles. Alarmingly, he is almost a Fascist in his thinking and his talk. What I find frightening is that he is on over 300 radio stations throughout the country. Couldn't you just see someone like this in a black uniform, arm band, and jackboots? He exemplifies every negative term that I can think of, and how the station can present someone like this to the radio public gives me cause for concern."

Schneider went on to say, "This man is obviously pompous, simplistic, stupid, not informed, arrogant, bigoted, a sexist, insensitive, his knowledge is given to him from headlines and what his handlers prep him on, he is intolerant to minorities." Tiring of adjectives, Schneider ended the sentence with, "etc., etc." "Forgive the diatribe," he said in closing, "but as a thinking person and a liberal, I know that he must disturb you as much as he disturbs me. It is disgraceful that the station sees fit to carry the program."

Bob Agnew felt no disgrace. He was ecstatic. His memorandum announcing the arrival of Limbaugh had identified the show as part of his plan to "wake up a sleeping giant," and KNBR's ratings were soaring with the new show. As radio stations across the country added the Limbaugh show, Agnew's attitudes were consistent with those of most managers. "I would put anything on the air as long as it made me money," KSRO general manager Terry DeVoto told me in 1991 as he explained Limbaugh's presence on that Santa Rosa, California, station. Stations began vying with each other for the rights to the Limbaugh program. It was originally offered on a barter basis. A radio station received the show for no cost, giving some commercial time to Limbaugh's network, which was then sold to national sponsors. But as competition for Limbaugh developed, some stations offered cash in addition to the commercial positions and Limbaugh's producers responded by demanding cash from many affiliates in addition to the commercial time. There was some initial grumbling, but the change in terms—costing, according to broadcasting trade journals, as much as $100,000 a year—was borne by needy stations.

David Remnick joined the tangle over Limbaugh with a passion-filled commentary featured in the Sunday *Washington Post*.[5] His credentials were impeccable for an attack on Limbaugh. He had headed up the *Post* Moscow bureau, had written an award-winning book about the fall of the Soviet Union, and had recently returned to America and a job as a staff writer for the *New Yorker*. "Limbaugh," Remnick wrote, "is defending the successful against the impudent demands of the poor; by making all that funny, he gives the comfortable a way to think that greed and a cold-hearted wit comprise a cohesive ideology." Remnick identifies the Limbaugh style as "pure demagoguery," charging correctly that "Limbaugh is neither curious nor brave," that "he would rather tell his audiences fairy tales than have them face the world; he would rather sneer at the weak than trouble the strong."

Yet listeners and consequently radio station owners and operators seemed insatiable when it came to filling the hours with Limbaugh. By 1994, many stations, including KARN in Little Rock, were following three hours a day of Limbaugh with more talk based on his rants and raves. At KARN it was titled "Respond to Rush," an hour a day filled with snippets of Limbaugh's monologues followed by a local host introducing the comments of callers who were unable to get on the air during Limbaugh's nationwide live broadcast.

"What is the difference between Rush Limbaugh and the Hindenburg?" goes the joke cited in the *Flush Rush Quarterly*. "One is a flaming Nazi gasbag and the other is a dirigible!"

═══════

"I have no defense for anything I say," Howard Stern explained himself to *Rolling Stone* magazine.[6] "I just bullshit my way through life." Using the same technique employed by Limbaugh, he refuses to take responsibility for his influence on the audience. "Do I worry about what the audience's reaction is going to be?" he said in response to a question from interviewer Rock Marin. "Absolutely not. You have to assume that they're reasonably intelligent enough to know that a guy on the radio shouldn't be formulating every opinion of theirs. I couldn't give a shit what the audience's reaction is going to be. I just hope they keep tuning in."

Once the FCC began fining Stern for violating restrictions against broadcasting "indecent" material in 1990, the total bill quickly grew to over a million dollars. But Stern's employer, Infinity Broadcasting, fought the fines, and Stern used the commission as a target for his broadcasts, casting himself as a victim of government-sponsored censorship. In an attempt to assuage critics, Infinity announced it was adding a seven-second delay device to Stern's broadcast, to enable the company to edit offensive material. But the complaints continued.

As stiff as the fines seem, Stern's show is so lucrative for Infinity that paying them could be considered an acceptable cost of doing business. When WLUP decided to cancel Stern, Infinity sued the Chicago station. Consequently the terms of WLUP's contract with Stern became public court records, providing an opportunity to see an example of how much revenue Stern was able to generate for his employer at just one of the more than a dozen radio stations carrying his show. The contract was a three-year deal, providing for WLUP to pay Stern $750,000 the first year, $850,000 the second, and $1 million the third. In addition, Stern was to pick up 5 percent of the net WLUP earned from advertising sold in Chicago for broadcast during the Stern program.

Besides charging stations not owned by Infinity for the rights to broadcast the Stern show, Infinity sells commercial time in the program. In 1994 it cost $10,000 for Stern to read an advertiser's copy live on the air, with the spot airing once a day, nationwide for a week. It's a bargain, according to his satisfied clients. Ron Tiongson, in charge of advertising for Dial-A-Mattress, told Paul Farhi of the *Washington Post*[7] that ads on the Stern show brought over $3.5 million in sales to his company. "People call up and say, 'Howard told me to call.' It's amazing," said a pleased Tiongson. Bruce Barron, who buys and sells cars in New York City, lauded Stern too. "No one brings in customers like Howard Stern," he gushed. "He speaks the truth. People listen and people believe him."

FCC rules and regulations define "indecent" programs as those describing "in terms patently offensive as measured by contemporary community standards sexual or excretory activities or organs." And, complains the commission, it is Stern's "repeated pattern of violations" that is especially offensive. As the conflict between Stern and the commission heated up, the FCC chairman at the time, Alfred Sikes, was suffering from prostate cancer. Stern responded on the air with the wish "that Al Sikes's prostate cancer spreads into his lungs and his kidneys." This was not just some off-the-cuff, ad-libbed remark that Stern later regretted. On the contrary. Although his employer apologized, Stern told the *Washington Post,* "Every time I feel myself thinking, 'Maybe I shouldn't say that,' I consciously say it. That's the point of the show. Maybe it's wrong to wish cancer on some guy, but say it anyway, say your true emotions."[8]

From the FCC's files is this example of a Stern broadcast that meets its criteria for being labeled indecent: " 'AIDS baby, come here,' " he said. "You know, the big know-nothing Barbara Bush. Can't even speak up to her husband about abortion. Anyway, so I'm reading *People* magazine, then I get upset by that, so I lay down, and I figure, well, I gotta masturbate."[9]

The conflict in the Stern case is between the free speech guarantees of the First Amendment and the federal government's role as regulator of the public airwaves. "Indecent" material, the term used in the FCC decisions against Stern, is identified as less risqué than "obscene" material. Radio programming that meets the obscenity test—explicit portrayals of sexual activities—can be kept off the air completely; "indecent" material can be restricted to broadcast times when children are presumed not to be in the audience.

Las Vegas radio listener Al Westcott became one of the most active complainants to the FCC about Howard Stern. Self-described as a product of the sixties, with long gray hair and a beard, Westcott seems an unlikely foe of Stern's. Westcott traced his distaste of the program to an on-the-air conversation that included a description of a pair of Stern's sidekick Robin Quivers's dirty underwear, offered as a prize to a listener, soaked in salmon oil and Hershey's chocolate. "I thought that was offensive," Westcott told the radio trade magazine *Radio Ink*.[10] "I thought it was inappropriate for kids." Westcott filed a formal complaint with the FCC. Although Stern and Infinity claimed in response that children did not listen to Stern's show, Westcott pointed out that with Stern claiming millions of listeners it is highly unlikely such a huge audience is free of children. Westcott sought a restriction of the Stern program to night hours when he, the FCC, and court decisions presumed there was less opportunity for youngsters to be listening.

Westcott told *Radio Ink,* "I would guess that if the bulk of the American public could sit and read the transcripts of the Howard Stern show, they would say that it is indecent and, in fact, some might even consider it obscene." Westcott rejected the suggestion that for him, or anyone else, the solution is to change the station or turn off the radio. "I own these airways, our children own them. It's not so much upon me to change the station as it is for broadcasters such as Infinity and Howard Stern to adhere to the obligation they inherently took on when they decided to be a licensee through the FCC."

Just before Christmas 1993, Al Westcott was credited by another trade sheet, *Inside Radio*, for a piece of doggerel that circulated into Las Vegas facsimile machines. Titled " 'Twas the Week Before Christmas," the rhyme named dozens of Stern sponsors in Las Vegas and urged a boycott of the businesses:

> *'Twas the week before Christmas,*
> *I was running around*
> *Trying to buy presents*
> *All over town.*
>
> *I turned on the radio*
> *And I was amazed,*
> *The things that you hear*
> *On the radio these days.*
>
> *The talk was of niggers*
> *And Jews that grab money,*
> *I thought to myself,*
> *This stuff's not funny.*
>
> *I listened for sponsors*
> *And then I exploded.*
> *Kentucky Fried Chicken, Kenny Rogers, Circle K,*
> *Circuit City, Photo Finish, and TWA.*
>
> *When you shop at these sponsors*
> *You give them the cash*
> *For porno and racism*
> *And Howard Stern's trash.*

Others critique Stern not for his dirty language but for the tone of his broadcasts. When Los Angeles morning radio star Rick Dees overtook Stern in the southern California ratings, Dees took the opportunity to challenge the role of his shock-jock competitor. "I think people are curious about evil," Dees told *Radio and Records* columnist Joel Denver,[11] "and I think he's evil. To go on-air and assassinate people's characters and annihilate individuals is permissible under the law, but to do it and not know that there will eventually be a price to pay is being an intellectual pygmy." Dees described his own success as being based on the opposite of Stern's presentation. "We stand for making people feel good in the morning, not hurting people, and not exposing them to hate. People get exposed to hate and Howard enough."

After a *People* magazine story about Stern's book, Mark Wyatt wrote to the magazine from Fort Worth. "I happened to catch Howard Stern's radio show several days ago. He was joking about Vanna White's miscarriage and how funny it would have been to see it happen live on TV. I couldn't believe what I was hearing. Isn't there enough hatred and cruelty in the world without Howard Stern promoting it in the name of humor? Anyone who would pay this man two cents for his drivel needs to get a life—and more importantly, a heart."

Stern's retort to his critics is simple: No one is forced to listen to him on the radio; if they are offended, listeners should change the station. He readily and proudly acknowledges that he does not allow his own daughters to listen to his work—making a distinct and appropriate differentiation between government control and parenting.

# 7 Talk Radio in the Shadow of the Stars

*Languishing in the minor leagues, what is a poor* talk show host to do, watching the runaway successes of the Limbaughs and the Sterns, to draw attention to the act?

Carving out a secure local niche is one device available to talk show hosts. Barbara Carlson used that approach on KSTP in Minneapolis and St. Paul. Well known in Minnesota before she settled on her broadcasting career, the former Minneapolis city councilwoman and the governor's ex-wife sounded as though she took lessons from Howard Stern when she told *People* magazine, "I'll say things that most people won't say. It's the way I've always been." Among those things: She treats her depression with Prozac, stapled her stomach, and enjoys announcing, "I love oral sex."

"I'm not a female Howard Stern," she protested to *Broadcasting and Cable* magazine.[1] "I'm outspoken and outrageous with a wonderful sense of humor and I'm able to tell the truth."

She invites her Friday guests to join her in her home hot tub as she broadcasts. "I like to relax, and people relax in water," she explains. "I thought if I could get my guests in a hot tub, they would act differently, and they do." The stunt also provides Carlson with great publicity photographs, as did her decision to decorate herself with a tattoo of her radio station's call letters. Adorned now with KSTP on her buttocks, Carlson seems content to remain a local Minneapolis product. "This is where I've lived and loved." She grins. "It's always fun to be a big fish in a little pond."

========

Floyd Brown tried to create a place in talk radio for himself by attacking Bill Clinton and wishing he were Rush Limbaugh. By mid-1994 his right-wing show was on a few dozen secondary stations around the country and Brown was working hard to both increase the number of outlets for his program and find more prestigious stations in larger markets with which to affiliate. Whether he wanted to become a radio star or was just using radio to further his political philosophies was hard to judge; likely—as is the case with many talk radio hosts—he wanted both.

In his promotional material, Brown called attention to one of the achievements he was most proud of in his relatively young life (Brown was born in 1961). He claimed responsibility for producing the so-called Willie Horton commercial for George Bush's 1988 presidential campaign. The ad played on racial fears to attempt to portray Democratic contender Michael Dukakis as soft on crime. "I'm very proud of the Willie Horton ad," Brown told me. "What it did was crystalize for people Dukakis's position on crime." Brown's current material is equally inflammatory.

In 1992 Brown produced a book attacking the then Democratic presidential candidate Clinton, titled, *"Slick Willie": Why America Cannot Trust Bill Clinton.* An example from the book's pages: "In looking for the cause of world problems, Bill Clinton learned to blame America first." Brown closes the *Slick Willie* acknowledgments with, "Finally we all wish to thank Rush Limbaugh for inspiration and 'equal time.' We listened as we wrote."

Brown also publishes a newsletter called *Clinton Watch.* Inflammatory headlines and unsubstantiated innuendo fill its pages. "*Clinton Watch* investigators reveal that Vince Foster's death may not have been suicide," was the March 1994 headline. The scoop in this article? Quotes from a paramedic who was supposedly first on the scene where the deputy White House counsel's body was found and who told Brown clues seemed "strange." The April 1994 *Clinton Watch* headline is lurid: "Clinton Drops His Pants for Paula to See." The story rehashes allegations of Clinton's extramarital activities and use of his gubernatorial connections to accomplish them. On the back page, Brown made an appeal for new subscribers: "If you want to find out if your suspicions about Bill and Hillary Clinton are true, then you need all the facts. *Clinton Watch* has made those facts available." The cost of the newsletter? "A year's subscription is available for a donation of $39.95." The terminology is intriguing. The "donation," the fine print reads accurately, is not tax deductible.

Brown's organization operates under the umbrella name Citizens United. Another product is a newsletter called *Citizens Agenda.* This one costs twenty-five dollars a year. Its back page, too, is adorned with a letter from "chairman" Floyd Brown. "Dear Citizens United Patriot," Brown addressed his followers. He suggested that his radio show, *Talk Back to Washington,* was responsible for the investigation of the involvement of the Clintons in the Whitewater land development in Arkansas. *Talk Back to Washington,* wrote Brown in the solicitation for financial support, "has paved the way in the journey to expose Whitewater, but only because of your help. Your dedicated support has allowed us to keep researching and uncovering the facts that seem to grow more plentiful every day. It is true that the more we know, the less we know. But with you standing by me, I know Citizens United will soon be able to uncover all there is to know about Whitewater and the Clintons."

In Volume 3, Issue 4 of the newsletter *Citizens Agenda,* Brown's assistant Fran Shane tries to tie the Federal Communication Commission's Fairness Doctrine to Whitewater, suggesting in a front-page article that were the Fairness Doctrine still in place any investigation of the Clintons and Whitewater would be stymied. "By exposing it on *Talk Back to Washington,*" writes Shane about his boss, "Floyd Brown made conservative talk show listeners the

first to hear the illicit details of Bill and Hillary Clinton's past."
Key to the propagandistic nature of the entire Citizens United act is
the use of the word *illicit*. At the time, the Clintons were charged
with no crimes and certainly had been found guilty of nothing
"illicit." That article ends with Shane attempting to attach Brown
firmly to the success of Rush Limbaugh. "If you want to continue
getting the truth about Whitewater from trusted conservative
sources like Rush Limbaugh and Floyd Brown," wrote Shane in
an appeal that readers lobby Congress against the Fairness Doctrine, "then your call is more important than ever!"

Using Limbaugh-like, fast-paced radio production techniques,
making use of rock music and quick cutting from sound effects to
people's voices, Brown's radio show begins with an announcer saying, "Here's your chance to tell Congress, President Clinton, and
our leaders in the nation's capital what you really think about the
state of the Union. Do the politically correct thought police have
you singing the blues? Then join us for Floyd Brown's 'Talk Back
to Washington,' a group therapy program for those who love
America. Stand by for your host, Floyd Brown."

Later, in my office pitching his show, Brown explains himself as
"basically in communication and idea marketing."[2] He tells me
that he wants to be a radio star and use the radio to sell products
such as his newsletters while furthering his vision of a conservative political agenda. "The purpose of the radio show," he says,
looking boyish and enthusiastic in his conservative brown suit and
Mayberry, R.F.D.–style haircut, "is to market ideas." He considers his audience "conservatives" and tells me with relish and a
smirk that "they are a market with a lot of income and they buy
product."

Brown likes to talk about his family to explain his own politics.
His grandfather was a Wobblie, and his father and brother were
hard-working woodsmen in the forests of Washington state who
sacrificed so that young Floyd could enjoy the benefits of a University of Washington education. "What happened was the Democratic party lurched leftward in the sixties and my family stayed
put." That left them, he explains, Reagan Republicans. The result

motivates him to fight what he fervently joins Pat Buchanan in calling a culture war. "I am a radical," he says. "A radical wants and is willing to work for and demands change." High on Brown's list of things to change is what he calls the "permissiveness of society."

---

Nikki Reed was on the air at WNIS in Norfolk, Virginia, when she realized she was pregnant. As so many talk show hosts do, she shared this very private news with her public.

"I had a baby in mid-August," she tells me when we talk a month later. It was her third child; she already had a two-year-old and a three-and-a-half-year-old. "I had this particular baby placed for adoption," she says, "and I decided to go public with the story."

She explained that the older children were from a previous marriage. She was twenty-nine and engaged to be married to the husband of the third child when she became pregnant. Then the relationship went sour.

"I decided to carry the child at first with the intention of keeping it and just having three kids running around. As time went on and my two-year-old and my three-year-old were not growing up as quickly as I wanted them to, I realized that I couldn't handle all three as a single mother." There were other reasons for the adoption. "I wasn't really getting along very well with my ex-fiancé and I did not feel comfortable with the idea of this child being shuttled back and forth. There was also the money issue. I didn't really feel like I could afford a third child. I just felt the best situation for this child—well, for any child really—would be in a two-parent family. I kind of slowly came to the conclusion that I felt adoption was the best answer, although I had a difficult time bringing that up with my ex-fiancé."

While she was figuring out how to tell him of her plans for their child, he called Reed and suggested adoption. She was in her eighth month when they made the decision. "I found a family in New Jersey—a stay-at-home mom and a father." Reed is about to tell me how terrific her baby's family is for the child. We are talking on the air,[3] and I'm appalled by what I consider her cavalier dismissal of her child. But as a student of talk radio, I'm also fascinated by Nikki Reed as an example of the bizarre type of people who end up as talk radio hosts.

I can understand that a case could be made to support her choice for her child. But why would she feel compelled to share that personal and difficult decision with the world? Is it because the ego needed to drive the demands of a talk show occurs in people who are compelled to talk about themselves no matter what the subject matter? Is it because the ego needed for a talk show host comes with a personality that fails to recognize how strange it is to treat a child as just more baggage? Or maybe it's because a talk show host must continuously seek new material, and if it happens to be autobiographical, no problem—the needs of the show are paramount. These are my thoughts as Reed carries on with more details.

"I really liked their personalities," she says about the New Jersey parents she auditioned. "I asked them all kinds of questions, everything from how do you feel about homosexuality and teaching the kid about sex to discipline, and how are you going to afford a college education, you know, those types of things." It sounded as if she were interviewing these replacement parents as she would guests on her talk show.

"Why," I ask her, "didn't you think about all this before you became pregnant?"

She hesitates, nonplussed, and suggests, before answering, that the question is ludicrous. "At the time I had a very good relationship with this person, and for reasons I'd rather not go into"— there is still an element of self-censorship left in Nikki Reed—"the relationship fell apart. It was my fault, it was a mistake that I had made."

"And, why would you take something so personal and decide to make it public?"

"For several reasons," she says easily. "First of all, it was on the heels of the baby Jessica story." Baby Jessica was the girl who was removed by court order from her adoptive parents. "The issue of adoption had gotten a lot of bad publicity, and, I feel like my story is a very positive one. I went through times of pain, but overall I'm satisfied with the decision I made. I felt it was time to hear a positive story about adoption.

"Secondly, I want to promote open adoption. I know—in fact I chose—the adopted parents for my son. That gave me a feeling of satisfaction. It wasn't as if I was just giving my child up to an agency. For me, I felt more positive doing an open adoption, letting my child know who his parents are, where he came from."

As I listened to Reed tell about the birth itself and the actual transfer of the baby to the adopting parents, she sounded more like a talk show guest than a talk show host. And, of course, she was my guest that day on the air—an example of the cross-pollination that develops within the media. Why shouldn't host Reed also take a turn as guest Reed? And why shouldn't guest Reed—the woman who gave up her son for adoption—be as forthcoming about herself as the guests who routinely bare their souls and achieve some sort of gratification from a public explanation of a moment of epiphany in their lives?

━━━━

At KFI, Jane Norris was holding down weekend talk shows while Rush Limbaugh helped the station beat KABC for the title of most-listened-to talk station in Los Angeles. As do so many talk show hosts, she found Limbaugh both a frustration and fuel for her own program.

"I would fight to the death to retain Rush Limbaugh's right to say whatever he wants on his radio show," Norris tells her listeners on August 22, 1993, as she begins the show with what is known affectionately in the industry as her *churn*—an opening monologue designed to generate telephone calls from the audience. Norris is a fast-talking and intense woman, sporting a chin-length blond pageboy with bangs over her eyebrows. Her eyes are large and flash as she emotes over the air; her mouth looks small—but never lacks words.

Norris caused a national stir in 1991 when she devoted two hours of her KFI show to a discussion of Bree Walker's pregnancy. Walker was anchoring the news on KCBS-TV and is afflicted with ectrodactyly, a rare genetic deformity of the fingers and toes. Norris asked her listeners to advise Bree Walker on the appropriateness of bearing children, children with a fifty-fifty chance of inheriting the disability. "Would I bring a child into the world knowing that the child had a very good chance of having this deformity—webbed hands? I have to say, I don't think I could do it."

Walker was incensed. "I felt terrorized," she told the *New York Times*,[4] "I felt my pregnancy was terrorized." She complained to the FCC and evoked great sympathy from her viewers. KFI's studios were picketed. Although Norris managed to generate calls for an exciting two hours of talk radio, she was left with the reputation as the woman who used her radio voice to tell Bree Walker to abort her baby, even though Norris never made such a recommendation.

The show was a dramatic example of how the talk radio audience often does not listen carefully and easily misinterprets what is said on the air. People often come to conclusions about radio shows based on what they are told was on the radio, not on what they hear themselves. Stories about material heard over the air are retold by listeners, and then retold by nonlisteners. The result is often gross misinterpretation.

"I didn't say Bree Walker was wrong." Norris tried to clarify the matter later.[5] "I didn't say she was immoral, I didn't say she should have an abortion. I personally think it's an unfortunate choice on her part [to have the child]." She told me she felt wronged by the publicity that Walker developed against her, and was confused that her opinions could be so thoroughly misconstrued. Our conversation took place more than two years after the show on the Walker pregnancy; Norris was still troubled by the negative effects of it.

Another interesting phenomenon occurs when the audience hears the performer but misses the content. "I heard you on the air the other day," is a greeting radio personalities often enjoy, until they hear the rest of the sentence. "You were great, you were talking about . . ." Then the fan falters, searching for the memory. "You were taking about," comes out again, often followed by, "Well, I can't remember what it was, but you sounded great." Radio is a fleeting medium. The impressions a skillful talk show host leaves in the audience can be lasting. But at the same time, radio is forgiving of transgressions, both factual and moral. It is rare that a radio talk show host must face transcriptions of a program's content. Usually the audience is not taping for posterity; no one is taking close notice. Such cursory consumption, combined with the ad-libbed nature of the genre and the virtual absence of governmental restrictions of radio content, allows hosts almost limitless license to speak without inhibition.

As she did with Bree Walker, Norris opened her telephone lines for reaction to Limbaugh. "I don't care if I agree with his opinions or disagree with his opinions. I don't care if he's an ideologue for the Republican party. I don't really care what he presents. If it's effective, and it's interesting, and people want to listen to it, then I think he has a right to be on the airwaves as often and as on as many radio stations as he can possibly get on. It's only good for talk radio, it's only good for the radio industry, it's only good for broadcasting in general. I would challenge those who would seek to limit his free rein to the airwaves of the United States of America. I would challenge them to put up their own candidate, to put up their own talk host." It is significant that she uses the words *candidate* and *talk show host* interchangeably.

The mention of Limbaugh is all the audience needs to go into action. The phone indicator lights begin flashing. Norris is ready to roll.

"Matt is calling in from Fullerton, a first-time caller." The jargon *first-time caller* is heard repeatedly on talk radio shows. The goal is twofold: to proclaim to the general audience that involvement in the show continues to grow and to give comfort to potential new callers. "Welcome to KFI."

"It's a great show," Matt tells her, "and what I'm hearing right now is that the politicians are afraid of hearing what they're doing wrong. And whether it be Rush Limbaugh or Jane Norris or whomever, they don't want to hear about it. And they want to put a stop to it." A discussion of the proposed new Fairness Doctrine was an element of Norris's churn.

"People fail to realize that this is an entertainment medium," Norris says, defending her business.

Matt asks her the question baffling radio programmers and audiences alike since the advent of Limbaugh's nationwide success. "Why isn't there a liberal entertainer out there being a counterbalance?"

"Well, there are liberal voices that will reach the airwaves," she tells him. "You're just going to have to wait for Jane Norris to hit syndication. I'm telling you, that's just the only answer. Thanks for calling in. Mark is calling from San Diego. Hi, Mark, welcome to KFI."

Talk show listeners who call talk shows love to talk about talk shows. "I think it would be a good idea if talk radio went to the print media for hosts."

Norris is caught off guard and musters only, "You do?"

"Yeah," says Mark. "People who write are generally more clear thinkers."

It is the bane of broadcasters to be saddled with criticism such as Mark's. Norris does her best to accommodate it. "Well, you know," she says sweetly, "I would agree with you, and a lot of people do come out of the print media and go on talk radio. But once again, they would have to have a desire to do this. Not everybody does, you know. Usually journalists who write don't really want to express themselves [on the air]. They consider us, the broadcast media, a bastard child. I hate to tell you that. They consider us déclassé. They look down on us, okay?"

"When you look at some of the TV newsreaders," Matt says, "it's understandable."

"Hey, man," says Norris, "they're not all rocket scientists.

They're there because they're pretty. Thanks for calling in. Heather calling in for the first time from West Hollywood. Hi, welcome to KFI. How are you doing?"

"Hi, Jane. I don't think the way to counter Rush Limbaugh's influence is by limiting him, but rather by presenting suitable competition. However, I find the power and influence he has frightening, because he's a demagogue who appeals to our, I don't know— I really feel he appeals to our weakest sides, to our selfishness. A lot of things about him I really despise. However, he obviously has a right to say what he wants to say. But I think there's a danger when people like him get access to the airwaves and start thinking only about the very next minute, only about next week. A lot of the things that Clinton wants to do, for example, are going to require long-term sacrifices that will pay off eventually."

"It's a very good comment, Heather, and I appreciate you making it. Thanks for calling in." She takes the next call. "D.J.'s calling from Hollywood, first-time caller to the program. Hi, D.J. How are ya?" Norris treats her as a friend.

"Good, thanks," he tells her. "I just wanted to take issue with one of the things you said. You said it takes years of experience to be a good talk show host. Okay, I want to know what qualified police chief Darryl Gates." Gates was subsequently fired from his KFI position, but at the time had just retired from the LAPD and accepted work as the afternoon host at the station.

"Now, D.J.," says his new friend Norris, "you should know the answer to that, before I tell you what it is."

D.J. is fast, asking, "Because he's a white Republican?"

"No," says Norris, "he has celebrity appeal. The man's a celebrity. He's got that built-in celebrity appeal. You know, if Cher wanted a talk show, she'd probably get one too. I mean, Whoopie Goldberg wanted a talk show, she got a talk show. Chevy Chase wanted a talk show, he got a talk show. When you get a certain amount of celebrity you get certain benefits. It's not fair, but . . ." Norris dispatches D.J. without saying good-bye and starts the next scene with a hearty, "Welcome, Randy from Hollywood. Thanks for calling KFI."

"Hi, Jane," he says. "You must admit that the Rush Limbaugh show has become a three-hour-a-day, five-day-a-week campaign spot."

"Let me just interrupt you for just a second," she says, taking the talk show host's prerogative. "Then you would be in favor of censoring him? Or you would be in favor of requiring him to put on guests who differ with his opinion? How would you bring balance to the Rush Limbaugh show?"

Randy is ready for her question. "I'll tell you how. I would not be in favor of censoring him. I don't believe in that in any way, shape, or form. But I think he should be required to have articulate guests who have opposite views, and let that be the censoring mechanism because Rush Limbaugh doesn't take a whole lot of calls. He's mostly talking and giving his personal doctrine."

The specificity of the analysis coming out of the audience this day is impressive, as is the detail with which so many audience members have studied the talk show industry and the various performers.

"You know something that's really interesting," continues Randy, "this is what scares me. It's not Rush, but the shallow mentality of greater America. Most of the people in middle America just don't think. I mean, look at the popularity of Paul Harvey over the past forty years. He's certainly no great journalist, but the people just go along with him."

Randy bounces from point to point much like a talk show host. Often it seems not much in the way of talent and technique separate the hosts from the better callers. Sometimes during my late-night talk show on KCBS in San Francisco, I would simply connect the callers together and allow them to run their own talk show without me. At KABC, when it owned the talk market in Los Angeles back in the early seventies, program director Jim Simon picked a rowdy caller from the audience, proclaimed his title as "Superfan," and gave him his own talk show.

Randy continues to probe talk radio and its history. "One of the most revealing things in the annals of conservative talk show history was back when David Duke was running for president. Rush

Limbaugh had to suddenly backpedal. And Rush said something that I keep very precious on tape. He said, 'Well, of course a dittohead is a very shallow-minded dork that can't think for himself. And we can't go along with these people. That's just for show business.' So Rush actually said that about his own fans on his own program." Or so Randy says on Jane Norris's program. One of the beauties and tragedies of talk radio as it is practiced in America is that there is rarely a fact-checking department at the radio station, and even if the news department or the producer's office is available to check facts, the talk show hosts rarely employ either.

Did Limbaugh say what Randy asserts? If he did, what was the context? Such questions need to be asked about most so-called pieces of information offered over the radio in a talk show milieu. Norris pauses for a moment and considers the charge. "That they're shallow-minded dogs?"

Randy seizes the opportunity she offers him. "Dorks," he says again and again, finally spelling it out, "D-O-R-K-S. And Rush put down his own fans."

Randy is off the air without any formalities. "David calling in from Garden Grove," announces Norris. "Welcome to KFI."

"We don't like Rush Limbaugh because he's Rush Limbaugh," says David after identifying himself as a conservative, "we like his views. Because those are our views."

"Thanks very much," says Norris after they talk for a spell, adding, "Good call." *Good call* is another phrase from the lexicon of talk radio that allows the radio god to anoint the common caller with special status over the airwaves.

"Rosemary calling in from Rollin Heights." Norris skips rapidly through the jammed switchboard. "Welcome to KFI."

"Hi," says Rosemary. "I wanted to comment about your previous caller who commented that Rush Limbaugh calls his listeners dupes. Rush Limbaugh, demonstrates absurdity by being absurd, and what he was doing was mimicking what the elite say or think about the people who listen to Rush Limbaugh." Limbaugh has been educating his vulnerable listeners for years, explaining, for example, that they are being victimized by some amorphous "elite."

Norris cautions, "Rush Limbaugh used to say, 'You don't need to think, I'll do your thinking for you.' "

"That was demonstrating absurdity by being absurd," is Rosemary's ready response.

"I don't know," says Norris. "I think he believed that."

"I don't think he did," says Rosemary.

"Well, thanks for calling in today,' says Norris, allowing Rosemary the last word. "I appreciate your call. John calling from Irvine. Welcome to KFI."

"Well, thanks for having me on," he says. He then insists he doesn't listen often but felt forced to call because the direction the discussion was taking was annoying him. "I think a lot of people are missing the entire point here. It's marketing. You put it in entertainment terms. Limbaugh has niched himself out a very, very qualified audience. Some are probably smarter than others, but he certainly puts his opinions forth and people are buying off on those opinions."

Norris agrees with John that Limbaugh's business success can be attributed to his sympathy for the segment of society that yearns for a return, as she puts it, "to 1952." She pushes the telephone button. "Jeff is a caller from Imperial Beach. Welcome to KFI."

"Oh, hi," says Jeff. "Any high school debater could show Rush Limbaugh up for what he is," Jeff claims with easy arrogance. "Rush Limbaugh is an embarrassment to broadcasting."

"Have you ever tried to call his show?" asks Norris.

"Many times."

"And what happened?"

"Well, I can't get through," says Jeff. "But I call the second stringers on your station and argue with them and they all try to be just as outrageous as he because he's influenced radio in an embarrassing way and that's what needs to be pointed out. You're missing the point, Jane. I'm a huge fan of yours but I find myself disagreeing with you. Rush Limbaugh cannot be defended." Talk radio, says Jeff, is not an entertainment medium.

"Yes, it is."

"It's an advertising medium," says Jeff, agreeing with John from Irvine. "It's a marketing medium." Jeff is upset; he's yelling as he complains about Limbaugh. "He has had full tilt at the American masses for the last five years and he's been totally unfair. Somebody has to say that—"

Norris interrupts him, saying, "I love you. Your blood pressure is going through the roof here; you need to calm down."

"No." Jeff is not finished. "There's nothing wrong with my blood pressure. He puts out misinformation, which is unfair. He's a liar and a fraud, which is unfair."

Norris says good-bye after suggesting Jeff complain to Limbaugh's network and request that they hire another voice to counter Limbaugh—hers. The calls keep coming, but the hour of talk about talk radio is finished. "I love your opinion," says an exuberant Norris, "but I need to take a break for the news. Thanks, all of you."

# 8  Howard Stern Only Talks About Sex

*The dedication in Howard Stern's best-selling* book, *Private Parts,* concludes, ". . . and most of all, to my wife, Alison, who stuck with me through thick and thin, who never gave a shit about material things or put any pressure on me, who let me finger her on the first date, and who loved me before I had a radio show." That sophomoric, lascivious attitude pervades the volume. "Writing a book just might be the hardest thing I've ever done," the book begins, "besides trying to get laid in college." The first chapter is subtitled "Lesbians, Lesbians, Lesbians." It includes a transcript from one of Stern's radio shows, an exchange between Stern and a woman identified as Lisa. Lisa tells the story of her initial lesbian experience.

"She started caressing you," the book quotes Stern as prompting Lisa, "and then she did everything to you."

"Yeah," says Lisa.

"Did you do anything to her?" asks Stern's sidekick, Robin.

"She instructed me for about an hour."

"Oh, I can picture that," drools Stern. "Oh, man! My head's exploding!"

"Then she leaned over and kissed my mouth while she gently cupped my breasts." *Private Parts*—according to publishing industry accounts—sold more books almost immediately after its release in 1993 than any offering in the history of Simon and Schuster. In addition, the book became a bestseller faster than any previous book marketed by the venerable publishing house.

Long before America suffered from Howard Stern's fantasies, one Warren A. Sugarman, back in 1971, wrote a letter to the San Francisco office of the Federal Communications Commission. A carbon copy went to radio station KSAN.

*Gentlemen:*

I am not in the habit of writing letters of complaint—this is my first. However, I am fed up to the teeth with overpermissiveness and people "doing their own thing" to the point of my discomfort or inconvenience. I am not a prude nor a bluenose, BUT—:

Last night my wife and I retired earlier than usual and decided to try FM radio for a change (and a change it was!) We happened on KSAN-FM and tuned into a talk format show run by a "Doctor Hip." The subject of the show—with two instudio guests and countless telephone calls—was "Oral Sex." The guests on the program were proponents of this practice and spared no details nor restroom wall language in their conversation. I would be more graphic in my recounting of the program, but would probably be subject to arrest.

Suffice it to say that every crude term in the book was on the public airwaves. In seventeen years of marriage there have been few times my wife and I have blushed at each other, but this was one of them. We could (and should) have turned off the station, but just couldn't believe what we were hearing and then wanted to find out what kind of station we were hearing it on. I have no opinion one way or the other about the subject of discussion, but feel that a radio station is hardly the place to missionary for a particular sexual practice and the language was less than fit for public airwaves.

If it is possible, I would suggest that you procure a tape of Sunday evening from about 9:30 to 10:30 and get an idea of what goes on.

The FCC did just that and Metromedia, KSAN's owner at the time, and its lawyers went into action to deal with the radio history that was made the night of November 7, 1971. The first response came from Willis Duff, then the general manager of the radio station:

*Dear Mr. Sugarman:*

Thank you for your courtesy in copying us on your letter to the Federal Communications Commission. First, be assured, that Dr. [Eugene] Schoenfeld's program is not an exercise in "doing our own thing." Rather it is a continuing experiment in using the radio medium in the field of public health.

Dr. Schoenfeld is a recognized pioneer (via his columns, magazine articles, books, speaking engagements, etc.) in the field of disseminating practical—and direly needed—information and advice in those medical and psychological areas formerly considered taboo. The title of David Reuben's book "Everything You Always Wanted to Know About Sex, But Were Afraid to Ask" is a breakthrough of social observation simply by the inclusion of the phrase, "But Were Afraid to Ask." KSAN and Dr. Schoenfeld have tried to generate programs in which one need not be afraid to ask.

Inevitably when involved in the subject of sex, and specifically such subdivisions of the subject as oral sex (likewise venereal disease, homosexuality, etc.) there are bound to be trespasses into areas embarrassing to a certain percentage of our audience.

Generally the language used on Dr. Schoenfeld's program stays well within the bounds of medical terminology—a form of circumlocution that renders the most discomfiting subjects acceptable. In the program of November 7th, the variations from this practice with the use of the common vernacular are perhaps questionable from the point of view of taste, but not from the point of view of communication. (We know, for instance, that only a small percentage of most groups knows what "cunnilingus" means.)

Please be assured that Dr. Schoenfeld's program is under constant review here at KSAN and that we strive for that difficult balance of candor and good taste, while discussing subjects that are rarely discussed in the media. We, in no way, intend to "missionary" for any particular sexual practice.

I personally apologize for embarrassing you and your wife.

Duff signed the letter, "Cordially," but he was unsuccessful at placating Sugarman, who quickly wrote back:

While I find your position interesting (no double meaning intended!), I remain at a loss to comprehend your logic.

I have always been opposed to censorship of the media, of litera- ture, of expression, but can see no relevancy to the use of such terms as "sucking cock" or "eating pussy" on public airwaves. Likewise, I can hardly agree . . . that Miss St. James' friends' opinions that she "tastes good" [fall] under the classification of "education." The only education I received from her critique was a sudden distaste for yoghurt.

I do, however, agree with you that taboos should be removed from subjects such as sex and further agree that our culture is mak- ing progress in those areas. I feel strongly, though, that there is a happy medium somewhere between Latin terminology and the lan- guage found on bus station restroom walls.

I could care less if you do in fact wish to missionary for any sex- ual practice. I have been looking for something "new" for years. All my original ideas have been depicted graphically on pyramids and cave walls. All I ask is that you or any public medium use a mod- icum of good sense (if not taste) in your choice of syntax. My eleven-year-old daughter is hung up on your "music" and I'd hate to have some of your experts guide her emotional and/or social devel- opment.

So what was on that Sunday-night talk show that so troubled Mr. Sugarman? It took Duff some work to sort out an answer, and to learn that Sugarman had missed the most innovative program- ming of the evening—the broadcast of a live sex act that preceded the program Sugarman and his wife heard. On November 7, 1971, as Howard Stern was beginning his freshman year at Boston Uni-

versity and two years before Stern first tried his mouth on the
radio at the school's station, Dr. Eugene Schoenfeld, also known as
Dr. Hip, showed up at the KSAN radio studios for his regular air-
shift. At the time, KSAN rollicked with a free-form music format,
regular newscasts, and weekly talk shows. The station broadcast at
94.9 ("Jive 95" was our slogan) on the FM dial. (Since the demise
of that loose format, 94.9 has been filled with popular country
music.) Dr. Hip was famous with much of the KSAN audience for
his *Berkeley Barb* newspaper column, which addressed readers'
health concerns with directness and language that appealed to the
California counterculture of the times. He approached his radio
show with the same candor and vigor.

"Last week we were speaking to a lady from a Berkeley clinic
for treating sexual problems," Schoenfeld begins his show that
infamous night. "This week, I thought we would talk not about
sexual hang-ups but about more or less normal sexuality—whatever that is. We're going to talk with Margo St. James about ways
of making it a bit better. I guess that's a way of capsulizing what
we're going to be talking about: making good things better."

Schoenfeld introduces his guest to the radio audience—a guest
famous for founding a trade union for prostitutes and for engaging
in high-profile self-promotional stunts dealing with her own sexuality. "I work for pussy power," St. James explains to Schoenfeld.

"Pussy power," acknowledges Schoenfeld. "What is"—he
pauses and tries again—"how would you define that?"

"Pussy power is woman's sexual potential. It's infinite actually,
I think."

Schoenfeld then asks her, "Well, what's wrong?" because she
had been billed as coming on the air to explain a routine she calls
sexercise. "Do you think this potential isn't being exercised, so to
speak?"

She then launches into her analysis of the problem. "True,
yeah," she says. "The frozen pelvis abounds in this country and
they just shed their girdles, this last generation, and the women's
muscles are still unworked. Very few women have what men refer

to as 'snappy pussies.' " St. James knows she is pushing the boundaries. "What do you call 'em on this show, anyway?"

Seeking to ground the discussion in safer language for radio, Schoenfeld suggests, "Well, on this show we'd probably say that you believe most women don't have full development of the muscles which surround the vagina."

"Right," agrees the frolicking St. James as Warren Sugarman settles down for a night of radio listening with his wife.

Schoenfeld asks, "What kind of exercises would a lady do to strengthen the outer muscles?"

St. James is ready with an answer. "I think the best thing for her to do, of course, is practice alone at first, and insert a finger so she can tell when those muscles are closed, when they're tight and when they're not, and do this until she reaches a point of awareness so that she can tell just by thinking about that muscle what it's doing." The conversation continues for several minutes about specific techniques for such exercise or, as St James says, "what's necessary to have a true snapper." She advocates dancing and running. "I love to run; I feel very free when I'm running. I especially like running on the beach in front of your house."

"Um," deadpans the doctor, "I like it, too. I like to see you running down the beach."

"I'd like to be able to run naked down your beach," offers St. James, "but so far I haven't done it."

"There are people there with telescopes," cautions the doctor, "who get uptight at things like that."

"Yeah," she agrees.

"But I wouldn't care," he advises and plays a commercial. The show meanders along, and Schoenfeld offers the audience a chance to ask St. James questions.

"You were talking before about loosening up the lines of communications," starts the first caller, a man. "It's kind of hard to talk, you know, but I really feel that this would be an appropriate time for me to find something out here."

"All right," Schoenfeld encourages him, "what would you like to find out?"

"About cunnilingus."

"What about it?" prods the radio doctor.

"Is the woman there? I forget her name."

"Her name is Margo."

"Margo," the caller asks, "what is it that's really the best way to get that real good, you know, relationship in that act, so that I can really know that I'm getting the full amount of it, 'cause I feel I'm not now."

"Well, how do you do it? Do you do it sixty-nine or one at a time?"

By now Warren Sugarman is paying closer attention to his radio.

"Ah," sighs the troubled man on the line, "well, it's kind of hard. Sometimes it's sixty-nine and sometimes it's not, you know. I kind of have to get into it so that I can really get her interested in the same way, you know, so that she just doesn't stay off to the side. I feel that if I could, you know, manipulate it in the right way—because sometimes I feel that she's riding wrong on me and she's not really into it, like she's detached or something, you know, and maybe I could do something to turn her on more."

St. James needs more information. "You're confusing me," she says. "I don't know if you're talking about balling or eating."

"Yeah, right," the caller explains, "that's what I'm talking about—eating it."

Host Schoenfeld jumps in at this point to facilitate understanding between his guest and the caller. "It sounds as if he wants to know, when he has a feeling that his lady isn't really into it, he wants to know what he should do."

"And then," hopes the caller, "she'd ball me back."

"Oh, okay." St. James knows what to say now. "Okay. I think one of the most valuable techniques insofar as keeping a woman in condition to enjoying a full vagina is the insertion of a finger at the same time that you're giving her head."

"Right." The caller and probably most of the audience are paying close attention.

"And you know, don't be too vigorous."

"I know, I know," is the caller's enthusiastic response. "You've got to watch the teeth."

"Well, yeah," agrees St. James, "and stubble if you shave."

"I do have a moustache," the caller worries.

"Well," she soothes him, "a moustache is fine. I think if you practice in the queen's position, which is you lying between her legs on your stomach, that you could concentrate on the same spot. Two people concentrating on the same spot should get better results if you're having trouble that way—with her attention wandering."

"Right," he says, "those were a couple of good pointers, definitely."

But St. James isn't finished. "Try to create a vacuum with your mouth."

"Yeah."

"Not a very big vacuum," she says, "just a slight one."

"Yeah, I've already done that with my chin, to a certain extent."

"Well, your chin isn't too good to use," she cautions, "especially if you shave, and it's bony, and—"

"That's the trouble, yeah," he interrupts. "So the lips are always better then."

Warren Sugarman and his wife are listening closely now as St. James instructs. "It's not too good to move your head around too much, unless she's really in heavy throes of passion, and then you can get more excited and more vigorous, but keep it gentle. Exercise your tongue so it doesn't get too tired, so you can do it for at least a half an hour, you know."

"Yeah, right." He's happy. "Hey, thanks a lot!"

"You're welcome."

"Okay. 'Bye-'bye."

Dr. Schoenfeld chimes in with, "Hope you can use that information to good advantage."

They take another call on another subject before St. James returns to oral sex. "A complaint I hear from men who are reluctant to participate in oral sex," she tells Schoenfeld, "is that it smells bad to them."

"Well, the lady must have an infection, then, if that's true," he answers, "because, normally, one of the purposes of the secretions and the odors is to attract men. In other species we can see this very clearly—in the dog when the bitch is in heat and many males are flocking around."

"Yeah," says St. James. "I think if they just got down there and burrowed around for a while, they'd adapt. They'd get used to it. I know people that dig it. Some guys say the funkier the better, you know. It's really real. You know, I believe in bathing and I know the hairs collect smells and all that. You have to wash the hair very well. Women should take a taste test of themselves every once in a while," she recommends, "and eat a lot of yogurt."

At this point Warren Sugarman is taking notes for his FCC complaint letter.

"I think yogurt has the same bacteria that should be present there in order for it to taste good," opines St. James, allowing that she's "never tried putting yogurt in directly, but it might be something."

"It might be something," acknowledges the doctor without judgment, simply asking, "plain or blueberry?"

"Straight plain yogurt," she says, "none of that sugared stuff. Lay off that sugar. Healthy yogurt. Unpasteurized, if they can get it."

The doctor moves past the theoretical yogurt douches and asks, "What about the many women who are leery about participating in oral sex?"

"Well, I must admit," she says easily, "that eating pussy is easier than sucking cock."

As Warren Sugarman starts writing his letter, Dr. Schoenfeld gives a worried look to his operating engineer at the radio station and asks, "Is that all right?"

"It's all right," says Bonnie Simmons, the engineer, just back from the dentist and claiming later to be filled with painkilling Percodan.

"You could have said 'penis,' " complains Schoenfeld. All of this dialogue is still on the air, entertaining and informing most of the audience.

"Oh," says St. James without complaint, "Penis." They continue their talk.

"Why is it easier?" he wants to know. "A lot of men complain that it's not easier because the clitoris is so small they have trouble finding it."

"Oh, well, they just have to look," says St. James, "if they want to find out where it is, you know. A lot of 'em are afraid to look."

"You recommend strong light?"

"No, but just enough to maybe see—a little, teeny, tiny bit."

"What would you say," inquires the doctor next, "to a woman who said, 'Gee, I'd like to try that, but I feel somehow there's something wrong with—' "

St. James helps him, "So demeaning and debasing and all."

"There's something wrong," the doctor continues, "with putting my mouth on a penis. This is reinforced, of course, by so many things. Like in a way, the worst curse you could say, right, is a ten-letter word that busted Lenny Bruce, right?"

"Yeah, right, yeah," offers St. James, "ends in -er, right?"

Schoenfeld makes it clear that he knows how close he's coming to trouble. "Yeah, right," he tells St. James, "and it's not going to bust us, okay? That's one of the worst things that you could call someone. I think because of that kind of attitude a lot of ladies are reluctant. Do you find that an unpleasant chore?"

"No, not at all," she tells him. "I certainly did in the beginning, though, when I harbored some hostilities toward men. But I got to the point where I almost would—when I was hooking—I got to the point where I would rather suck a guy off than ball him. It was less intimate in a way, but more intimate from another aspect, you know. But at least it was away from his face, which is where most people communicate. So it was really less personal and probably I felt it was cleaner than his mouth—some of my customers even drank and smoked and smelled foul and tasted terrible."

"Yeah," Schoenfeld concurs, "cigarettes and alcohol can really turn you off."

"That's really bad, yeah," says St. James. "But I got so I really liked it and I like it still."

It was time for another commercial, followed by the first woman caller of the evening. Warren Sugarman is probably turning up his radio as she says, "I wanted to ask Margo what kind of exercises you can do so that you don't get tired when you're sucking your man off. Like, my mouth always gets tired."

"Hmm," considers the guest expert, "sometimes you can hardly avoid that if he's got a big one and if your mouth has to stay open too wide for a long period of time."

"Well," asks the caller, "do you know if there's anything to do? I have a fairly small mouth and, you know, it gives him pleasure and I like to do it, but I get very tired. Do you know if there's anything I could do for that?"

"You could practice on carrots and cucumbers," suggests St. James, "something like that, you know, to strengthen your mouth muscles."

This was captivating and riveting radio. It served the listeners with valid information that they sought, and it served the needs of KSAN—a commercial radio station seeking ratings—because this was the kind of information that lured listeners to stay tuned to the station. And it offended Warren Sugarman. After a year of legal battling, Metromedia prevailed—KSAN's license was not jeopardized.

What the FCC and Warren Sugarman did not learn was that prior to her candid interview with Dr. Hip, St. James and host Paul Krassner acted out fellatio in the radio station studio while Krassner was broadcasting.

"Five minutes before I was due to sign off," Krassner remembers in his memoir *Confessions of a Raving, Unconfined Nut*, "in walked Gene Schoenfeld, whose 'Dr. Hip' advice program would follow mine, and his guest, Margo St. James. I couldn't help but notice that she was trying to unzip my fly, which was held up by a safety pin, and I realized that she intended to give me head while I was on the air."

The story is an integral chapter in the history we KSAN alumni keep alive about the radio station's lore, and details include an extra microphone being dragged over to the critical spot so that St. James's efforts could be broadcast to the audience.

"Be careful, the zipper's broken," Krassner writes that he told St. James.

"She unpinned and unzipped me," his account continues, "then began to perform fellatio. 'Would you please say something so that feminists who are listening will understand the context?' She looked up and said, 'I'm doing this of my own volition.' I maintained my composure, and continued talking. The radio audience had no way of knowing for sure what was actually happening. I finally said good-bye to the listeners—'It's been a pleasure being with you'—then gave the proper station identification. 'This is KSAN in San Francisco,' I announced, 'the station that blows your mind.' "

=====

Defining obscenity and pornography is always tricky. For Warren Sugarman, Dr. Hipp's program crossed the line. On stations around the country, the *Don and Mike Show* plays over car radios during the afternoon rush hour. Don and Mike and Don Imus, like Howard Stern, are under contract to Infinity Broadcasting, along with G. Gordon Liddy and the Greaseman. Infinity owns radio stations across America as well as the Mutual Broadcasting System (radio home of Larry King and Jim Bohannon) and the NBC Radio Network (the carrier of Bruce Williams). In one broadcast Don and Mike solicited callers to get on the air and describe which of their wife's relatives they'd like to kill. "Come on," encouraged the team, "wouldn't you like to put a gun in somebody's mouth and pull the trigger, just for the sport of it?"[1]

=====

The physical airwaves over America belong to the public, so radio stations are licensed by the federal government and operated with restrictions not faced by print media. The relationship between First Amendment rights, free enterprise, and obscenity as defined by the FCC, all in the context of the raging national success of shows such as Stern's, Don and Mike's, Don Imus's, and the Greaseman's, is confusing.

Exactly what cannot be said on the radio is elusive except for seven specific words, identified by the Federal Communications Commission and made famous in a routine by comedian George Carlin. WBAI in New York City played a recording of the routine, was cited by the FCC for violating its restrictions, fought the commission in court, and lost. Now known collectively as the "seven dirty words," even they *(shit, fuck, piss, cunt, cocksucker, motherfucker,* and *tits)* can be broadcast if their use can be proven not to be gratuitous.

=======

Much less offends other listeners. "Dear Management," Lorraine Black wrote to WRC on November 2, 1993, in script easily identified as that of an older woman. "While [it] was informative," she complained about a computer show, "I was offended by the female's use of 'damn' in her conversation. She immediately said, 'Oops.' " Judging from the rest of the letter, Ms. Black must not listen to Howard Stern or Don Imus, or any of the dozens of copycat shock hosts operating around the country. She probably does not know they exist, or she would not be wasting her time complaining about a computer show. "I feel that this kind of slow invasion of a talk show with little slips of the tongue (profanity) cannot be tolerated." Black herself put "profanity" in parentheses, adding "It's like a slowly spreading cancer that eventually kills the body." She concludes her complaint, "I do hope she is reprimanded this time and fired if it continues."

=======

On a weekend morning back in the early seventies, a journeyman radio news reporter was asked to fill in for a talk show host who was late for his program. With that personnel adjustment, radio history was made. Don Chamberlain took over the KNEW microphones in Oakland that morning with a few simple questions addressed to the vast potential audience of bored and frustrated San Francisco Bay Area housewives.

"What is the most unusual place you've ever done it?" asked Don with his charming voice, a cross between probing newsman and lascivious dirty old man.

Within hours, Don was fired by KNEW management. By the middle of the next week, the pile of positive mail to the station was so high that he was rehired, removed from the newsroom, and given his own show. Named *California Girls,* the program enjoyed a decade-long successful run. It laid the groundwork for a cadre of copycats and the still-successful Dr. Ruth.

# 9  Larry King: Too Busy for Homework

*By the beginning of 1994, Larry King was making* it abundantly clear that he was bored with his radio show, a show that made him a household name, a name he was able to harness to develop best-selling books and a CNN television show. Early in the morning of January 17, King, along with most Los Angelenos, was shaken awake by the earthquake that devastated the nation's second largest city. While radio, television, and print journalists were rushing from around the world to report on the disaster, Larry King was running for the airport. He wanted to get out of town quickly, back to the relative security of Washington.[1]

The earthquake hit on a Monday. Larry King missed his show that Monday and again on Tuesday, blaming his absence on the shaking ground under him. He finally returned to the air from the Mutual studios in Crystal City, Virginia, on Wednesday. Official word from the network was that the show was impossible to produce from L.A. because damage to the Mutual studios in Culver City affected the line that King would have used to hear his callers. That excuse was just a lame attempt at damage control. Network producers knew that King wasn't on the air from Los Angeles because he was bored with his radio show. One of the exciting realities of the radio medium is that it is so simple. A hustling talk show host can conduct a talk radio show from the field with nothing more than a telephone. King could have done his show from a telephone booth.

"I have one regret about that earthquake," a senior producer at Mutual told me a few days later as he railed about King's dismissal of his radio duties, "that the cocksucker was not in that apartment house in Northridge." He was referring to a building that collapsed, killing many. "I'd love to see him fucking dead."[2]

Abandoning the earthquake story was just the latest in a string of abuses King was heaping on his radio handlers. He was demanding to work only half time, and when he bothered to show up for work, he sounded bored and unprepared, stumbling through his three hours on coast-to-coast radio. Radio stations carrying his program were watching their ratings sink; the network was losing affiliates.

"He really believes his shit don't stink," spat out the Mutual producer. "He really believes he made Bill Clinton president."

A few weeks later King made it clear he was disgusted with his callers, the lifeblood of a telephone talk show. A man called from Mount Olive, North Carolina, complaining about King's attitude. The Carolinian called King snide, sarcastic, impatient. King agreed with the criticism, blaming his audience.

"Since I switched from nighttime radio to daytime radio, while they're making a lot of money"—presumably he was speaking about his network—"and I love radio, although a lot about radio disappoints me, I love the business I'm in. I love the fact that it's such an educating, entertaining business—it's become a lot contrived and calculated and it's not my kind of stuff," whatever that means. But King continued to set up his attack, his voice rising. "And from that, with all these right-wing, and not just right-wing, wacko radio people on, I mean everybody and his—" He interrupted himself for a joke. "I ran into a guy who didn't have a show. What this has produced is, as with most volume, lower stan-

dards. I'm pretty high on standards," he congratulated himself and
went on for the kill.

"The call-in quality of the afternoon caller that this show
receives—"

Mount Olive interrupted with, "You think is going down!"

"Heh, heh, heh," said Larry King, "has reduced considerably to
the nighttime caller. So, I know the caller is only 1 percent of the
audience. I've never called a show. I've never written a letter to the
editor. I know they are not indicative of the entire audience. I
know there are millions of listeners. But I'll tell you something.
The quality of the caller has diminished to the point—" For a
moment he loses his train of thought, or his ability to articulate it.
"Am I disappointed in the quality of the caller," he asks himself,
answering, "Yes." He asks himself another. "Is my reaction to
them normal for me?" Again, King responds to himself. "The
answer is yes, since I am not a phony."

=====

King enjoys calling his the first nationwide talk show. It is not.
Herb Jebco was probably the first to host such a show, on KSL
out of Salt Lake City in the 1970s. But the image King created with
his audience is—like that produced by Limbaugh and most other
successful talk show hosts—larger than life, based on blatant self-
promotion. For example, King simply told listeners that his was
the first coast-to-coast show. Most had no reference point for dis-
believing him. In my role as WRC program director, I dispatched a
colleague of mine, radio producer Evan Haning, to spend an afternoon in the fall of 1993 talking talk radio with King, taping the
session for promotional announcements to air on WRC.

"Yeah, it did start with us," King told Haning about national
talk shows. "Back in 1977, late in the year, a guy named Ed Little
who ran the Mutual Broadcasting System came to me in Miami.
He'd known my work there, and he said, 'I think national talk
radio can work.' I said, 'You've got to be kidding,' because talk
radio is so localized. He said, 'But I think if we get a good host,

and touch a lot of bases [it can work]. The country's so close that Phoenix is interested in the same thing that Washington's interested in. Let's try it all night, and we'll roll a little dice and we'll try a three-year contract.' The show debuted on January 30, 1978, from midnight until five-thirty on 28 stations, and before we switched to daytime, we were up to 430."

In fact, in 1977 I was working in the Mutual news department. C. Edward Little was the president of the company and Mutual did indeed hire Larry King. But it was not to conduct the first national talk show or even to conduct Mutual's first national talk show. Such historical details may seem somewhat inconsequential, but in businesses such as talk radio and journalism historical revisionism is an abuse of credibility. Before Ed Little contacted King for the Mutual job, longtime talk radio host Long John Nebel was talking through the nighttime hours over Mutual, assisted by his wife, Candy Jones. It was when Nebel died and Little needed a new host for the show that he sought out King.

"Yes," King told Haning as they talked at Mutual's Crystal City studios in suburban Virginia, just across the Potomac from Washington, "I guess it was the forerunner of all this massive amount of network talk now." As he talked about his past, he decided to claim not only being the first but also being a hero. "And I guess in retrospect, it was one of the saviors of AM radio, because most people who want to hear music, they listen to FM. When I want to hear music, I listen to FM. And AM—a lot of wonderful stations around the country were feeling the heat. Talk is one of the answers." Although more and more FM stations are succeeding with a wide variety of talk radio styles, King is correct. The poorer fidelity of AM radio is not a hindrance to spoken word programming.

"Talk's expensive," he said, continuing to explain his value to broadcasting, claiming syndicated shows such as his allowed the rubes in the provinces to transcend their isolation. "You can't expect Des Moines, Iowa, to have six great talk show hosts living in its city. So taking people who are pretty good at what they do, from New York or Washington or Los Angeles, is a good idea."

A consistent criticism of King is that he handles his guests cautiously, that his questions are almost always softballs. "I don't know what softball means," he said defensively when asked about his interviewing technique. "I ask good questions. I've been asking them all my life. I'm an interviewer. In fact, I never thought of myself as a talk show host. I've always done the Larry King show, been doing it since 1960. I ask questions. In fact, throughout the sixties, I never took a phone call. I would do three to four hours of radio every night, with three or four different guests. I like long phone interviews. I listen to the answers; I ask short questions. I leave myself out of it."

He called attention to how people making news or needing publicity—such as Ross Perot—have made use of his show. "We certainly made a lot of news over the last few years. Softball I guess would be, 'Tell me about your latest movie.' I've never said, 'Tell me about your latest movie.' I am interested in what people do. I am not a confrontationalist, that is, I don't like arguing. I never learn when I hear arguments. Arguments are okay, they have a place, but they get to be kind of predictable. I like what I do. I do what I do the best I can do it. I can't judge what others think. But I've never thought of the term," he protests one more time. "I don't even know what softball means."

Softball or not, King was correct that his show affected the national agenda. During the 1992 presidential election campaign, King was soaring as a multimedia celebrity. His radio show was just an adjunct to his life as a television interviewer with his own CNN show, a newspaper columnist for *USA Today,* a best-selling author, and a hit on the speaker circuit around the country. After Perot announced his candidacy on King's television talk show, talk radio was abuzz with Perot's rise to fame. "Not long ago we were treated something like Rodney Dangerfield, we didn't get no respect," said WRKO host Jerry Williams after the Perot appearance with King. "Ross Perot changed that."[3] The rest of the media were forced by the Perot announcement on the King show, and the interest of talk radio hosts and their callers, to pay attention to Perot. Perhaps if King were more confrontational and adversarial, guests such as Ross Perot would not feel comfortable about joining King on the air and the national debate would suffer one less outlet.

In *On the Line,* his book on the effect of talk shows on the 1992 election, Larry King called the influence of his and similar programs part of a political revolution. "It grew out of the public's distrust of, and disgust with, their poll-driven leaders—and their perceived coconspirators in the traditional press," wrote King in the book's introduction. He asserted that "the public saw the traditional press as snide, frenzy-driven trivializers who were contributing to the erosion of their democracy. Waning confidence in the media rivaled the public's anger at Washington."

In his analysis of the media effect on the 1992 election, *Los Angeles Times* correspondent Tom Rosenstiel worried about encroachment of personalities such as King on news gathering and dissemination. "The rise of King and other quasi-journalists," wrote Rosenstiel in his book *Strange Bedfellows,* "leaves the process more open to manipulation, innuendo, and rumor. The masters of talk have clout, but they operate by different standards."

Quasi-journalism is an intriguing description for the work done by King and his fellow talk show hosts. When he was defending his abandonment of the Los Angeles earthquake story, King protested loudly about being shackled with the burdens of journalism. Mutual's president at the time, Jack Clements, supported King's dodge. "He's not a newsman," Clements told the *Washington Post*'s radio writer Jeffrey Yorke.[4] In *On the Line,* King analyzed his role without apology while acknowledging, "Because I am not a journalist, I do not always ask the follow-up question a reporter would ask."

King's colleague Rush Limbaugh exercises no such dodge. On the contrary, while he denigrates traditional mainstream journalists as without credibility, he embraces the title for himself. On one broadcast,[5] after he signed a controversial agreement to be an advertising spokesman for Florida orange juice, Limbaugh claimed he had received what he called a "news tip" about an attempt to get him out of Florida. It wasn't clear whether he was referring to an attempt to keep his radio show out of Florida, end his relationship with Florida citrus growers, or physically keep him out of Florida. "As a good journalist," Limbaugh rhapsodized about himself, he was going to refrain from passing along further details about the incident to his radio audience until he confirmed the so-called tip.

The *Washington Post*'s press critic Howard Kurtz, in his book *Media Circus,* called Larry King "a great schmoozer who makes no pretense of being a newsman." Kurtz cited questions King asked President Bush during the 1992 as "friendly questions." If King needs a definition of "softball," he should take a look at his own questions for Bush, collected in Kurtz's book: "You like campaigning?" "Is Millie writing another book?"

As King talked with Haning, he insisted that his interview techniques are designed specifically to develop details about the subject. "I can't remember the last time I used the word 'I' in an interview," he said. "It has no place. In fact, you cannot give me an example where 'I' has a place other than self-aggrandizement, other than feeding your own ego. Why should you have to say 'I'? Another thing, why should you have to ask a question in five sentences? Any good question should take one or two sentences. And if you're really good, and really curious, I mean really curious, I would like to do a show where the door opens, and the guest sits down, and that's where we all learn who the guest is."

That statement was classic Larry King. King attempts to make his lack of preparation an asset. He has announced repeatedly that he engages in no research before interviews, no study of the personality or subject matter involved. His excuse is that by ignoring the type of preparation most interviewers—most journalists—consider crucial to a successful exchange with a source, he approaches the guest with the same type of questions the audience, supposedly similarly unprepared, would ask given the chance. "The basic things that I think everyone would like to know are the very things that the news reporters miss," King explained in his autobiographical book *Tell Me More.* "They're afraid to look dumb.

Dumb questions. They're dumb because the person asking the question is admitting he or she doesn't have the slightest idea what the answer is."

His philosophy is a creative excuse for avoiding study before interviews. But it cannot remove the reality that his work is journalistic in nature. King and both his backers and critics can protest as much as they wish, but King and other talk show hosts who deal with political and social issues cannot hide from the journalistic responsibilities of their endeavors simply by claiming that they are not journalists.

Although King refuses to call himself a journalist, he describes the journalism of his shows in *On the Line*. " 'Talk show democracy is certainly not without risk or flaws," he wrote. "Our callers ask better, more serious questions than some in the press give them credit for. But some candidates and their handlers still think of talk shows as a way to avoid tough press grillings. Talk shows should supplement the campaign press, not replace it. There's room enough for everyone."

King told Evan Haning as their talk continued, "I just learned who's the guest on my show today, right now. And I'll be going on soon. I like that. I'm curious. I think you have to be intrinsically curious [to be a good interviewer]. If you're overly ego-involved, you're not a good interviewer. You do not want to sit next to me on an airplane, because I'm going to find out an awful lot about you on an airplane. But I also want to know why the pilot wants to fly the plane, why the bus driver wants to drive the bus, why the movie projectionist wants to show movies. What do they do all day? What does the movie projectionist do in the mall? When he punches [the film] up, does he stay with it, does he watch it? What's the pay in that job, I wonder. What are the rewards?"

More insight into King's show and his personality came from the next question: What type of person does King think listens to talk radio, to his show? "You know," he said, "I never met a good host who thought much about that." The answer is baffling. How can a performer or a journalist not be curious about who is out there and why they are listening? "It's hard to explain," said King.

"You do the show for yourself, in that if I start going on saying, 'What would the listener like?' I then start becoming the hack, like the hack novelist thinks, 'What does the reader want to read?' The good novelist writes for his or her pleasure. So I ask what I'm curious about, and hopefully enough of the listeners are curious about it too, to want to listen. Hopefully, I appeal to an intelligent audience."

King used a story to illustrate his point. "Jackie Gleason told me once, 'I could have intercourse Saturday night at eight o'clock live on CBS and I will win the rating period. So what? What does that prove?'" It is a lesson King said he followed with his radio show. "I've never copped out. I've never had to do other than what my talent takes me to. I've always had management support. I've never needed a gimmick." He obliquely attacked Howard Stern, "I don't have to talk about sex." He similarly went after Rush Limbaugh. "I don't have to get on a soapbox. I don't have to put down people. I can be funny.

"But do I think about the audience? I hope the audience enjoys it. I can't strangle them and make them enjoy it. I hope they're intelligent enough to appreciate what is really good conversation and good curiosity at work. And I have always been very proud of the show in that I think that every day we produce the best guests in America, good callers, good questions, the show moves along, and it's not predictable. I like diversity. That's my cup of tea. I feed off it. But I don't sit with a picture of the audience in my head."

King said he looks for four qualities in a guest. "If they can explain what they do very well, if they have a passion for what they do, if they have a sense of humor about what they do, and a little bit of anger about what they do. If you're listening to me talking to someone with those four traits, you will not hit the dial."

He's a great schmoozer, said Howard Kurtz about King, and much of that schmoozing takes place in Washington and King's favorite restaurant, Duke Ziebert's. "I think it's the prettiest, probably along with Paris, the prettiest capital city in the world," he said about his adopted city. "Washington's the best place I've ever lived. I've lived in New York and Miami and here. I love it. I like the people, I like the importance, I like being around where the action is. I love lunch," he said, stressing the word. "Lunch is the best time of day. I would never want to work at lunch. I feel sorry for people who have to work at lunch. Who would ever want to be on the air when it's lunch? Important things are happening at Duke's. Deals get done at lunch. Decisions are made at lunch. This is a great lunch town. Washington is super lunchville."

With no prodding, King rhapsodized about Duke's. "It's a hangout; it has the pickles on the tables and good rolls; it lends itself to good conversation. The spacing between the tables is excellent. The lighting is excellent. Duke is a wonderful raconteur. And they're a dying breed in America, the Duke Zieberts. You know when they leave us, there are no replacements. Basically, Duke's has an atmosphere. Food critics often miss that. See, food critics come in and say, 'The carrots were a little overcooked.' It doesn't matter if the carrots were overcooked if Marlin Fitzwater is eating the carrots with you."

The Larry Kings—the softball-throwing schmoozers—are a dying breed in America, too.

═══════

The rivalry that develops between hosts—real and staged—is often amusing. Los Angeles host and feminist lawyer Gloria Allred calls Limbaugh's style of humor "harmful to women." Limbaugh ignores invitations from Larry King to appear as a guest on his show. Stern encourages his fans to call other talk shows and insert Stern's name gratuitously into conversations with competing hosts. And a radio actor on the Imus show makes regular appearances as Rush Limbaugh, mocking him with stinging parodies of his hate-mongering. "I like friends with white faces and a burning cross that you know chases the blues away," the actor sang on February 14, 1994, to the tune of a popular country music song with the catchy refrain, "I've got friends in low places."

Even when supporting Stern's fight against the fines the FCC was levying against Stern for his so-called indecent broadcasts, Imus was attacking his competition. "Stern should be able to say whatever he likes no matter what puddle of putrescence he happens to be wallowing in at the moment," said Imus on WFAN and his growing group of nationwide affiliates in January 1994. But at the same time Imus made it abundantly obvious that he was no fan of Stern's. "This nitwit couldn't have distinguished the Bill of Rights from his utility bill until somebody pointed it out to him about twenty minutes ago. To cast him as some guarantor of the Constitution is so preposterous, it's laughable. The plain truth is that Howard Stern is a vile, misogynistic, xenophobic punk who panders to the worst instincts in the worst people and even to the worst instincts in some people who should know better."

Stern and Imus have been swinging at each other for years. In his book Stern recounts his ratings war with Imus. "My ratings roared and I dragged Shit Stain down to a one share." Stern quotes Imus in the book as saying, "If Howard Stern beats me, I'll eat a dead dog's penis."

For a *New York Times* story about "The I-Man," commemorating his return to the air after suffering a collapsed lung, Imus told reporter Richard Sandomir, "People perceive me as Howard Stern. It's not the case. I'm Howard Stern with a vocabulary. I'm the man he wishes he could be."[6] Those remarks elicited an immediate response from a *Times* reader and a talk radio aficionado who calls himself Hans Frederic Strumpfhalter and identifies himself further on his letterhead as "Citizen of the World." As is the case with many letters from talk show listeners, this one carries no return address, but it is symptomatic of the extent to which talk shows and their hosts affect listeners.

*Dear Mr. Sandomir,*

   I read your article about the radio personality, Don Imus, with a great deal of relish. You are obviously on the station's payroll, you are getting a blow-job from Charles McCord [Imus's sidekick news reporter], or you have no concept of reality.

   Don Imus is an abusive washed-up has-been, who has little talent and commands no respect, no ratings and poor sponsorship, which is the ultimate test in the marketplace.

Your pandering to this has-been may be an omen that your career will soon go the way of the Dodo bird and Don Imus. You challenged nothing that vomiting, urinating drug addict said. I hope he urinates on you. You can eat his vomit, you unworthy sycophant.

The FCC doesn't go after Don Imus because he is not a threat. Howard Stern is viewed as a threat because he makes you think about the phoniness of our society. Howard Stern is an iconoclast that upsets people. He is cerebral. His so-called vulgarity is merely a hoax that makes you look at other things that are vulgar. Movies like "Friday the 13th" are normal, but Penis and Vagina jokes are going to destroy our society? With metal detectors being placed daily outside our schools, Howard Stern is a real threat that the government needs to quash? Right??? Everyone has a penis or a vagina. Children joke about it with their parents as a natural part of life. But obviously, while you are getting sucked off by Don Imus, you don't have any balls! You should be ashamed of yourself.

Go fucketh thyself, pansy!!!

The letter is signed, "Sincerely yours."
An industry joke addresses this competition.[7]

Larry King dies and goes to heaven.

"Welcome," St. Peter greets King.

Larry says, "I'm excited to be here. I had this guy named Limbaugh on my back."

"No problem," says St. Peter. "No problem if he comes here. Heaven is a big place."

St. Peter then takes Larry King on a tour. Up on a hill King sees a beautiful mansion. They go inside. Over an ornate throne is a huge sign reading RUSH LIMBAUGH.

"Oh, no." King groans.

"Larry, don't worry," St. Peter comforts him. "This is God's throne. He only thinks he's Rush sometimes."

"What do you make of the success of Rush Limbaugh and Howard Stern?" a caller asked Larry King during his radio show as his ratings continued to descend during the year he worked afternoons.[8]

"They're both freakish phenomena," deadpanned King, "in that one appeals to the right and to the anger in America and does so in a fashion of putting down many of the people who I regard as easy targets. It's easy to make fun of the homeless, they don't have a good weapon back." Finished with Limbaugh, he acknowledged success on the radio by competitors is good for the industry. "I like people in the business to do well." Then he went for Stern. "I have yet to figure out what Howard's talent is. I mean, I know some funny people. I knew Lenny Bruce well. I don't get it."

======

Limbaugh claims similar ignorance. "I only know what people tell me about Howard Stern, which isn't much," he told *Playboy*.[9] "Honestly, I do not listen to other radio shows. I never have. I don't want to get ideas from anybody else about how to do something."

"He's such an asshole," Stern told Mim Udovitch for an interview in *Details* magazine[10] when she asked him about Limbaugh. "And judging from his history—he was in radio and the most creative idea [he had] was to be a disc jockey. When that didn't work out for him, he left radio. And then about four years ago, he figured out all the freedoms I pioneered and went: 'Oh, now I know what to do, I'll give my views on things.' I think I may have spawned him, that big fathead jerk. How much do you think that head of his weighs? It's the size of a fucking pumpkin."

======

On the evening of November 7, 1993, one of the most dramatic announcers in broadcasting, Don Pardo, with the accompaniment of an equally dramatic drumroll, told a nationwide audience, "Live, from Chicago, it's the 1993 Radio Hall of Fame Awards saluting radio's biggest stars on radio's biggest night and recalling the magical moments that Americans have experienced on the journey across the radio dial!" What followed, at first, was a typical self-congratulatory industry awards presentation.

Larry King was the master of ceremonies for the evening. "Good evening. It's a great pleasure to be here," he said. "I bring you greetings from Ross Perot." A year after the presidential election he was still trading on the fact that Perot had used King's show to announce his own candidacy. "He called me this morning," said King, "and asked me to extend his best to all of you, but we have to be out in half an hour. He just bought the building." Some laughter followed.

But the real joke was still to come. About halfway through the program, King introduced the next award presenter. "We thank you all very much for joining us," he said. "To present the award to the syndicated personality of the year, we call on a lady who has become one of the legends in the business. I worked with her years ago in Miami. We both worked at WIOD. We were on back-to-back. She's gone on to phenomenal success. Her show now airs in almost two hundred markets in the United States and internationally, She's one terrific lady. Here she is, the lovely Sally Jessy Raphael!"

"Considering who the recipient is," Raphael began her comments about Rush Limbaugh, "he calls women like me 'femi-Nazis,' so I will read this as written for me." The crowd grew quiet, not expecting Limbaugh to be criticized as he was being honored by his industry. "Please note," Raphael said about the award, "that it does not express my opinion" There were some scattered cheers.

"Ya gotta admit," she said before reading the citation, "putting Rush Limbaugh, Sally Jessy Raphael, and Larry King on the stage means that radio makes strange bedfellows." She then blithely and dryly read the hyperbole about Limbaugh as written by the awards committee. About halfway through the prepared material, when she first read Limbaugh's name, the crowd cheered. She stopped them, saying coldly, "Twenty-five seconds more of copy. Give me a moment."

The next day, Limbaugh used his program to lash back at Raphael, suggesting "her noses were out of joint." (Rumor in the industry is that she is the recipient of plastic surgery.) And a few days later,[11] Bruce Dumont, the Radio Hall of Fame president, appeared on WRC in Washington to answer questions from talk show host Mark Davis and the radio audience about the incident. The Radio Hall of Fame was established in 1988 and operates under the auspices of Dumont's Chicago Museum of Broadcast Communications. Dumont is host of a weekly syndicated radio show, *Inside Politics*.

"Sally Jessy Raphael was aware who she was going to present," a somewhat irritated-sounding Dumont said. "Her producers had communicated to our producers how excited she was about the prospect, because she and Rush taped in the same studios and they're both multimedia properties. Every piece of information that had been communicated from her producers to our producers was how excited she was. I spoke personally with her producer on Friday, before the broadcast. She said, 'Well, Sally's still going to present to Rush, right?' I said, 'Yes.'

"Sally Jessy Raphael sat at my table for dinner for ninety minutes prior to the broadcast." After Raphael presented the award, she left the ceremony. "She went backstage as was custom. All of the presenters were to be photographed with the inductees. She did not stick around to have the photograph taken with Rush; she went back there, had a photograph taken of herself, then grabbed her coat, took her husband, hopped in the limousine we had provided her, and was off to the airport."

Radio is, for the most part, a business of crass publicity seekers. Dumont suggested Raphael was just using the moment to call attention to herself.

"I think it's possible that this was a setup because it's the beginning of sweeps week, and what you have people talking about is her program and Rush's program." Items about her remarks were printed nationwide the next day. "A lot of people are talking about it."

Dumont said the guests at the awards dinner were shocked.

"People who came up afterwards and identified themselves as not being fans of Rush, they said they felt sorry for him. They were embarrassed that she chose to use that platform to make her comments. If she really felt strongly about it, she could have declined the invitation, she could have asked to make another presentation. She could have made her comments to the reporters who were there beforehand or afterward. This was the beginning of sweeps week. And so, who are people talking about? They're talking about Sally Jessy Raphael, which could help her ratings, even if she's viewed as a rude and boorish, immature person. As is often observed, there's no such thing as negative attention in our business." (In fact, Dumont's own talk show had received a sudden splash of national publicity because of the incident, tempering his irritation with Raphael.)

Mark Davis invited his listeners to join the fray. Radio listeners lined up to offer their opinions about what radio hosts were saying about each other at radio awards banquets.

"Ed, you're on WRC," Davis announced. "Welcome to you."

"Thank you, Mark," said the caller. "Mark, I beg to differ with you and Bruce. Mr. Limbaugh is very fond of low blows. Only this time he was on the receiving end. And I applaud Sally. She did stoop to his level, but rational people have been pummeled for too long by that goon who screens his calls so effectively that only his dittoheads get on the air to have a mutual admiration society."

Davis defended Limbaugh. "When was the last time that Rush embarrassed someone publicly at an event—"

"Every day," Ed interrupted.

"Sir, please listen to the entire question," demanded Davis. "When was the last time Rush publicly humiliated someone, off the air, at an event meant to honor them?"

Ed parried well. "Fortunately, I don't hang around with demagogues like him, so I don't know."

"So if there's somebody that you don't like,' said Davis, "it doesn't matter how cruel people are to him?"

"He's a hateful person and he instills hate in people. We don't need that."

One of talk radio's workhorses, Joel A. Spivak, a veteran of the Washington, D.C., airwaves and a colleague of the abrasive Joe Pyne at the old KLAC in Los Angeles.
PHOTO: VINCE RACOBALDO

Joe Pyne was screaming about politics and offending listeners while Rush Limbaugh was still in high school.

Washington, D.C., talk radio listeners who seek an alternative to the screamers on commercial radio enjoy the calm and balanced programs offered by Diane Rehm and Derek McGinty on the public WAMU. Both shows command respectable audience shares.

REHM PHOTO: CLAIRE FLANDERS
MCGINTY PHOTO: HILLARY SCHWAB

"I'm not a right-wing wacko or a convicted felon," yells Tom Leykis about his credentials at the start of his daily syndicated show.

PHOTO: VINCE RACOBALDO

**W**atergate burglar G. Gordon Liddy enjoys looking tough in publicity pictures for his new career as talk show host.

**M**orton Downey Jr. (*left*) and comedian Jackie Mason during a live broadcast from Golden's Restaurant on West 51st Street in New York City.

PHOTO: AP/WIDE WORLD PHOTOS

Howard Stern, who calls himself the "King of All Media," is dismissed by some listeners as nothing more than a dirty-talking juvenile prankster. But just before Christmas 1994, he used his radio show to talk one of his fans out of jumping off a New York City bridge.

PHOTO: AP/WIDE WORLD PHOTOS

Rush Limbaugh looking serene about the empire he's built.

WBAP's Mark Davis holds on to Rush Limbaugh's huge Dallas/Ft. Worth audience with his local show following Limbaugh's daily. PHOTO: RANDY SANTOS

Bob Grant, whom many consider a right-wing hatemonger, broadcasting from the WABC studio. PHOTO: AP/WIDE WORLD PHOTOS

**P**residential candidate Pat Buchanan working to take back America at Mutual.

**P**at Buchanan's periodic jousting partner, the liberal Barry Lynn.
PHOTO: PORTRAIT SPECIALTIES, INC.

**D**on Imus enjoys the reputation of being the intellectual's shock talker.

Another attempt at dislodging the right-wing hold on talk radio comes out of the loud mouth of feminist lawyer Gloria Allred over KABC.

Convivial Jim Bohannon behind the microphone at Mutual's Crystal City, Virginia, studio.

"I love oral sex," Barbara Carlson likes to croon over KSTP in Minneapolis. Her KSTP tattoo is hidden in this photo.

Jim Hightower, trying to carve out a niche for himself as a populist, broadcasts with a drawl from Austin, Texas, over the ABC radio network on weekends.

"Well, he's obviously instilled hate in you," said Davis "because this is a hateful attitude you hold. And if you don't like the show, that's fine."

"He starts that hate," Ed continued, "and it brings on the same. He's a goon, he's a demagogue."

"And that makes it okay to be cruel to him?"

"It makes it fair to use the same weaponry he uses back at him," Ed said.

Bruce Dumont jumped into the wrangle. "She knew it was an induction ceremony. She knew what the script was." Dumont said Raphael was furnished an advance copy of what she was expected to say about Limbaugh. "She accepted the plane ride, she accepted the limousine ride, she accepted the free dinner, she went up to the microphone, and then she decided to make the comment she made."

Ed added, "I think she decided from the outset."

"If she felt so strongly about it, sir," Dumont told him, "she could have declined the invitation, she could have asked to make another presentation. We would have abided by that, and she didn't do that. So I think that's hypocritical."

But Ed was not moved by Dumont's argument. "Then you would have had some other confederate up there doing what you would consider the right thing. But what she did was the most effective, and I think it was fantastic. I'm sorry your affair didn't go the way you wanted, but I don't think you should be holding somebody like Mr. Limbaugh up to such a high regard."

In fact, Dumont was smiling in the studio, happy with all the attention he and his show and the Hall of Fame and the museum were receiving.

"Hi, Frank," said Davis to the next caller. "You're on WRC. Welcome."

"Hey, good morning, Mark, and good morning, Bruce," said Frank to his radio friends. "Thank you for taking that previous call and for your example of showing how churlish and boorish and classless, not only Sally is, but the other side. I really appreciate it."

Davis tried to construct a perspective for the ongoing dialogue. "We care about the personalities in our lives," he said about Raphael and Limbaugh. "When a couple of them wind up in a bit of a quandary, it captures the public imagination. Now we only have about a thousand of you on the line, so let me just offer everyone some comfort. We're going to give all the callers all the time they need. I want to give all of you on the horn an opportunity to get your two cents in, so we're going to kick back, relax, and take as many of your calls as we can. All right, John, you're on WRC. Bruce Dumont's here. How are you doing?"

"I'm doing fine," said John. "I'm glad I had a chance to sit in my car here and listen awhile so I can calm down. After hearing Sally, I couldn't agree more with you regarding the characterization of her performance. It really was despicable. But I'm sitting here trying to figure out what benefit there might have been out of this. We now know that Sally Jessy Raphael has no personal integrity. To do what she did would be the equivalent of somebody introducing the valedictorian at some high school, saying here's the valedictorian but I really don't think this person deserves to be here. I know this is the high spot of their high school career, but they're really a piece of trash, you'll listen to them if you have to, but that's what they are."

Davis took another call. "Barbara, you're on WRC. Welcome."

"Yes. Hi, Mark, how are you?" Barbara sounded happy to be one of those chosen to talk on the radio. "I'm sorry, I don't agree with you. Anyone who puts the face of a dog on his TV show, and says this is a picture of Chelsea, when he's on the receiving end and Sally knocked him off of his pedestal, I say give the lady two dozen red roses from me!"

"Well, that's hate," offered Davis.

"No, it's not hate," Barbara responded. "This man is a closet bigot. He is a closet bigot."

"It was disgusting," Davis agreed with Barbara about the Chelsea Clinton insult, and he proceeded to criticize other Limbaugh broadcasts.

"Tracy, you're on WRC," said Davis. "How're you doing?"

"Fine, how are you? I just have to say, her conduct was shameful, completely unprofessional. She did nothing to further the feminist movement, because she came off looking bitchy. If she wanted to dedicate a whole hour of her show to how she can't stand Rush Limbaugh, that's fine, that's fine, but this was his moment. And if she had a problem, she should have backed off."

The calls kept on coming in to the radio station until Davis changed the subject. It was another example of how successful Limbaugh has been in marketing himself. The high-profile persona he has created seduces his fans to defend him. *Success* magazine titled an article about Limbaugh[12] "I Am the Product." The talk on the Mark Davis show following the Hall of Fame incident was more proof of just how skillfully Limbaugh has created his commercial and influential position in the talk radio industry and the American popular culture.

# 10 The Listener Profile

*Vital characters in the talk radio business are the* millions in the talk radio audience—without them there could be no telephone talk shows.

The intense relationship my aunt had with her late-night radio companion Michael Krasney is mirrored in the lives of most talk radio listeners, and plenty of listeners to Krasney's show. As he said good-bye to his KGO audience, the faxes filled the station.[1]

"You have informed me without beating me up," wrote Joanna Wooley. "You have entertained me, educated me, given me hope and made me laugh."

Roxanne Neito checked in with, "You were my anchor, my sanity at day's end. You were my teacher and friend. You have, by your kindness and class, validated your listeners and made us feel we counted."

Another fax from Gary James read, "You brought to your program an intellectual depth that I have not encountered elsewhere. What truly set you apart was the unfailing patience, kindness and civility with which you treated all your callers. You never took a cheap shot. It was the warmth and humanity of your program that I treasured most."

"You were KGO for me," wrote Susan Pemberton. "The worst of this is that the management doesn't seem to care what listeners want."

Just a few weeks later Krasney found another microphone; he went to work for KQED, the noncommercial news and talk radio station in San Francisco. And KGO continued to seek its audience by operating as a radio version of a tabloid newspaper. "How it feels," yells out the headline in one of KGO's print advertisements.[2] "Whatever happens," continues the copy, "you'll always hear it here first." The illustration is of a sooty, concerned-looking firefighter staring away from the camera, presumably at the burning building from which he just saved the scared infant he's clutching. "And you'll always feel the emotion," continues the cloying message before offering the reader a chance to participate in the tragedy. "Once news happens, you get to listen to how people really feel. And you get to talk to the people who make the news."

Another print ad for KGO irked *San Francisco Chronicle* columnist Jon Carroll. It portrayed a skinhead and a black man yelling at each other as a policeman looks on at them. "When people talk," announces the ad, "you'll always hear it first." Carroll was disgusted and used his column soapbox to denounce tabloid talk radio. "Yessir, really angry people screaming at each other—that's my idea of a good time," he wrote. "Ignorant conflict! Great radio!"

But it is not only the nonthreatening talk radio hosts such as Krasney with whom the listeners develop love affairs. "He was morally outraged without being morally superior," said an Alan Berg listener. Another remembered, "He had something beyond the courage of his convictions. He had the courage of his perceptions." Still another said, "I've gone back and forth. I've admired him and hated his methods. But he had an impact on people, and that's why we call people important, not because they were good or bad. He made people think about who he was and what he was doing."[3]

═══════

Who are these people? Who is listening? Who is calling?

"Barb in Vienna [Virginia]," I welcome a woman to one of my talk shows, "you're on WRC."

"Good morning," she says.

"Good morning," I say, and then glancing at my computer monitor realize that the poor woman has been waiting on hold for about an hour. I ask her what motivates such patience; isn't there something else she wants or needs to do with her time?

"I have a cordless phone," Barb tells me and laughs, "so I have been tidying up the house. We have three kids and my husband already went to work. I'm just getting myself ready for work."

Remember that Barb and her calling colleagues represent only a small fraction of the general population. As previously stated, the Times Mirror Center for the People and the Press determined that only 11 percent of Americans say they've ever tried to call a talk radio show, just 6 percent say they've made it on the air, and only 3 percent say that they made it on the air during the year preceding the survey.

"This is Mike, I'm in my car," says another caller. I've been spending some time on the air asking the audience why they listen to talk shows. The growing number of private automobiles equipped with cellular telephones is adding to the vigor of the talk radio audience. Frustrated commuters are joining shut-ins and insomniacs waiting for a chance to talk on the air. "Being a salesman," says Mike, "I live in my car. Driving is my life and I get a lot of good opinions from the different people who are on, either the talk hosts or their guests. It keeps me informed about what's happening in the world at the current moment and the different opinions of everybody."

I ask Mike if, especially given his forced confinement in his car, he's addicted to talk radio. "Do you get in the car and turn it on because it's part of your day—have a cup of coffee, get in the car, and there are your friends on the radio?"

It's an image Mike likes. "Definitely. On my car radio I have two AM stations. One is yours and one is the other [talk station]. I go back and forth and enjoy."

Fred calls and says he likes talk radio because "you can call in and ask questions."

What about the other callers on the air? How does he relate to the barrage of anonymous voices asking questions, making statements, passing along information, misinformation, and disinformation? "When you listen to another caller," I ask Fred, "do you just give him or her the benefit of the doubt and figure that what they're saying is what they really believe?"

"Absolutely," says Fred, pointing out that he himself calls talk shows and speaks honestly and from his heart when he gets on the air. "I don't think people call in just to harass or pull the wool over people's eyes, just to sound good."

It is a fascinating concept that a large share of the audience accepts with trust input from anonymous callers. "They've got to be informed. They've got to be smart," a listener tells me about the callers he enjoys, because "I find it very stimulating for my mind. I like to listen to people who are challenging—with differing opinions—for my mind."

Part of the explanation for this blind acceptance of caller credibility must be that people are seeking replacements for the loss of direct personal contact in modern society. We rarely shop at a local market where the owner knows our names; we shop at huge supermarkets where the checkout clerk is a stranger. Few of us sit around a coffee shop chatting over the morning paper with our neighbors. We grab a cup of coffee to go, drink it in the car during a boring commute, and tune in to the radio for company.

Jerry Williams, the WRKO (Boston) host with one of the industry's longest running careers, made a sad commentary when he described talk radio as "the only avenue left where people can express themselves."[4]

"I feel sort of like I accomplished something," said Elizabeth Harris, a Chevy Chase, Maryland, businesswoman, explaining why she called the Diane Rehm show, a serious forum for discussion on one of Washington's public radio stations, WAMU. "You know," she told the *Washington Post,* "it's a contribution to the discussion. We always get so much fed to us in the media that it's fun to be able to respond."

"Exciting," is the reason Russ Bouvin of Washington, a retired military officer, gave the *Post* for his repeated calling of talk shows. He said he called the Limbaugh show frequently and enjoyed the anonymity. "I'm not an outward-going person in public that much. I like to listen to people in public. I get a thrill," said Bouvin about being on the air, "sort of like I'm doing something that matters."[5]

There are all sorts of listeners supporting talk radio. The back of Howard Stern's office door is adorned with photographs sent in by female listeners, who use the pictures to make a graphic statement of what they would like to do with their radio god. "Many are topless," reported the *Washington Post*'s Richard Leiby after a visit. "Many bottomless. Some display their talent for using large implements for self-gratification."[6]

In the skies over Missouri, June 24, 1994, President Clinton announced not only that he was a talk radio listener, but that talk radio was a problem for him and his presidency. He was on the phone from Air Force One, talking over KMOX (St. Louis) with hosts Kevin Horrigan and Charles Brennan. Their show aired just before Rush Limbaugh's.

"Do you get the sense that the American people are becoming more cynical, becoming less tolerant?" Horrigan asked the president.

Upset was obvious in the tone of Clinton's answer, as he seemed to confirm the notion that talk radio influences the national mood. "Absolutely. Much of talk radio is just a constant, unremitting drumbeat of negativism and cynicism." Then he put talk radio hosts' influence on a par with that of the president. "After I get off the radio today with you," he complained, "Rush Limbaugh will have three hours to say whatever he wants. And I won't have the opportunity to respond. And there's no truth detector."

A few months later, President Clinton made himself available as a guest on a few select talk shows. "He thinks national talk radio has become dominated by a right-wing viewpoint that he feels is skewing the national debate," explained Jim Hightower after an off-the-air chat with the president during which Hightower said Clinton praised the left-leaning orientation of Hightower's weekend talk show. "He is getting beat up by it," Hightower told *Broadcasting and Cable* magazine, "and I think he's glad there is some kind of progressive viewpoint there to counter the cacophony that people are hearing in their right ear."

# 11 Broadcasting Hate and Sleaze

*Simply making noise and fomenting trouble is not* an adequate recipe for a successful talk show—even for those equipped with a well-known name. Since the days a couple of generations ago of Joe Pyne screaming over the radio and crashing the telephone down in callers' ears, talk radio continues to attract real crackpots as hosts, many much further over the edge than the controlled and calculated rants and raves of a Limbaugh or a Stern. The failed career of Morton Downey Jr. is an example; his legacy has been reduced to a few stories about his more ludicrous violations of good business sense and good taste, along with broadcasting industry memories that his failure in Sacramento left a job opening that Rush Limbaugh was hired to fill.

But failure is often a credential for future employment in radio—or at least it is often no obstacle to a new job. Notorious failure by a talk show host, especially a talk show host with name recognition, is interpreted by some managers not as evidence that the host is no good but that the host was poorly directed. In late winter 1992, Morton Downey Jr. was wandering around Washington, followed by television news crews making pictures for stories about Downey's return to talk radio on WRC, one of the long list of radio stations that risked their reputations by hiring him in hopes that his shock talk style would boost their ratings.

"How do I differ? I'm a radical centrist," he told Channel Four television interviewer Arch Campbell, who asked him in 1992 how he intended to compete with Rush Limbaugh and G. Gordon Liddy. "A radical centrist is a guy who sees some good in some of the wild liberal ideas that are out there and some good in some of the wild conservative ideas that are out there, and believes that if we can get the Arabs and Israelis talking, we can certainly get the liberals and conservatives talking."

His tone continued to be lofty as he traveled the publicity circuit during his attempted radio comeback. "Radio is different from television," he explained to a TV interviewer on Fox Morning News, flashing his trademark wide-open mouth filled with over-sized teeth. "On radio you can use the theatrics of the mind. I do my talk show in the hopes that we're here to keep the big boys honest." He described the talk show genre as an opportunity for Everyman. "It allows the people who don't get on radio and television a platform," he told the interviewer. Asked about his past performances as a shock television host, Downey described his role as heroic. "I wanted people to get so angry at each other that they just blurted out the truth. And we got a lot of truths told on the show."

The questions were asked with respect, and Downey used the platform to announce that there were no barriers separating his work from anyone on radio or television who uses the title *journalist*. "I think anyone is a journalist who can converse with someone else," he said earnestly. "I think the journalistic fraternity and sorority has become so closed because they all think they're very proper and pompous and they're the ones who will tell you what's going on. Well, journalists don't know what the hell is going on any more than the average person on the street does, and the average person on the street is like the town crier. So I'm a town crier, I'm not a journalist."

But by late summer, Downey's Washington show clearly was

not connecting with the audience. The positive publicity that greeted his arrival in the capital was over, as was the novelty of his abrasive routine. Ratings were poor. The struggling radio performer often arrived late for his program. He turned on his microphone to vent his anger at his late train, his colleagues at the radio station, life in general, and listeners who called him in particular.

"Dianna, are you there?" he introduces a caller to his program in the late summer, months after his Washington show debuted.

"Yes," she says.

He's sounding charming, "Yes, dear, what were you going to say?"

"I was going to say I agree with Lee." She's referring to an earlier caller who was critical of Downey's performances.

"Okay," says Downey.

"And I think you have been—" she starts to explain her upset.

But Downey realizes she is not a fan and cuts her off with an ugly vengeance. "Wait a second," he barks. "Wait a second, you ugly bitch. Punch that off," he tells his engineer, an order to cut the connection with the caller. "Bitch is what I called her," he says to his audience and rants on, "I wasn't thrown off TV, and when you want to call me a Jew-hater, find out first if I'm a Jew. I don't hate Jews, I just hate old baggy bitches like you. Good-bye."[1]

That exchange prompted a reprimand from management, as did his use of the term *asshole* in another broadcast. Memos were sent to his file that eventually helped lead to one more of his many canceled talk shows. It is instructive to compare that radio exchange with Downey's philosophy about carefully choosing words as stated in his book *Mort! Mort! Mort!*. "Words *can* hurt," said Downey through the writer who cowrote his book, "even more so than sticks and stones. They are weapons that today's media can wield without mercy." Downey, the man who easily allows "ugly bitch" to roll out of his mouth while dismissing a caller, seeks a high moral niche for himself as he analyzes his business in his book, claiming the press is "fond of proclaiming their *right* to free speech, yet loath to acknowledge the *responsibility* that goes with it. Freedom of the press is basic to our unique experiment in democracy, but so is the responsibility to police oneself. The *right* to say just about anything must be subjugated to the *responsibility* to be fair, compassionate, and decent."

On occasion, Downey found himself the target of his own insulting techniques, as happened when Howard Stern interviewer "Stuttering John" caught up with him. Afflicted with a severe stutter, John Melendez was assigned to seek celebrities and ask them potentially embarrassing questions. "Are you drooping yet?" he queried Raquel Welch. "Will you be sleeping with any other presidential candidates?" he wondered to Gennifer Flowers. He asked Oliver North, "Did you ever have a nightmare where your penis gets caught in a paper shredder?" and Imelda Marcos, "If you ever pass gas at home in front of others, do you blame the family dog?"

When Stuttering John cornered Morton Downey it was to ask, "Would you let your wife dance topless in clubs for money if you really needed it?" Downey responded with words first, saying, "I wouldn't ask my lady to do that. I've got too much class." Then he grabbed Melendez and shoved him out of his chair, adding, "Play that, you silly little ———."[2]

Another example from the Downey file, still kept at WRC when I arrived there, shows the counterproductivity of turning over the airwaves to the self-centered and infantile type of troublemaking practiced by the Downey-style performers. After a commercial for a Washington, D.C., hospital that included warnings about the early signs of a heart attack, Downey mocked the advertiser, saying, "Now every damned hypochondriac who listens to this show is rushing to get over there, because they think they are having a heart attack. You probably ate a lousy grape or something, and they're gonna have you dropping dead from that commercial."[3]

Downey's boss responded to this thrashing of an important client with a memorandum that provides further insight into the bizarre workings of the talk show world, a world that manages to combine the legitimacy of journalism with the crass hustling of carnival midways.

"Very simply," reads the official memo to Downey, on WRC letterhead from the program director in charge there before my tenure, "don't fuck with our commercials. I can't afford the loss of revenue. Leave the commercials alone. Twelve minutes [of your program] belong to me. Don't fuck with them."

But Downey continued his antics. On February 26, 1993, he took a call from a listener named Ken. "How are you, buddy?" asks Mort.

"I'm doing great," says Ken, and, joking around, tells Downey and his guest at the time, "You people are getting on my nerves, you old people. I'm tired of all these old guys with lots of money taking all the young babes and I don't get none, you know what I mean?"

"Wait a second, Ken," says Mort, "you say these old guys are getting women only because they have bucks?"

"Yeah, they only want you for your money. She cannot possibly be attracted to you old guys. You're going to fail them sexually."

"Let me ask you an honest question, Ken," is Mort's response. "How many times can you get it up and get it on in a night?"

"In one night?" asks Ken.

"Yeah," says Mort.

"I lost count."

"Okay, you lost count. But let's say you're a real stud and you can do it ten times, all right?"

"At least, yeah."

"Yeah, sure, right," says Mort. "How old are you, Ken?"

"Twenty-five."

"Chances are you're good for approximately six minutes a shot, all right? That's beyond the norm for you young guys." Ken laughs, and Mort continues with his dissertation. "So six minutes a shot times ten means you've got an hour of sex for this woman, whereas the old—"

Ken starts to interrupt Mort, saying, "No, no, no, you're wrong—"

"Wait a second, listen to me," Mort says. Ken is still saying no and Mort starts to yell. "Zip it. Zip it, creepface. Listen to me just a second, all right? Let me tell you something, you little bearded fink. I can tell you've got a beard because you're sucking on it with your tongue." Somebody in the studio laughs. "Now, let me tell you something. An older guy can probably only get it up maybe twice, you know, maybe twice." He's yelling again. "But each time he's good for an hour!" Ken laughs and Mort keeps yelling. "So you got two hours going there. So the guy satisfies the woman. I know exactly what you go through," he tells Ken, "because boy Neil tells me"—he's referring to his producer—"every time he has sex with his girlfriend she always ends up saying, 'Oh, that's all right, honey. Don't worry about it. It happens to all—' "

Ken tries to speak again, interrupting Downey's imitation of a woman's voice.

"Aw, zip it you piece of dreck, yeah," says Mort as he hangs up, the dial tone filling the airwaves. "I got rid of him."

On another occasion, Downey trashed one of his radio station's clients while reading commercial copy for Wall Street Clothes and its special price for pants. Downey suggested that the slacks on sale were of such poor quality, "You'll bust through if you get a hard-on."[4]

The Downey file from WRC is fat with such violations of productive business practices. Included in one folder is a list of verbatim quotes excised from Downey broadcasts. In reference to a woman supporter of President Clinton, he asked, "Were you laid by the guy?" He dismissed another woman with, "She's just a bitch." Also on the list, these choice one-liners:

"Picking boogers and eating them."

"Farting in the kitchen and burning your member on the stove."

"Men who like big-breasted women, rubbing them to get excited."

========

Morton Downey's last show for WRC in Washington came into the station via satellite. By early 1993 Downey had packed up his act one more time and moved to Dallas, hoping to establish a radio network modeled on the Limbaugh success story. While Downey was on the air from Dallas, broadcasting over WRC, one of his few affiliates, and engaged in a harangue about homosexuals, I pulled the plug and finished the shift myself, inviting listeners to call in and discuss talk radio.

When Downey next surfaced, it was to call me "that faggot-fuck from San Francisco." San Francisco is where Downey's roller-coaster ride through stardom crashed once before; he claimed he was attacked at the airport by skinheads who cut his hair and drew swastikas on his face and his clothes. Downey said he was standing at a urinal and "was grabbed from behind and pulled into a stall" by two or three skinheads who said to him, "Now it's our turn to take you apart."[5]

Police immediately became suspicious of Downey's story. Airport Police Sergeant Gary O'Connell said, "Downey was incoherent and incooperative. He had very slurred speech and said he was drunk. The officers saw the swastikas on his face, pants, and shirt, but they were very neatly done."

Downey returned to his hotel room at the downtown Meridien (he was in San Francisco to promote his TV show) and invited news photographers to take pictures of the swastikas. The next day Sergeant O'Connell said the marks on Downey's face as shown on TV and in the newspapers were "not the same markings our officers saw on his face when they investigated the incident."

After a few days, police came to the conclusion that Downey's story was probably a hoax. No charges were filed against him; he had not pressed the case with police at the airport when they first investigated his complaint.

"If I'm lying I'm obviously already in mental jeopardy and need a rubber room," he said later on the Phil Donahue TV talk show to a studio audience. Downey conceded that he was drunk at the airport, that he had downed five vodka-and-cranberry-juice cock-tails at a party that evening.

A member of Donahue's studio audience offered this comment: "If I had five vodka and cranberries I would have put a swastika on backwards also."

The swastikas marked on Downey were mirror images of the Nazi symbol, inviting the interpretation that Downey had been looking in the airport restroom mirror when he applied them on his own face.

=======

Tom Leykis is another from the sharp-tongue, in-your-face school of talk radio. Leykis is infamous for killing Barney the dinosaur on the air (through sound effects) and beating up his girlfriend (his own girlfriend, not Barney's). We met on the White House lawn the day of the health care carnival; he was broadcasting on WRKO in Boston. A few months later he was syndicated nationally by Westwood One. "I did kill Barney on the air," he said, proud of the radio play he had constructed. "And a lot of people—I've got letters from all over the country from people thanking me."

Several months later, in Worcester, Massachusetts, Derrick McMahan was arrested and charged with assault and battery. His college roommate had dared him to attack a drug store employee dressed up as Barney, betting ten dollars that McMahan would not commit the crime. According to Worcester police, McMahan jumped out of the car he was riding in with his friend, and, swearing loudly, tackled what turned out to be a woman in the Barney suit, and struck her repeatedly. Even after her Barney mask fell off, he continued to pummel her in the face.

"Why are you doing this to me?" Deborah McRoy later told the *Worcester Telegram and Gazette*[6] she pleaded with her attacker. She was employed to draw attention to the opening of the store. McRoy said his response was, "Because we hate Barney." Among the witnesses was a little boy who McRoy said offered to help. "I'm going home to get my gun, Barney," the little boy told her, "and I'm going to shoot him."

=======

Tom Leykis, along with his colleague Les Kinsolving from Baltimore, is in a complaining mood on the morning the White House lawn is filled with talk show hosts. "We paid for everything," he says about his travel and his broadcast operations from Washington back to Boston. "The White House hasn't wined and dined us. I mean, hey, the columnists and the anchors—Connie Chung and Dan Rather—all had lunch with the president this week. We are the low rung on the totem pole. Certainly they want to include us in, they want us to be talking about health care. But the danger is, of course, that we're now going to take a closer look at what Clinton is proposing. We're seeing it close up. We're seeing how this whole thing operates, and frankly, I don't know that people are here being bedazzled. Certainly we're not here under lavish circumstances."

Perhaps—seems his suggestion—it takes a limousine and some smoked salmon to influence the content of America's talk shows, not just the facade of the White House. I ask him about talk radio audiences. If talk radio hosts such as Leykis are considered blowhards, I propose, then the listeners might well be described as malcontents.

"People like to say that that's our audience," he says, rejecting the theory. "I don't believe it because the audience is so large now for talk radio. I don't believe it's a bunch of malcontents and women knitting in their rocking chairs and what have you. This is a big, large, active audience of all kinds of people from all backgrounds."

Leykis sees this growing audience as an indication that the importance of talk radio in American society is increasing. "I think talk radio is an important part of democracy. I think the hosts are not an important part of it, because our job is just to act as a catalyst for conversation. Believe me," he says, showing a firm understanding of the vagaries of the industry, "I've been in five or six major cities doing talk radio and when I go, somebody else comes in, picks up the conversation. Within two days, the callers are calling in saying, 'I like your show and I don't know who that other guy was who used to be on.' That's really what it's all about."

A few months later, a couple of days before Christmas, Tom Leykis and his fourth wife stumbled back to their Beacon Hill home after midnight from the WRKO Christmas party. They made it up into the bedroom and, according to the police report filed by thirty-four-year-old Susan (Tom was thirty-seven), that's when the evening really fell apart. She says he threw a glass at her, hit her in the head, and then jammed her head into the bedroom fireplace and threatened to kill her.

Susan Leykis managed to call the police. They arrested Tom and charged him with assault and battery with a deadly weapon and threatening murder. They reported "scratch marks on the victim's left forearm" and "a large bump on the victim's head."

Immediately his lawyer dismissed the matter as inconsequential. "This was an absolutely minor domestic tiff that almost went unreported," is how lawyer Jeffrey Denner characterized the struggle, saying it "got out of hand because both sides were drinking at a Christmas party and clearly have some private issues they need to work out." Through Denner, Tom "absolutely and categorically" denied threatening to kill Susan and claimed "no intention of hurting" her.[7]

What makes this story of interest to a study of talk radio is not that a low-level celebrity and his wife drink and fight. The Leykis affair exemplifies the double standard that pervades the relationship between the talk radio host and the audience. A few months before the fireplace dance, *Boston Globe* columnist Bella English talked with Leykis about his strident show. "When I asked why he allowed sexist, vulgar language on his show," English wrote in the paper shortly after Leykis was arrested, "he told me he was not in 'the censorship business.' "

In fact—although he was quickly back on the air after being released from police custody—Tom Leykis used his producer to screen out callers who wished to chat about the host's marital problems. This from a man who, as critic English reported in the *Globe*, "loves to brag on the air about making some of [his wives] sign a prenuptial agreement that if they got pregnant, they'd have an abortion or split—as long as he doesn't get stuck with any horrid little babies or child support payments."

It was not only on his own show that Tom Leykis attempted to muzzle talk about himself. On the Compuserve computer network, there is a bulletin board called Radio/TV Talent. There, professional broadcasters engage in cyberspace gossip, talking shop. After the Leykis story hit the national news wires, some initial correspondents on the bulletin board wrote messages expressing doubt about the veracity of Susan's charges in the police report. Others responded with suggestions that given Tom's notoriously volatile public personality, there was no reason to believe the charges were untrue. Those comments generated a new rush of messages from Leykis supporters who insisted that speculation on a public computer bulletin board about Tom's private life was unfair and inappropriate. Finally, Tom himself joined the fray, threatening to sue anyone who repeated on the bulletin board erroneous information relating to that debauched Christmas party and its aftermath.

"I am amazed," Leykis tapped into his on-line computer for all the world to read,[8] "that this group of broadcasters which makes its living off the First Amendment doesn't understand a thing about the concept 'innocent until proven guilty.' Many folks on this forum take umbrage at an expressed concern that what is electronically published here be factually accurate!" Some bulletin board users were suggesting that speculation in a public forum about Leykis's guilt or innocence was inappropriate, maybe even illegal. It was an absurd theory. If ever figures in our society could be identified as public, talk show hosts are those public figures— people who get on the air day after day and engage in first-person conversations with anonymous callers over the public airwaves. The Supreme Court has established clearly that the standards for proving libel and slander against a public figure are almost impossible to meet. Actual malice must be established. Not only must Leykis, given his profession, know that standard, but for any talk show host to cry that he or she is being maligned in the public arena is absurd. Talk shows hosts—including Tom Leykis—are in the business of personal attack. All day, every day, all across America.

"Let me assure all of you here," Leykis continued his bulletin board assault, "that I will take any and all legal steps to assure that my reputation and career are protected from you folks who don't care what effect your idle comments may have. I am an innocent man. Today is my second wedding anniversary. My wife is sitting here in tears reading your silly messages speculating about a minor domestic dispute that took place in the privacy of our own home, a dispute that never should have involved the courts or the press."

Leykis's whining is almost funny considering the ease with which he and most other talk show hosts around America leap at the opportunity to speculate about minor and major events involving any person, place, or thing they imagine might be potential ingredients for their insatiable talk show appetites.

"How many of you can say you've never had a domestic dispute?" Leykis's message to his peers that day was a long one. "This could happen to any of you (assuming you even *have* a relationship!). None of you were here and none of you will *ever* know what happened. Nothing criminal, I can assure you." Next he goes for sympathy. "Susan is already mortified at what has happened. She wants the whole thing dropped. But you guys just want to keep hammering away at something that, beyond the fact of an arrest and an unsubstantiated allegation, is none of your damned business." There is something especially amusing about seeing a talk show host—someone who by his very job description meddles daily in other people's affairs—complain about privacy invasion.

Talk show hosts often attempt to generate a particular on-the-air personality to suit the job requirement they perceive exists. This modification can range from completely abandoning one's true philosophical beliefs for the sake of the show's point of view to simply trying to keep embarrassing personal histories and experiences from the audience. The ease with which skillful talk show hosts are able to obfuscate their own true personalities and create a radio life for themselves adds to the overall credibility problem of talk radio. Why, for example, should a listener continue to believe a Tom Leykis's cry that he "is not in the censorship business" after it is made clear that when his own life is the one being examined, censorship is exactly what he seeks to accomplish?

Consider these transcripts: A caller to WABC in New York asks, "Is it possible that the lower intelligence of blacks is responsible for the complete lack of morality in the blacks?" A caller to WTEL in Philadelphia is allowed on the air to spew, "The Jew-Commies only parade around with this [Lech] Walesa to trick the Western banks into giving them money and then they transfer these funds to Israel or New York." Across town on WWDB in Philadelphia another caller wants listeners to know, "It's normal practice for Italian people to squeeze every cent they can out of you. Underhanded dealing seems to be very prevalent among Italians."[9] Hate and sleaze on talk radio comes not only from hosts, but from callers allowed by hosts to fill the airwaves with poison.

Just before the 1994 elections, *New York* magazine directed nationwide attention toward WABC's afternoon talk show host Bob Grant with a cover story[10] headlined "Why he hates blacks" that charged Grant with turning "fear and loathing into fun and profit." The article blamed Grant for providing a platform for hate and feeding his callers' worst instincts with his own venom. *New York* offered a litany of examples. Grant called former New York mayor David Dinkins "the men's room attendant." President Clinton was characterized as "the sleazebag in the White House"; the president of the National Organization for Women, Patricia Ireland, "that ugly dyke."

Bob Grant had been broadcasting over WABC since 1984, building a huge audience by pandering to the paranoia and prejudice of his listeners. His immediate boss, WABC program director John Mainelli, looked the other way with the recurring talk radio excuse that the show is just business. "Inform entertainingly, entertain informatively," was how Mainelli explained his philosophy to *New York*. The article was merciless, calling Grant "racist, alienated, bullying, embittered, hyperbolic—the white equivalent of gangster rap."

Jesse Jackson followed up quickly, trying to organize a boycott of Grant's advertisers. "This is foul speech calculated to hurt," Jackson said during a news conference he called outside the WABC studios. "This is hate and venom. We have a moral obligation to fight back."

Program director Mainelli, after conferring with his corporate supervisors at ABC's New York headquarters, worked hard to manipulate the attack on Grant into a public relations bonanza by using it to turn even more attention to his controversial host. He broadcast the Jackson news conference over WABC; he denounced the *New York* magazine article over the air; and he told the trade journal *Radio and Records*,[11] "I'm loving it. I love to defend what we do because I believe in it. I feel we're a lone voice in the wilderness crying out against political correctness."

Wrapping the station in the First Amendment without considering taste and responsible behavior, Mainelli suggested, "I don't know if all publicity is good publicity. But this will certainly make more people aware of what we do. It also makes us look like one of the few media outlets that has stood up to this political correctness. And I think that's good."

Some advertisers canceled as a result of the article and the resulting controversy; Mainelli said he replaced them with new clients who paid higher rates.

The newly elected New Jersey governor, Christine Todd Whitman, who was supported by Grant during and after her election, chastised him publicly, at first saying she would no longer appear on his show as a guest, then saying she would accept his invitation, but only to discuss race and intolerance. "It's not just happening here," she told Grant on the air about intolerance. "It's happening on a lot of shows. But because you have been a supporter of mine, and we agree on a lot of issues—on taxes, on government and criminal justice issues—it became even more important that I show I'm consistent. I need to speak out because language affects behavior and I know that you have a great deal of influence. You have a very loyal listenership, many of whom believe in what's said on the air, and they take it to heart. And the problem that I have is that we allow that talk, some of it very divisive, by categorizing groups of people because of who they are: race, religion, age, and then thinking that when the radio's turned off somehow that all that's forgotten. And my concern is that it's not, that people take that home with them and it makes it very difficult for them to work and live in the multicultural, multiracial society we have today."

Grant listened to her lecture and expressed no remorse nor any intention of changing his act.

But, despite John Mainelli's skillful manipulation of the attacks on Grant from the governor, Jesse Jackson, and *New York* magazine, not all ABC executives supported the talk show host. One of them told me privately that the *New York* article was correct, Grant is obviously a racist, but that the magazine should have used different examples. Instead of being preoccupied with Grant's insults to public figures such as David Dinkins, this manager suggested critics should be more concerned with how Grant treats callers who oppose him and who speak with accents that suggest they are foreign-born or black. "These are grass-roots callers who respectfully call to disagree," complained the executive, "and Grant hangs up on them, yelling, 'Go clean my toilet!' and 'I don't need my shoes shined.' That is racist. The mayor can take care of himself."

———

The call letters *KSFO* resonate with long-time San Franciscans because for years it was the radio station that epitomized the city over the air. Self-billed as "the world's greatest radio station," its audience was huge during the sixties and seventies. "Hear the sound of the city on KSFO," extolled one of its jingles, and the message was accurate. KSFO was one of those radio stations that industry used to call "full-service." Some music was played, the disc jockeys—especially legendary star Don Sherwood—gossiped, joked, and were major players in San Francisco's social and political life, and the Giants baseball games were broadcast over the solid 560 AM frequency.

By the mid-nineties, the station was foundering with a mix of talk shows—its good old days vanquished by a fragmenting audience. The elimination of the FCC rule forbidding one owner from buying more than one AM or FM station in any given market allowed ABC, the owners of talk monster KGO, to purchase its San Francisco competition, and just after the start of 1995, KSFO shocked listeners with its new incarnation: hysterical, strident, divisive programming proclaimed "hot talk" and pretending to be representative of conservative politics.

The success of Rush Limbaugh freed the radio industry to feel licensed to broadcast even more outlandish talk material on the fringes of good taste, political responsibility, and fairness. KSFO's new morning announcer, J. Paul Emerson, a simplistic screamer with marginal command of English grammar, is an example of the post-Limbaugh generation of political talk radio shock announcers. During his debut month, I listened—with some astonishment—to the deterioration he brought to public discourse.

With regularity that matches most radio stations' traffic and weather reports, Emerson calls his targets "assholes" and "slimebags" and "buttheads." Over five years after the fall of the Berlin Wall, he warns his listeners about the "Commie Vietnamese," the "Commie Chinese," and, bizarrely, the "Commie Russians." The Japanese are on his list, too. "We're going to end up having a war against the Japanese," he broadcast over the San Francisco station he was fired from before he joined KSFO. "Until the day I die I will hate the Japanese." After the killer Kobe earthquake, he mocked those sending aid to the victims.

Flag-waving Emerson yells that he is "pissed-off" and daily recommends that someone with whom he disagrees be "lined up against a wall and shot." The president of the Chrysler Corporation is an example. Emerson yelled for several days that "the president of Chrysler should be shot as a traitor for taking jobs to Mexico." When the peso was devalued and the Mexican economy stumbled, Emerson screamed his disgust with "Mexican dictators," saying, "We ought to go down there and shoot those sons of bitches" instead of providing financial support.

Emerson called for the quarantine of people suffering from AIDS on the fiftieth anniversary day of the liberation of Auschwitz. A caller managed to blurt out before being dumped, "People like you established those camps."

"Shut up, you asshole," was Emerson's response, explaining he could not be so equated because, "I don't hate homosexuals, I hate the disease AIDS."

Later that morning, another caller joined the fray and with relative calm suggested that Emerson's hateful programming is dangerous. With a credible argument he suggested that broadcasting such venom could not be considered simply business, but that—just as in Germany in the thirties—the greedy businessmen and women who believe they control announcers like Emerson and who believe they simply use them for commerce will lose control of their dupes as social and governmental institutions are bypassed and crushed by demagogues. Mid-morning host Tom Kamb—almost as wild on the air as Emerson—was behind the microphone to field that call, and he yelled back with a barrage of personal insults directed at the caller, never addressing the substance of the caller's rational complaint. Kamb ended the call with a belligerent severing of the connection and a final torrent of abuse, "Don't call me again, Roger!" Kamb's voice was cracking, as he screamed, "Change the station!"

The new KSFO used the First Amendment as an excuse for its hateful words, and its hosts suggested that those opposed to what they heard on its air were anti-American censors. The station gave away miniature American flags as a premium to callers.

Hate, scapegoating, and stereotyping fill the airwaves of Atlanta's important news source WSB, too. The station hired ratings-success Neal Boortz away from crosstown rival WGST. Boortz now takes home over $200,000 a year for spewing out barrages like this one I heard in January 1995—his response to the arrest of three boys for attempted robbery. The boys were picked up at their mother's home. "When police came to her welfare house and knocked on this welfare queen's door and took her little predators away, this woman, who by the way was about the size of a phone booth—she obviously puts her food stamps and welfare checks to good use—she was screaming like a stuck pig because the police were taking her little predator welfare tickets away!" I was driving through Atlanta, listening, driving past streets named for Martin Luther King Jr. and Ralph Abernathy while Boortz continued, talking as if he were speaking directly to the mother, telling her that her children will "go into the system and they'll be home in a few days, and when they grow up, they'll probably kill somebody! Maybe even somebody you know!"

"It is a prized American privilege to speak one's mind, though not always with perfect good taste, on all public institutions," Justice Hugo Black wrote in an important Supreme Court decision regarding the free speech rights of Harry Bridges and the *Los Angeles Times* (*Bridges* vs. *California,* 1941). Had he been listening to J. Paul Emerson or Neal Boortz or any of the rapidly growing post-Limbaugh radio talkers when he was working on his opinion, he probably would have still voted for free speech, but undoubtedly with a grimace of distress.

═════

Sleaze on talk radio often takes the form of commercial hustling. Broadcasting history is thick with snake oil (or billy-goat gonad) salesmen. Dr. John R. Brinkley, armed with a medical degree earned in a month at the Eclectic Medical University in Kansas City, created a sensation in the twenties with his cure for impotency. The technique called for transplanting slivers of billy-goat gonads into the scrotum. To further his practice and its income, Brinkley applied for the first Kansas commercial radio license and went on the air over KFKB late in 1923. Business boomed. But by the early thirties, under pressure from the American Medical Association and the Federal Radio Commission, Brinkley left for Mexico and established a new radio outlet across the border from Del Rio, Texas, the 75,000-watt XER. With it, a new industry was born: radio on the Mexican border, blasting into the United States, usually with messages—from those shrouded in religion to the overt commercial—that resulted in listeners remitting money to the broadcasters.

In *Border Radio,* a rollicking account of border-blaster radio,

Gene Fowler and Bill Crawford transcribe a sample of Brinkley's pitch over XER, seeking customers for his billy-goat transplant clinic:

> Life offers few sights more tragic than that of a splendid, successful man, keen of mind, robust of body, transformed into an old weakling, tottering on the brink of senility, his mental powers waning, his body constantly fatigued. Contrast the castrated animal, of any species, with the natural male or female. Note the difference, for instance, between the stallion and the gelding. The former stands erect, neck arched, mane flowing, chomping the bit, stamping the ground, seeking the female, while the gelding stands around half-asleep, cowardly, and listless, with no interest in anything.
>
> You people who are all the time grunting and groaning, never fit for anything, you are entirely to blame for your condition. You probably have used poor judgment. The great trouble with our world today is a shortage of thinkers, men who can stand on their own feet. If you are a red-blooded he-man with a real backbone, we will hear from you. Delay is oh, so dangerous. Many untimely graves have been filled with people who put off until tomorrow what they should have done today. It is, you know, your health or your funeral.
>
> Dr. Brinkley is anxious to help you if you are man enough to help yourself. You only can make the answer. What is it, please?

By the late thirties, the AMA was successfully prosecuting Brinkley in American courts, and the Mexican government closed down his radio station. But Brinkley and his pioneering radio colleagues spawned imitators both along the border and throughout broadcasting that continue to successfully extract cash from the audience.

Especially vulnerable are listeners seeking financial advice. Since the deregulation of the radio industry in the eighties, the time each hour that may be filled with commercial messages is no longer limited. Although commercials are supposed to be clearly labeled as such if their content is not obvious, commercials masquerading as information programming fill the airwaves, in violation of Federal Communications Commission rules and regulations.

Some financial advice programs are hosted by hustlers who buy the air time from radio stations and use the talk show format and their own charismatic personalities to camouflage their pitches to sell their own services. A lucrative trick is to then subcontract a portion of that time to "guests" who appear, again in the guise of the familiar talk show format, to peddle their products and services while posing as experts. This practice is not illegal if the audience is informed. Skillful performers can obey the letter of the law while confusing many listeners into believing that they are being offered an opportunity to learn important information instead of simply being exposed to a fast-talking sales pitch.

In a sobering 1991 exposé of radio financial advisers, *Money* magazine advised, "Given the number of scoundrels behind the microphones, keep one hand on the dial and the other on your wallet."

# 12 The Workhorses of American Talk Radio

*Travus T. Hipp looks out over the snow-covered* mountains of the Nevada desert and unleashes still another one-liner: "Like Zapata," he announces to whoever may be listening—well before the Zapatista Liberation Army attacked the Mexican establishment in Chiapas—"I am in the hills—forever in the hills."[1] The talk show host hasn't always been in the hills; California radio listeners with memories that span back to the late sixties and early seventies know the Hipp *nom de guerre* from San Francisco and KMPX, the old KSAN, and what Hipp calls the "relevant talk radio at that time, which has, like most good rock and roll, disappeared from the airwaves."

Until the landmark casino closed down, Hipp could be found broadcasting live from the Ormsby House in Carson City, filling the desert airwaves with the sounds of all-American anarchy, mixed with heartfelt commercial endorsements for advertisers he clearly patronizes: "Whether you're looking for fine steaks or Long Island duck, stop by the Misfits Supper Club in Dayton, right behind the Old Corner Bar. You tell 'em Travus T. Hipp told you to stop by for the finest meal in western Nevada, and if you don't get it, tell me about it." But politics constitute the main course on Hipp's show broadcast on KPTL, and he gets just as passionate about the local race for county commissioner as he does about the Gulf War.

"Hi, you're on the air!"

"Good morning, Travus."

"Hi, Jay." Hipp recognizes many of his regular callers, and hearing the show is like listening in on neighbors chatting and arguing.

"Jim Brady is the poster boy of gun control." Jay is mad that Congress approved the seven-day waiting period for gun sales. "He's the pest they wheel out. I'm talking about the sympathy number."

"People with guns don't need sympathy," responds Hipp. "Gun control is not about Bambi-bashing. I've got a gun because I may someday need to do something about my government."

The show cartwheels, taking on American support of Israel, inadequate boat-launching ramps on Nevada lakes, and everything in between. Off the air and over a glass of milk and a bowl of vegetable soup in the casino coffee shop, Hipp keeps talking: radio and his self-exile to Nevada.

"Nobody uses talk radio in San Francisco," he says. "It's become totally meaningless. I get to define talk radio in western Nevada. I make it work for the audience as a tool for political change." Hipp talks about his listeners as neighbors and coconspirators. "My people come to the legislature, form phone trees. Activism is still possible, both from my position as a host and for those who use my show. We're a small enough state that you can get a handle on the powers that be."

Hipp gets excited talking about the important function he's convinced talk radio can play in modern society, a role he sees neglected by the practitioners of the business in San Francisco. So does he wish he were back in the big time, plying his wares?

"Not at all," is the immediate comeback. "It's also the lifestyle. I live in a small town. Clean air. Mountain vistas. I can shoot guns to my heart's content, drive fast on dirt roads, and generally carry on in a manner that's not allowed in California. That's what Nevada is for."

This is clearly a theme that Hipp's thought out and been over before, that of the San Francisco expatriate. "For many years San Francisco was a bastion of independence and freedom. That tolerance and libertine atmosphere is no longer the rule. San Francisco is no longer a party."

Not that he wouldn't come back, confesses the fourth-generation San Franciscan with an intrigued glint, "If there were a station dedicated to talk radio and having fun . . ."

Periodically Hipp climbs into an old Toyota station wagon adorned on its side panels with a fading NBC trademark and the call letters of a defunct Nevada radio station and heads down to California, poking around for more prominent and lucrative work. He bought the news cruiser from the radio station, and as he hoists himself out of the little car, his leathery and lined face, long braid, and cowboy boots combine incongruously with the KOLO NEWS sign painted on the side of the battered little car. His nonconformist looks and the corporate car combine as an example of the type of cultural clash that Hipp revels in and seeks both on and off the air.

On one of his California jaunts I caught up with Hipp at the Savoy Tivoli, a landmark café and bar in San Francisco's North Beach. We've know each other since his KSAN days, often hosting the meandering Sunday-morning talk show there together. His long brown hair, now adorned with plenty of gray, is braided into a red Tibetan string braid he picked up years ago on a trip to Nepal. The extended braid is wrapped around his beret.

"We were too far ahead of the trend to make a dollar on it," he says, musing about talk radio's phenomenal success since the early days of talk we shared at KSAN.[2] "The society at large needs some sort of communications mechanism. Thirty years ago there was a lot of protest and the younger 20 percent of America invented a number of systems of networking at that time to stay in touch with each other." Hipp is warming up. On and off the air he loves to hear himself talk; he loves to draw public attention. "Today you have the same feelings of disassociation and anger in probably 80 percent of the population, and just as we did when we were protesting students, the middle-aged-redneck fringe and the it's-all-a-flying-saucer-cannibal-hoax fringe and the gun-nut fringe and everybody are finding some way of staying in touch with each other"—here Hipp's voice rises with a theatrical inflection of satisfaction—"through the medium of radio!"

So goes his theory of talk radio and its late-twentieth-century success. And in many respects he is correct. The radio talk show shares similarities with the barber shop, the coffee house, the bar, the general store cracker-barrel, the backyard fence. It is a meeting point for socializing—from idle chatter to rabble-rousing to serious philosophizing, and even calls for political and other types of action. But there are important differences, too. Remember, the talk show experience is almost always an anonymous one. The vast majority of listeners are passive; they never call. And those who do call often face a long wait on hold just for the opportunity to spend a few minutes—at most—on the air, engaged in a conversation that continues only at the pleasure of the host. Such an arrangement is a bizarre replacement for the sense of community that a chat around the barber shop routinely offered earlier generations of Americans.

Shallow and removed from physical interaction, talk radio nonetheless passes for important social intercourse for many Americans, and consequently the new power of the talk radio stars infuriates Hipp. "If Rush Limbaugh and his audience of knee-jerk fascist assholes are the mean measure of the American political mentality at this time, which they are in terms of talk radio, then we're all in deep shit. If they aren't, then the question becomes one of why hasn't any other element of the political spectrum or responsible society done something to take this cat out."

For Travus T. Hipp, the answer is simple: conspiracy. He interprets the right-wing veer of talk radio as the natural result of deregulation in the broadcasting industry. "Radio licenses, even AM licenses, cost an arm, a leg, and your ass. The people who can

afford to pay those kind of prices for radio licenses are, by the very
nature of their business, investors. They are capitalists. They are
people who have a vested interest in a peaceful and controlled
business environment."

I interrupted his speech long enough for him to take a drink of
the Red Hook ale he was nursing. The Grateful Dead was blasting
out of the speakers. We were sharing one of the Tivoli's sidewalk
tables—chipped, round black marble—watching the Saturday
night scene passing on upper Grant Avenue. I suggested that his
conspiracy theory was too complex, that the broadcasting business
is simpler and more selfish than he figured. Radio stations would
turn their microphones over to a Lenny Bruce and a Gus Hall if
they felt Bruce and Hall could host talk shows that would earn the
amount of money Limbaugh and Stern generate.

"If they had their choice between Lenny Bruce and Adolf Eichmann," was Hipp's disgusted response, "they would go with Adolf
Eichmann." He is convinced that talk radio is rigged. "The entire
debate as it is presently centered is semantically incorrect. We're
not talking conservatives and liberals. Limbaugh et al. invented
that bifurcated terminology. What he made are conservatives who
are neofacists. Ask Barry Goldwater. He'll tell you. He wouldn't
touch those cats with a ten-foot pole. Barry Goldwater is a conservative. Limbaugh is a fascist."

The other half of the problem, Hipp explains correctly, is that
too many of those people opposed to or offended by Limbaugh
allow him to identify them as liberals. "Nobody likes liberals, man.
Liberals are the wimps of the fucking world. Liberals vote and
march, but they don't fight. And liberals are incapable, because
they are too nice and too polite, of taking on a gutter-fighting little
asshole like Rambo." He likes to refer to Limbaugh as Lush
Rambo as he attacks Limbaugh's credibility, education, and political sophistication.

Hipp's face contorts with disgust and frustration. "The question
is, knowing that he will not rise above this particular level of bad
information, disinformation, and demagoguery, why doesn't any-

body else do it?" It is a question that plagues the radio industry. Where is the next Limbaugh-like success? That refrain is usually sounded because networks and radio stations want to discover another cash machine—not because they share Travus T. Hipp's concern that alternative viewpoints to Limbaugh's enjoy an opportunity to reach the growing talk radio audience. "Nobody is counterattacking from anyplace to the left of center-liberal," is his continuing lament, "and center-liberals don't hold up."

The music at the Savoy has changed to a mournful jazz. Hipp looks out on Grant Avenue and reminisces about his boyhood. He grew up in the neighborhood back in the fifties, on the periphery of the burgeoning beat scene. I ask him if he believes that some of the vitriol he directs at Limbaugh is motivated by a little old-fashioned envy. After all, Hipp is on the air on one little Nevada radio station these days, while Limbaugh's meteoric rise now includes his media empire of hundreds of radio stations, his television show, and his best-selling books, along with such perquisites as stretch limousines and an overnight at the Bush White House.

"I can set that aside easily enough," insists Hipp, while acknowledging some jealousy. "It's been pretty obvious since the middle sixties, man, that our generation of drop-out psychedelia rebels and troublemakers was never going to be given access to the corridors of power and the levers of manipulation of our society. China did it, man. China took the cultural revolutionaries and said, 'Forget it, you're going noplace. Here's your apartment, get some menial labor, make hash pipes, call yourself an artist, do whatever you want. You're out.'"

I suggest his theory of marginalization is farfetched and his response is immediate. "That's because you've never been paranoid." It is just such glib and rambling ranting, combined with conviction, that makes an intriguing talk show host—and Hipp concludes with a quote from his dominant radio mentor, Tom Donahue, the architect of KSAN and the other so-called "underground" radio stations of the late sixties and early seventies. "There are," Hipp recites as I've heard him do so many times over the years, "innovators, operators, and undertakers. We, as innovators of the sixties, were unique and we are being punished for it to this day."

He drains his Red Hook and our conversation degenerates as we debate each other. I reject the conspiracy theory, using my own position as news and program director at the mainstream talk station in the nation's capital as my prime example; he insists I'm naive as he expresses some admiration for Limbaugh and his clones. "The point is that they are utilizing this medium and this format as their communications network. Because nobody else is challenging them in that usage, because there is no equivalent station over on the other side of the dial that is primarily left wing, there is no balance to it." He takes a bite of pepperoni pizza and keeps on pontificating without hesitation—his mouth full. "If a given issue comes up and the right wing screams bloody fucking murder on the talk radio station and generates 40,000 letters, the fact that there is no station which screams, 'Great job, Bill Clinton,' and generates 38,000 letters in praise, leaves the field to the right wing."

Hipp sounds evangelistic as he returns to his frustration with the lack of alternative voices to Limbaugh on nationwide talk radio. "Never mind who the audience is now. That's a temporary situation if you start dealing with the medium itself. The fact that it is currently dominated by mindless lumpen-proletariat right-wing redneck assholes is simply because those are the people who are on the air. You can take the audience that is out there now who are dissatisfied with society and government—the ones the right wing is recruiting—and offer them an alternative. They've started to think about politics. You can only stay ignorant in politics for a very limited amount of time, at which point if you have some alternative philosophical and political positions to offer, people will move past the politically inert mentality." When I ask him why he reduces all the questions I throw out at him to politics, he says, "Because in America, life is politics. There isn't a fucking thing out there that isn't politics."

A few days later we meet again, this time in the studios of KPTL, across from the Kmart parking lot and hidden away in a strip of offices on the south side of Carson City. I arrive just prior to noon, when *Travus T. Hipp and the Rawhide Realities Review* goes on the air, filling Carson City, Lake Tahoe, Reno, and the western deserts of Nevada with Hipp's sonorous interpretations of the news and life in general. "I don't begrudge him his success," Hipp tells me just before the show starts, bringing up Limbaugh again. "But I do begrudge everyone to the left of neofascist for failing to respond and utilize radio for their ends." Clearly he spent time since our last conversation considering who might be to blame for the lack of balance on talk radio across America. "I want to participate in how our times change." The words come out passionately. "Radio is the weapon I drew from the armory when we went into battle in the sixties. I never expected to make a million dollars. We're all fucking lucky to have work."

We settle down in the studio. Crystal, the disc jockey, is packing up her materials—the radio station mostly broadcasts music. The two trade hair-care ideas; his is longer, there is no gray in hers. Hipp's braid is still tied to the Tibetan string. This day, instead of wrapping around the beret, it hangs loose over his Buddha-like belly, a belly pushing against a stained blue flannel shirt. Over the shirt is a safari vest. Hipp stands expectantly at the microphone, his hands jammed into the pockets of corduroy slacks, as his theme song plays.

KPTL is a ramshackle place. Coffee is festering in a pot near the front door. Broken acoustical tiles decorate the studio ceiling; a messy box of worn phonograph records, some compact discs, and a few cartridge tapes litter the floor. A Patti Page album called "Golden Hits," issued by Mercury, is at the front of the stack of records. The album displays Page glowing in a strapless formal next to a music stand. Photographically superimposed on the cover alongside Page is a stack of old 45-rpm records on a thick plastic spindle. On the mobile-home-style wood-paneled wall is a bumper sticker that says KILL YOUR TELEVISION alongside tattered old record album covers—*Bob Dylan: The Bootleg Series* among them. The Emergency Broadcast System Checklist is hanging from a pushpin.

A derelict turntable, the tone arm off its support, is adjacent to the microphone stand, next to it is an empty tape dispenser.

Hipp slides a weathered tape cartridge into a player and pushes the start button as the ABC network news at noon ends. The tape is deteriorating from age and overuse. The sound of the theme song is muddy; a new listener would need to strain to understand the words. But Hipp's regulars hear it every hour. They probably can sing along, as he does, under his breath, the microphone not yet turned on, the words, written in 1978 by Mike Wilhelm (of the sixties band the Charlatans, who eventually opened an espresso café in San Francisco's financial district), filling the studio:

> *I can't read the morning paper,*
> *Because it just fills my heart with fear,*
>
> *And still would have you believing*
> *That it can't happen here.*

The refrain is the repetition of the words, "Hear the people!" and Hipp finally turns on his microphone, saying, "And right here is where you can hear the people!" He looks out the window. "Good afternoon. It must be Sunday. I'm Travus T. Hipp. The sun is shining in Nevada." He clearly loves to listen to himself, as does any successful talk show host. He hesitates only a few seconds before figuring out what he is going to talk about. He starts, "And, ah . . ." Then switches to, "I've been hearing reports . . ." But he interrupts himself again and says, "We have been . . ." Finally he settles on, "God grant that it doesn't turn into a drought. We have been particularly blessed, you understand. We had a brief little enough snow-to-make-sure-that-the-piñons-don't-die-right-away-kind-of-storm last weekend and now here it is back to blissful Bohemian weather. It's amazing, it's wonderful, and friends who have flown in where they had to wait with bated breath to see if the de-icing of their aircraft would allow them to get into the air are blinking in the sudden glare of this remote orb in the sky which has brought warmth and light. It has been a pig-whistler back on the East Coast, friends. Three times as many people died in the East Coast in the freeze-down that has gone on simultaneously with all of the silliness in shaky, quaky San Fernando."

His voice drops as he finally takes a breath and a new thought occurs to him, triggered by his weather report. "I wonder how my friends, the transvestite chorus girls in Kagel Canyon, are weathering this particular shake. They lived through the last one quite comfortably. There are areas down there in the San Fernando Valley which—"

Suddenly Hipp interrupts himself again and starts a new train of thought. He's had an idea, and he launches into a long soliloquy suggesting that the San Fernando Valley be returned to agricultural use. "You're not going to stop the San Fernando Valley from having earthquakes," he explains, his voice crackling with enthusiasm for this utopian project that seems to have just occurred to him. He sounds like a cross between a preacher and a campaigning politician, the words coming out in an almost Jesse Jackson–like cadence—but tinged with some frivolity. "You're not going to stop the San Fernando Valley from having earthquakes, but you could guarantee that very few things, except for a few potbellied Vietnamese pigs, would be casualties. The north San Fernando Valley is a great place to grow avocados or oranges. It is a lousy place to grow freeways and people! Relocate 'em! We're all supposed to move when it's time to move and the idea of rebuilding this incredible infrastructure dedicated to the 1953 De Soto as a commuter car in Los Angeles at the cost of billions of dollars that we don't have for anything else of any meaningful need"—his voice rises and falls with gleeful enthusiasm for his own words as he concludes—"is ridiculous."

Hipp works like a jazz player without charts—improvising his rants and raves, his comments and challenges to listeners' remarks, changing the subject whimsically. He chews on an orange while he listens to the callers, staring vacantly through the window at the desert hills of east Carson City.

# 13

## Politicians and Academics Ponder the Talk Radio Threat

*About an hour's drive north of the Golden Gate* Bridge, nestled along the Highway 101 corridor in still mostly rural Sonoma County, is California's Sonoma State University. The school is where Professor Carl Jensen headquarters his Project Censored, an ongoing study of stories his research determines to be underreported by American journalists and the print and broadcast outlets for which they labor. I became well acquainted with Jensen's analysis of the popular media in America when I taught at Sonoma State, and I sought him out as an expert witness for this study of talk radio because of my appreciation for his work—work that is a standard annual reference point for those involved in criticizing American media.

Jensen is no stranger to talk radio; he has been guest, critic, and target. In his book *Censored!* Jensen quotes KGO talk show host Jim Eason as calling him a "left-wing horse's ass." The jingoistic Eason, trying to outdo Limbaugh and cash in on war fever, achieved some fame during the Persian Gulf war by demanding on the air that patriotic newspapers print American flags for their subscribers. Some caved in to his offensive assault. Among those that did not was the *San Jose Mercury News,* whose editor, Bob Ingle, told the trade magazine *Editor and Publisher*[1] that the paper suffered over 200 subscription cancellations as a result of Eason's diatribe. The tabloid *SF Weekly* not only refused to print the flag, but editor Marcello Rodriguez challenged Eason to read the U.S. Constitution on the air during his program to prove his own patriotism and to remind him of his nation's roots. Eason refused to read more than the preamble, pleading time restraints.

Jensen and I meet in a café in Cotati in January 1994, his sparkling eyes accenting his enthusiasm for our inspection of the influence of talk radio on journalism and American culture. I begin the conversation reiterating my concern about credibility. The blurring of the line between news reporting and nonjournalistic entertainment that most radio talk shows indulge in fascinates and worries me because the audience appears so gullible. "It seems to me," I offer, "that during the talk show, the audience believes, for the most part, what the announcer says. Talk radio hosts enjoy built-in credibility, credibility developed for radio reporting by heroes of the business—like Edward R. Murrow working from the roofs of London during the Blitz. Now that trust, won over the years by radio reporters, often is being violated by talk radio hosts running fast and loose with the facts—and sometimes just lying over the air—and the audience believes the words just because they come from an authoritative voice on the radio."

Jensen sips his caffè latte and agrees with the premise. "I think the public cannot distinguish between Edward R. Murrow and Rush Limbaugh. They are using the same medium, and the public thinks that Rush Limbaugh is the successor to the Edward R. Murrows of radio; the people think they are both news commentators." But Jensen sees talk show hosts filling a role that is entirely different than the one filled by traditional news reporters. "These people, the Rush Limbaughs and the Larry Kings, they are not news commentators. Entertainers is what they are."

I question why the general public does not make the needed distinction between entertainers and journalists and instead is accepting the Limbaughs and Kings as reporters simply because they present themselves as purveyors of news. Theirs is self-announced and self-created credibility, accepted by a passive public. It's difficult for me to understand why the public is so unaware of the basic ingredients on the radio. "Why is the same consumer who test-drives a car before buying it or reads the label on food at the supermarket accepting with so little question what they hear on the radio?" I ask Jensen. "Is it because of the naiveté of the audience or the power of the medium, or both?"

"They are naive," Jensen says. "I will grant you that. Over the years, I think people have been so indoctrinated by Madison Avenue and propagandists that they have come to accept the messages regardless of their source, and regardless of how strange they might sound. Madison Avenue today says that in order to get the young people, they have to start propagandizing them at the age of three. Everyone grows up with radio, it's the constant media. Radio is very big when you're a teenager; radio continues on as you go into college and when you become a commuter. Radio is always there. Whereas, magazines, newspapers, television are not necessarily that constant a medium."

I say that I can understand how his theory could explain that Americans give what they hear over the radio the benefit of the doubt. But it is difficult for me to come to terms with the almost blind acceptance that the members of the audiences engage in as they embrace their talk show heroes.

Jensen tells me he thinks the portion of the audience believing without much question what is being broadcast is pre-prejudiced. Many select their favorite program based on a simple process: "They will tend to listen to people they agree with. So if you tend to agree with a Rush Limbaugh, then you believe what a Rush Limbaugh says."

I consider his point, a conclusion shared by the Times Mirror Center study on talk radio. "This blurring between entertainment and journalism that so offends the two of us," I offer, "is it really wrong or just a natural media development that must be accepted? Why do we—who are traditionalists in this regard—feel so compelled to oppose and judge this mixture of information transfer and sideshow act?"

Jensen's response is adamant. "If people cannot differentiate between a Rush Limbaugh and a Peter Arnett, we've got big problems, because Peter Arnett is responsible for what he says and does, whereas a Rush Limbaugh is irresponsible for what he says and does. To think that talk shows really drove the last election is an absolutely astounding thing."

I return the conversation to the blurring between fact and fancy. "Isn't it the consumer's responsibility to listen with enough sophistication to learn how to differentiate between what constitutes a credible news report and what is a talk show host just acting wild and crazy? How can we indict the hosts who are blurring the old distinctions as a device to provide themselves with a broader platform and higher ratings? They can then make more money with a larger audience. So isn't it the audience's, the consumer's, responsibility to differentiate?"

I tell the story of a talk show host who worked for me and regularly presented misinformation—and outright lies—simply in an attempt to incite a response from the audience, a response he hoped would translate into improved ratings. Whenever I would reprimand him about his lack of concern over credibility, he scoffed that credibility was not his business, that he was an entertainer.

"As a society, we have made a decision to give a platform to people to say whatever they wish on the radio, with no restrictions—even if they are intentionally misrepresenting things," I point out. "Is that right or wrong?"

"Oh, that's absolutely right," First Amendment–absolutist Jensen shoots back with no hesitation. "And thank God for that. As much as I abhor Howard Stern, I really resent the administration and the FCC and all the rest for trying to close him down. I totally disagree with that." Any policy must originate within the media itself, Jensen says. "The media have a responsibility as well as a right, which is inherent in the First Amendment. I tell them, and I really believe this, if they abuse that responsibility they're going to lose that right. If they abuse the responsibility, they are going to lose the right of the First Amendment, and the First Amendment will be taken away from the media."

I ask Jensen if he's being rhetorical with his warning or if he really believes that the First Amendment could be in jeopardy.

"Oh absolutely, absolutely."

"You believe the climate is right for that?" I persist, perhaps because I take the First Amendment so for granted that I have been lulled into complacency. While I am troubled by trends in the media, I never worry about losing the security of the First Amendment.

"I really believe there will be this incredible reaction over a period of time," Jensen says. "People will be pressuring Congress."

=====

People already are.

In 1987, as government deregulation swept the broadcasting industry free of most mandated responsibility to serve the public, the Federal Communications Commission voted unanimously to eliminate the Fairness Doctrine. The Fairness Doctrine dates to 1949, when the FCC enacted the rule in an attempt to offset any restrictions of free speech caused by the limited access to broadcasting stations. The intrusion was justified because broadcasting differs from print. It is distributed over the limited and public airwaves—public property that is properly regulated by the government.

The Fairness Doctrine was written to ensure that a licensed broadcaster would "devote reasonable attention to the coverage of controversial issues of public importance." There is nothing intimidating about that rule, nor about its correlative requirement that to accomplish the goal of covering controversial issues of public importance, "reasonable, although not necessarily equal" opportunities to express opposing views to those originally broadcast had to be offered to members of the public.

An example of how the FCC enforced its ruling came to the offices of radio station WGAY in Washington, D.C., on March 11,

1971, back when the Fairness Doctrine was law. "Gentlemen," wrote the Commission in the official language of the era,

We have been informed that at approximately 7:30 A.M. on March 9, 1971, Station WGAY-FM broadcast an announcement advocating support for the SST super-sonic plane and implying that persons opposed to the SST project supported the Soviet Union and, by inference, were anti-American. Complainant alleges that the broadcast of the announcement constituted presentation of one side of a controversial issue of public importance, and that in response to a telephone call, Mr. Chandler of your staff stated that he could not say whether the licensee had plans to attempt to present contrasting views on this subject.

Since the complaint raises a question of compliance with the Fairness Doctrine, you are requested within ten days of the date of this letter to furnish the Commission with your comments thereon. Please furnish the Commission with a transcript or recording of any such announcements which have been broadcast or which you intend to broadcast, state whether you believe such announcements to involve a controversial issue of public importance, and if so, what efforts the licensee has made or proposes to make to present contrasting views.

Attached for your information is a copy of the Commission's Public Notice on applicability of the Fairness Doctrine in the Handling of Controversial Issues of Public Importance. Your attention is particularly called to Ruling Number 17 (Letter to Cullman Broadcasting Co., Inc.), which states that the fact that advocates of one side of a controversial issue have paid for presentation of their viewpoint does not relieve the licensee from its responsibilities regarding presentation of opposing views, even if sponsorship cannot be obtained for broadcast of the opposing views.

The letter was signed by William B. Ray, chief of the Complaints and Compliance Division of the FCC. Being forced to air the remarks of someone opposed to the SST hardly constitutes the chilling effect on free speech that opponents of the Fairness Doctrine charge is the result of the requirements of the law. In fact, during the same period that Ray wrote his letter to WGAY, across the country at KSAN we were airing talk shows and news broadcasts which clearly were advocacy and participatory journalism. Adhering to the requirements of the Fairness Doctrine was never a problem for us; we enjoyed filling our shows with what we considered was the work of the loyal opposition to the government. We were certain that the comments of those with whom we disagreed only helped reinforce our own positions. We never felt that the government (and Nixon and his gang of dirty tricksters were in charge of the FCC at the time) and its policies were intimidating us into changing the content of our news or talk shows.

The requirements of the Fairness Doctrine are the requirements of good programming. As programmer Willis Duff wrote in one of his memoranda to the talk show staff at KLAC back in the sixties, "This is to reiterate our constant obligation to assure that both sides of all public issues are aired on this station. Both Communicasters and producers should strive to obtain listener reaction from all areas of the public opinion spectrum. In the unlikely event that both public and Communicaster opinion is unilateral on a specific issue, the opposite opinions should be solicited on the air. All Communicasters must seek out newsmakers and guests with top priority assigned to finding competent spokesmen for the positions in opposition to those of the air personality."

Of course, the note deals with the requirements of the Fairness Doctrine, but the last line indicates the self-serving reality of the FCC rule for broadcasters: "This will lead to more stimulating and provocative programming as well as a totally fair presentation of all specific issues."

Several times since the FCC dropped the rule in 1987, Congress has attempted to force the Fairness Doctrine back into effect by law. One of its principal sponsors was Massachusetts Democratic Representative Edward Markey, who insists it "does not allow the government to sit in judgment of the broadcaster's editorial judgment. It makes no requirement upon matters that are private or personal in nature, such as religious or moral views."[2] The first try at passing the proposed legislation came immediately after the FCC action to remove the rule; the congressional margin of approval was substantial, but inadequate to override a veto from President Reagan. When the bill was proposed again in 1993, the atmosphere was remarkably changed. Talk radio had come into its own; over a thousand stations were succeeding with a talk format. The *Wall Street Journal* decided to lead the charge against the bill by aligning itself with listeners mustered for the fight by Rush Limbaugh.

The *Journal* escalated the debate by misleadingly labeling the Fairness Doctrine the "Hush Rush Rule" and claiming that Democrats wanted to reenact the rule as a device to stifle Limbaugh, Pat Buchanan, Gene Burns, G. Gordon Liddy, and other right-wing practitioners of the talk radio trade. "What's really behind the Hush Rush Rule," announced the *Journal,* "is that Members of Congress just don't like the wide interest in public policy matter that talk radio generates."

The Fairness Doctrine would not silence Limbaugh and the others. It might place an expensive burden on broadcasters who choose not to present "coverage of controversial issues of public importance." But talk shows—and responsible broadcasters, no matter the format—do just that, and reimplementation of the rule would likely have no effect on talk shows that use controversy as fodder and solicit telephone calls from the audience. Radio station KSL in Salt Lake City made that clear in its public response to the lifting of the Fairness Doctrine in 1987. "KSL has always addressed the community needs and problems," the radio station announced,[3] "with news, public affairs programs, and editorials. We will continue to do so, with or without the Fairness Doctrine."

Larry King was one of the few nationally known broadcasters to come out in favor of reinstating the Fairness Doctrine, and he did it boldly, frequently advocating his position during his talk show and in his newspaper column. "Every responsible broadcaster I know likes the Fairness Doctrine," he stated with more than a taste of hyperbole, "because fairness is what the U.S.A. is all about."[4]

"That comment is just full of sophistry and bullshit," Limbaugh told Lou Prato for an article on Limbaugh's role opposing the Fairness Doctrine.[5] "The United States is not about fairness. That's Larry's side of it from the competitive side. Larry's got an exemption from it. The Fairness Doctrine would not hinder him." Limbaugh was leading up to his attack, using language he could not use on his radio program with or without a Fairness Doctrine "Larry doesn't say shit. He asks people questions. What Larry does is not at all what many talk show hosts do. So anything that would hamper the structure of shows which compete with him he would obviously favor."

The specific wording of the proposed new Fairness Doctrine made clear its intent.[6] It was a "bill to clarify the congressional intent concerning, and to codify, certain requirements of the Communications Act of 1934 that ensure that broadcasters afford reasonable opportunity for the discussion of conflicting views on issues of public importance." The draft points out that "despite technological advances, the electromagnetic spectrum remains a scarce and valuable resource." It draws attention to the fact that "there are still substantially more people who want to broadcast than there are frequencies to allocate." And it reminds the current lords of the airwaves like Limbaugh that, unlike print, "a broadcast license confers the right to use a valuable public resource and a broadcaster is therefore required to utilize that resource as a trustee for the American people."

As representatives of those American people, the sponsors of the bill establish in its wording that "there is a substantial government interest in conditioning the award or renewal of a broadcast license on the requirement that the licensee ensure the widest possible dissemination of information from diverse and antagonistic sources by presenting a reasonable opportunity for the discussion of conflicting views on issues of public importance." Finally, it is germane to quote from the bill that "because the Fairness Doctrine only requires more speech, it has no chilling effect on broadcasters."

Limbaugh, who devotes a chapter of his second book to drumming up opposition to the Fairness Doctrine, manipulated the debate about the bill, posturing himself as its intended victim, calling it an attempt at revenge by Congress. But the Limbaugh show is only a fraction of a licensee's broadcast day, leaving plenty of time for conflicting views.

Pat Buchanan too seized on the Fairness Doctrine as an ideal talk show subject; it generates interest in a show and, adroitly presented, tends to elevate the importance of the talk show host in the minds of the audience. "The Fairness Doctrine requires that if you discuss issues on a radio station," Buchanan told his periodic cohost, former American Civil Liberties Union lawyer Barry Lynn, and his listeners nationwide, "you are required to give other sides, other viewpoints. Rush Limbaugh is saying that this is the 'Hush Rush' law. There's no doubt that because of the growth of religious broadcasting, traditional conservative broadcasting, the Feds and the boys in Washington want a club over the head of the conservatives because they're doing too well."[7] Since attempts, by a majority of Congress, to reenact the Fairness Doctrine predate the success of Limbaugh and his ilk, the argument fails. "All of a sudden conservatives do well on these little radio stations,"— Buchanan's show was being carried mostly on smaller stations around the country—"and down comes this big club."

Barry Lynn disagreed and correctly pointed out that the Fairness Doctrine could not exert any influence over a show like Buchanan's. It is, he said, "just an enforcement of one responsibility and that is to raise issues of public controversy. Any station in the United States that has the Pat Buchanan and Company show on it probably has fulfilled its obligation under the Fairness Doctrine because you hear a multitude of sides of controversial issues that are of importance to the average community."

Lynn and Buchanan started taking telephone calls. Stacks of callers agreed with Buchanan's stated fears and accepted them as their own. Among the subculture of regular callers to talk shows is a growing element of listeners who parrot back onto the airwaves what they hear their radio gods preaching. Limbaugh is particularly adept at training callers in how to carry the Limbaugh mes-

sage further around the ozone. His tone is jocular as he instructs
his audience that a three-hour daily dose of his program, will teach
them what is important and how to think. They don't need to go
elsewhere.

The device works well. The host and a seemingly endless array
of callers laugh with each other about the absurdity of callers
blindly following Limbaugh—and then the callers enthusiastically
confess that they use Limbaugh as their news sieve.

"The media no longer have the respect of the general public they
once did." This is not simply Professor Carl Jensen's opinion; he
sees study after study reaffirming the same conclusion. "Reporters
are now looked upon as somewhere close to shoe salesmen."

It is just this deterioration of respect for the so-called mainstream media that is helping talk radio enjoy its fast rise in popularity. From Rush Limbaugh to hosts working at tiny radio
stations in tiny markets, most successful talk show operators
attempt to position themselves as some sort of alternative source
for the audience because of the listener participation. It is a programming element that seduces Jensen, too. "What I consider the
really good thing about talk radio," he says, "is that it is the public's major access to the media. Talk radio is also the public's
major access to a mass audience." Aside from letters to the editor,
an opportunity offered by some periodicals and most newspapers,
Jensen sees talk radio as the only medium available for what he
calls "massive public access."

But while talk radio appears to be one of the most accessible
forms of mass media, those who have access are often tightly controlled through the screening process. Many, many callers are
passed over because they do not speak rapidly enough, because the
points they wish to make seem redundant or less interesting than
those of another waiting caller, because they do not represent the
geographical diversity of the potential audience, because they
speak with an accent, or simply because of the whims of the call
screener.

I suggest to Jensen that the rigors of getting past the screening process discourage most listeners from bothering to try. Consequently, what is being presented as the voice of the people really is the voice of the bored, the shut-in, and those with nothing better to do than wait on hold for an hour. "Given the questionable value of the caller," I ask, "why listen?"

"Regardless of the facts," he says, "people perceive radio to be the major avenue of access to a mass audience. Because they don't know what is going on, they perceive that they can get it on radio."

"America really thinks talk radio is a town meeting?" I ask.

"Yes, I absolutely believe that."

=======

Norman Solomon established his credentials as a media critic with his encyclopedic book on the status of American media, *Unreliable Sources*. He works with the organization Fairness and Accuracy in Reporting, and produces commentary on the media for the Pacific radio stations. At a café near the San Francisco train station we discussed the ascent of the talk show.

As our chat starts I ask Solomon for his explanation of the right-wing tilt of talk radio. "It has to do with the notion that progressives are somewhat of a loose cannon," he says. "And then there is that issue of confluence between advertising target and editorial copy. Welfare mothers don't generally buy as much in terms of having disposable income as people who would not be so uncomfortable listening to somebody who is bashing welfare mothers. I'm not saying people listen just because they agree with the host, but I think having some sort of comfort level is significant."

Solomon refuses to accept the idea that radio programming should be controlled by simply satisfying what the audience and advertisers are perceived by station managers to desire. "To some degree there is the issue that people can't choose what isn't offered to them. In general, talk show hosts who have kept their jobs are not really that interested in new ideas. They're interested in pounding the old drums."

I ask Solomon my standard question about credentials. "Why are the hosts in their chairs?" He tells me about being a guest on the extraordinarily long-running Ray Briem program on KABC in Los Angeles. During a break, Briem pulled out his Arbitron ratings and showed Solomon that the Briem show was number one during southern California nights. That is the credential, suggests Solomon, the ability to achieve high ratings, without regard to content. "If you were spinning all of the dials in all of the localities of the country," he tells me, "the chances are, when you spin that dial and land on a talk show, the host has nothing to say particularly worth listening to. I think that's the average."

"But if that's the case," I ask him, "what accounts for the surge of popularity of talk shows?"

"I think that a lot of it has to do with spontaneity and a sense of authenticity. So much broadcast media now has this feel of being prepackaged and premeditated. Talk radio fits the bill because it's kind of like, after seeing thousands of prefab buildings you would want something that would look a little funky. Talk radio sounds a little funky. A lot of the more commercially successful hosts create an ambience of being funky, irreverent, not predictable. So much of what we get through mass media seems like we've seen it before—even the local TV news. I've seen that fire before." He laughs.

Solomon agrees with Jensen that talk radio can be dangerous. He quotes Jim Hightower ("Just because Perot is a phony doesn't mean the people who support him are phonies") to make the point. "I think we could extrapolate that and say just because so many talk show hosts are phonies doesn't mean that the people who hang on their every word are phonies."

I draw Solomon's attention to the inherent phoniness—or potential for phoniness—of talk shows. Many talk show hosts use phony names on the air. The callers are anonymous as they speak over the radio using only their first names, and no effort is made to check the veracity of what they are saying. "It's another layer of the bogus," is his response. "It's simulation. You could say, I suppose, that talk radio is to genuine public debate as phone sex is to genuine sexual relations, and that may be giving the benefit of the doubt to talk radio."

Solomon hears the key phrases echoed by talk show hosts and callers as clues to the mythology of talk radio. I point out how "thank you for taking my call," is repeated like a common mantra from the audience to the radio gods. "I think that really is a revealing comment," he says, "because it reflects the idea that one is being granted a favor for the chance to even speak and share one's ideas. The callers are the supplicants in a way and they often literally are able to continue to talk only at the sufferance of the host. Whether it is bad temper, impatience, sharp disagreement, or the need to go to the news at the top of the hour, it's still the idea that we all kind of hope to get in a few words on borrowed time—that us lowly vermin are actually being elevated to be on the airwaves."

Solomon is also offended by the priority so many talk show hosts offer calls from car phones, a distinction he considers a class bias. "You jet to the front of the line because you can afford to have a phone in your car and it is a kind of gee-whiz awe of people in that situation and with that technology."

But even as he criticizes, Solomon sees great value in the genre. "It is ironic that as bad as they are, talk shows are some of the most free-form, spontaneous, and open forums available. They can be relatively uncensored."

# Tilting at the Limbaugh Windmill While Buchanan Tries to Take Back America

*"Rush Limbaugh is a closet fruit," reads the graffito* in the men's room at Afterwords Café in Washington. The next line, written in a different hand, responds, "Don't insult gay people."

Rush Limbaugh has managed, through his larger-than-life radio persona, to make himself a real player on America's political and popular culture scene. The September 6, 1993, *National Review* sprawled him across its cover; the feature-length story was a debate over his viability as a conservative political leader and his potential as a presidential candidate. This movement from talk radio jester to potential politician motivated the editor of the *Flush Rush Quarterly*, Brian Keliher, into reaction. Four times a year Keliher mocks and critiques Limbaugh in his publication. "This guy is dangerous," he is convinced. "If he stayed within the realm of entertainer, that might be one thing. But to have him appearing on supposed news shows as a political pundit is frightening. He tells people what they want to hear, that the homeless have no homes because they are lazy, that teen pregnancy can be prevented by abstinence. The world is not that simple a place."[1]

*Flush Rush* is written in a breezy style ("Ever ready to let his mouth work without informing his brain," is the lead line in a typical story), but takes on the role of critic with thoroughness and sobriety. A sample of the value of the newsletter can be seen in a story called "Setting the Record Straight" from the Spring 1994 issue. The article cites Limbaugh as saying about the Walsh report on the Iran-Contra scandal, "They wanted to find illegal activity on anybody in the Reagan administration. They couldn't find any. These guys didn't do anything. There was no evidence, not one indictment, not one charge." The quote is typical Limbaugh, typical political talk radio. It is delivered as news information, taking advantage of the many listeners who accept talk radio's authority. It is offered without documentation. And it belies Limbaugh's insistence that his program is merely entertainment. The information may have been presented in a manner that made it entertaining, but it is political propaganda—as is most of Limbaugh's work.

*Flush Rush* simply went to the record and listed eight top Reagan administration operatives and their Iran-Contra crimes—the charges against them and the convictions they received in federal court.

Presenting titillating stories as fact is one of the worst characteristics of the Limbaugh show and plenty of those competing with him. Another example from *Flush Rush*[2] quotes Limbaugh as reporting on the air, "You know the Clintons send Chelsea to the Sidwell Friends private school. A recent eighth-grade class assignment required students to write a paper on 'Why I Feel Guilty Being White.' " Limbaugh is a skillful manipulator. He knows that one of the best devices available to him for reinforcing his credibility is to draw attention to the question of the veracity of what he is broadcasting. So he highlights the question of documentation by adding, "My source for this story is CBS News." And then for further emphasis, he attacks the disbelievers before they can question him with the finishing flourish, "I am not making it up." After such a performance, how many in his audience—especially an audience so thoroughly composed of "dittoheads"—would bother to doubt the report, let alone investigate further? Across the fruited plain, as Limbaugh would say, he managed to sow seeds of disgust for the president and his family, based on outright false information.

*Flush Rush* reprinted the work of Richard Roeper, a columnist for the *Chicago Sun-Times* who did the needed legwork to check out the details of the attack. Roeper contacted CBS News. It told him it never ran such a story. He contacted Chelsea's school. "There is no legitimacy for the story that has been circulating," Elis Turner, a Sidwell Friends administrator, told him. "We're anxious to let people know that this story is not true." Twenty-five percent of the Sidwell student body is not white.

Perhaps the greatest value the *Flush Rush Quarterly* offers to those interested in the influence of talk radio is through the page filled with transcriptions of telephone messages to the newsletter. The venom expressed against Brian Keliher and his work from the Limbaugh loyalists is disconcerting and lends credence to the concern that manipulative radio operatives like Limbaugh foment dangerous and unnecessary hostility.

"I believe in the First Amendment," said a caller to the *Flush Rush* voice mail on September 12, 1993, "but I don't know why you pick on Rush. I think you're a vindictive little bastard, probably a spoiled rich kid from the 'burbs. Get a job. Get a life. From what I saw of you in the paper with your spaghetti arms and pencil neck, you dumb bastard, I guess you're really frustrated, you little shit."

January 6, 1994, Keliher's phone received this message: "I'd like to have one of your *Flush Rush* subscriptions and I'd like to flush it right down your fucking liberal stupid motherfucking throat, you spineless motherfucking cocksucker. If I ever find you, find out where you are, you think you got death threats so far, I'm gonna punch you right in your fucking liberal cock-eating fucking throat. Good-bye, scumball."

The calls and letters repeat the same themes; the vindictiveness is unrelenting, threatening, ignorant. From the February 1, 1994, messages: "I think you're a bunch of pinko, commie, liberal, faggot motherfuckers. Take your fucking bitch fucking back to some other fucking foreign country, you fucking spotted-owl-fucking shit. Environmental asshole. Eat shit."

"The main critics of Rush Limbaugh," wrote J.W. of Fort Lauderdale, Florida, to Keliher, "are Jews, because he threatened their control of the mass media, including TV, radio, magazines, newspapers, books. So don't do the Jews' dirty work," he advised. "Support a moral, patriotic, Christian who is trying to save America from alien forces and ideas."

Controversy heated up in mid-1994 over the veracity of material broadcast as fact by Limbaugh when the left-leaning media watchdog organization Fairness and Accuracy in Reporting (FAIR) launched its own investigation of Limbaugh's act. The July/August edition of the FAIR magazine *Extra!* featured a compilation of over three dozen Limbaugh statements identified as lies and distortions by *Extra!* editors.

Some of the more egregious quotes cited:

"The poorest families in America are better off than the mainstream families of Europe."

"It has not been proven that nicotine is addictive; the same with cigarettes causing emphysema."

"The videotape of the Rodney King beating played absolutely no role in the conviction of two of the four officers. It was pure emotion that was responsible for the guilty verdict."

In his book *See, I Told You So,* Limbaugh blamed the gas lines in the seventies on "foreign powers playing tough with us because they didn't fear Jimmy Carter." *Extra!* pointed out that gas lines occurred in 1973 and 1974, when Richard Nixon was president.

During the Limbaugh television show broadcast on February 17, 1994, he charged that the Whitewater story was languishing underreported. "I don't think the *New York Times* has run a story on this yet," he said. "I mean, we haven't done a thorough search, but there has not been a big one, a front-page story, about this one that we can recall. So this has yet to create or get up to full speed." Then he claimed credit for bringing the Whitewater story to the public, saying, "If it weren't for us and the *Wall Street Journal* and the *American Spectator,* this would be one of the best-kept secrets going on in American politics today."

In fact, *Extra!* made clear, early questions about impropriety involving the Arkansas land development known as Whitewater were raised by the *New York Times* two years before the Limbaugh broadcast, in a March 8, 1992, detailed front-page story by Jeff Gerth.

Cartoonists Garry Trudeau and Dan Perkins offered their own assaults on Limbaugh's credibility in 1994 with "Doonsbury" and "Tom Tomorrow" strips detailing the inaccuracies catalogued by FAIR and the *Flush Rush Quarterly.*

Limbaugh quickly dismissed the FAIR critique, saying, "*Mad* magazine has more credibility than they do."[3]

In response to the FAIR study, the Benchmark Company, a radio research firm, launched its own study of Limbaugh's credibility. The telephone poll, identified by the company as part of Benchmark's ongoing research into talk radio, queried 538 adult talk radio listeners in a random cross-section of American cities. Sixty-five percent of those questioned reported that the *Extra!* exposé had not changed their opinion of Limbaugh. When they were asked if they took information presented by Limbaugh seriously, 25 percent said most of it, 37 percent said some of it, and 38 percent said none of it. To the question, "Does Rush always tell the truth?" 65 percent of the respondents said no while 28 percent of this small sample of talk radio listeners said that they think he always tells the truth.[4]

Benchmark president Robert Balon interpreted the results as good news to broadcasters. "The fact that many in his audience do not count every word he says as gospel has thus far not damaged the perceived entertainment value of the program." However, in a summary accompanying the study, Balon offered a warning to the radio industry. "The 41 percent of the respondents who feel Mr. Limbaugh had gone too far in his commentary on the Clintons is a significant number. It's possible," he cautioned, "that once a large group of listeners begin to perceive a vendetta that the broader based entertainment foundation upon which the show has been built could be placed in jeopardy."

Others studying the talk radio phenomenon are not so sanguine. After Limbaugh took at least some of the credit for Republican gains in the 1994 elections, Marvin Kalb, director of the Joan Shorenstein Barone Center on the Press, Politics and Public Policy at Harvard University, agreed with him, worrying that many Americans who do not know where to obtain reliable news are tuning to Limbaugh for their information. "He is not a newsman; he is a talk show host. An awful lot of people listen to him and believe he is the ultimate word of God," Kalb complained.[5]

Results of exit polling commissioned by Limbaugh's syndication company during the 1994 election suggested both Limbaugh and Kalb are correct and that talk radio did play a role in many voters' decisions.

=====

Resentment against Limbaugh, Stern, and the few other highly paid national stars of talk radio by some of the other hosts envious of their success is often tempered by the reality that their shows are largely responsible for the overwhelming popularity of talk radio in general.

"I love Howard!" says Travus T. Hipp. "I can say penis on the air now, thanks to Howard. It's a great step forward in broadcasting. C'mon, man," he says when I ask him if he resents Stern and Limbaugh, "you can't resent bad taste in America. It is America. Howard Stern is pluperfectly New York. And whatever New York is, is going to be broadcast to the rest of the world as the standard by which America is understood." Hipp expresses similar respect for Limbaugh. "This cat," he says about Limbaugh, "has walked into the middle of the arena, beating himself on the chest like Goliath and telling you he is the baddest cat in the world and"—he measures his words out in an irritated staccato cadence—"nobody has had the balls to stand up with a slingshot."

=====

The radio antics of right-wing journalist and presidential candidate Pat Buchanan over the Mutual Broadcasting System are designed to counter the one-sided rantings of Limbaugh, the Limbaugh wannabes, and the Limbaugh antidotes. Buchanan's gimmick is to match himself for debate with a rotating array of liberal cohosts. "He's as charming as he is hateful," was the report of one of those partners, Mother Jones magazine editor Jeffrey Klein.6 After three hours with Buchanan and guests such as Clinton Bollick, the lawyer who stuck the label "Quota Queen" on Lani Guinier, and Michael Bray, who spent time in federal prison for firebombing abortion clinics, Klein concluded, "Without taking any responsibility for stirring up hatred, Buchanan was quick to suggest that everything frustrating his guests and listeners was, more or less, the fault of the government—which is obviously run by liberals."

It is just such attempted manipulation of the audience that motivated Barry Lynn to join Buchanan as a regular foil. Lynn is a jolly and intense man, lean and gangly, his clothes looking perpetually rumpled, who spends most of his working day at the offices of Americans United for the Separation of Church and State, his think tank devoted to fighting the religious right. He is no stranger to talk radio. Prior to the Buchanan show, he performed on local Washington radio stations and second-string networks. We meet over salads at lunchtime in a suburban Maryland eatery.7

Lynn is ready with a pat answer to my first question: How does he rationalize sharing a podium with a reactionary philosopher such as Pat Buchanan? "I think there is such an extraordinarily high level of disinformation being communicated by talk radio in general around the country because it is so heavily oriented toward conservative political views, that any time you can get in there and expose the fallacies, the mythologies of those views, even on a playing field that's not completely level, you've got a leg up on sitting out completely." Lynn has been arguing with Buchanan on the radio for so long that his answers come out in run-on sentences, spoken with inflections that make them hard to interrupt. "You have to get in and play the game," he tells me intently, "or you lose by default, and I've never been willing to lose by default."

I agree with him. Too many radio listeners who complain about Rush Limbaugh and the followers he has spawned keep listening with frustration and inaction. "If you get in there and you say, 'These arguments are wrong and here's why,' and you can articulate with some semblance of credibility what those arguments are, you're a step up over being silent and simply moaning about it over coffee-table conversation with your liberal friends." Lynn is somewhat of an anomaly. There are few enough so-called liberals on talk radio, fewer still who manage to team up in a debate-style format with right-wing colleagues. "It is difficult to get liberals who are willing to put themselves on the program, even as guests," Lynn tells me. "I've constantly complained to my liberal friends, and heads of liberal organizations, that it doesn't do any good to ignore the fact that these programs are very popular and that they demand a response from our side."

Lynn is convinced that over the last generation the right wing in America has performed a superior job of training its spokesmen and women in the art of debate and the co-optation of talk radio. "The young Republicans are better," he says, using Congress as an example of the right beating the left, an example he says carries over to the media. "They're more practiced and they're more willing to be in the fray, more willing to appear before hostile audiences in order to learn the arguments of the other side and to learn catch phrases and mythological answers, some answers to the issues raised by the other side." Lynn expresses admiration for the right wing's skill in perpetuating points of view he finds abhorrent. "We've got to train people in their twenties and thirties as well as the Heritage Foundation is training people in their twenties and thirties to be good conservatives, to make precise, clean arguments on radio and television, because they're skunking liberals in this format because they are better trained to be effective."

Lynn's speaking cadence is tough and intense in the restaurant, just as it is on the radio, but with an accessible warmth. He comes across as concerned and sincere, but friendly. He sounds as if he is someone who could be your friend and colleague, especially com-

pared with the strident voice of Buchanan, who rarely sounds as if
he would have time to get to know any of the callers. (When I met
with Pat Buchanan at the Mutual studios, however, he was per-
sonable enough—anxious for constructive criticism of his show.)

Barry Lynn theorizes that one reason why there are relatively
few left-leaning talk show hosts and why the majority of callers to
talk shows skew right is that the left abandoned commercial news
and talk radio. "I think there is a sense in the liberal community,"
he says carefully, "that they have their radio in National Public
Radio, that that belongs to them." Lynn himself is unimpressed
with the NPR product. "I suppose if you like to hear six-minute
pieces about ballet on radio, which frankly has never turned me
on, if you like that, then NPR is just for you. I don't think NPR is
as innovative as it could be. It has enough staff to do almost any
damn thing it wants, yet it doesn't produce extraordinary investigative pieces. It's not groundbreaking as in fact it was two
decades ago when it was just getting started. But now I find it
often to be doing the same thing everyone else is doing." His criticism is accurate. "But liberals still think if they can listen to it,
they'll get their side of the news. I don't think there's much evidence of that. I think increasingly even the commentators on
National Public Radio are moderate to conservative."

By 1994, there were some exceptions at local NPR affiliates to
the tidal wave on the right. Michael Krasney had moved his liberal San Francisco show to the well-rated and powerful public outlet KQED. WAMU in Washington carried a couple of left-leaning
local and thoughtful offerings from Diane Rehm and Derick
McGinty. At the national level, NPR was producing *Talk of the
Nation* with Ray Suarez—a traditionally trained journalist—as its
host. "We're anti-elitist," Suarez was quoted in the *New York
Times*.[8] "If anybody wants to listen to smart conversation with
regular people, they'll see."

"People who want to promote conservative ideologies," Barry
Lynn reminds me, "don't just have the secular media, they have
the religious media. When you have 1,200 Christian radio stations
in this country promoting an agenda, often the same agenda, that's

another tremendous outlet to get people convinced that what they're hearing is the truth." Lynn points to James Dobsen as an example. Dobsen spews out his right-wing message wrapped up in religious terminology on some 200 radio stations. "When he says the same thing that the secular Rush Limbaugh is saying, and the same thing Pat Robertson is saying," Lynn worries, "that is a tremendously powerful force."

That power is real, not just as a money-raising force, but also as a political force. When the right-wing radio hosts assign their audience the task of calling Congress to lobby for and against specific legislation, the sheer number of calls can paralyze the telephone systems of members of Congress. While those opposed to the philosophies of the political-religious right may be appalled and even frightened by displays of their media prowess, they are evidence of a skillful use and understanding of the power of popular culture. "The results are very dangerous," says Lynn, "because I think it corrupts the level of political debate in the country."

But he believes the onus is on the left to rise to the challenge. "Remember, if you're going to have political debate, you have to have two sides, you have to have somebody on the other side, and if those people are hiding in caves or having meetings with themselves or sitting around with earphones listening to National Public Radio and thinking that's enough, then we lose by default. I don't think you should ever lose by default. If you lose I want to make sure there is a fight. I'm not going to complain as much as most people do about the levelness of the field. I just want to make sure they're going to let me into the stadium, and then I'll play."

Lynn believes once he's on the radio, his message will be heeded. "Maybe this is naive, maybe it's just out of that liberal tradition that I come from, but I think truth counts for something. You don't have to match them dollar for dollar, show for show, station for station, because truth counts more than fiction. Eventually it does rise to the top in a debate."

Travus T. Hipp identifies that concept as his theory of the self-correcting nature of talk radio. Hipp believes that hosts who are on the radio for a prolonged period of time, with daily exposure to a live and interactive audience, are finally forced toward an understanding of society based on reality. As an example, Hipp points to Rush Limbaugh and changes Limbaugh has made in his act over the last few years—such as acknowledging that he was wrong to mock those suffering from AIDS.

Barry Lynn does not question the influence of talk radio. "I think this is a very important source of information—good, bad, or ugly. It has an enormous influence on how people think." Yet in almost the same breath he admits, "I think if you listen to a lot of radio talk shows, you don't learn a damn thing. You don't even have any facts to help you put the facts together with your values and draw conclusions. You don't learn anything." But he refuses to call the shows simply entertainment. "They are not raw entertainment because they are frequently contributing to the general level of misinformation." The combination of ideology and misinformation broadcast on many talk shows, says Lynn, is what corrupts the national debate.

But in the midst of his frustration with the medium, Lynn conjures up a memory that makes it all worthwhile for him. "The nicest call I ever got was from a woman in Oklahoma City who called and said, 'I used to get in my truck after work and listen to country music.' She said, 'Then one day I was flipping around the dial and I heard you talking about an issue and I said, this is an interesting show. Now every single day I listen to this show on the way back to from work.' The capper was, 'I never knew there were this many interesting issues out there in the world.' To me," says Lynn, "that's the kind of person I think exists in large numbers if you give them an opportunity to hear and then make up their own mind based on some people who know something about the issues."

Despite allusions to public service, Pat Buchanan's and most talk shows are on the air to build careers and generate money. "I think Rush does a great job," Buchanan told Evan Haning shortly after the *Buchanan and Company* show debuted over the Mutual Broadcasting System in 1993. Buchanan, who had been a talk radio success in the early eighties in Washington, constructed his

Bruce Williams offers his same common-sense advice to the nation's ignorant night after night, coast to coast, border to border.

For over a generation Ray Briem has been the right-wing voice of the overnights in Los Angeles over KABC.

**D**espite her doctorate in economics from the Massachusetts Institute of Technology, Dr. Julianne Malveaux can sling words with the noisiest of talk show actors. She plies her trade over the listener-supported Pacifica Station in Washington, D.C., WPFW.

PHOTO: LEIGH H. MOSLEY

**T**echnological developments allow Jim Eason to broadcast his local San Francisco show from his hideaway in the Carolinas.

**D**ick Summer orients his show to women in the radio audience, talking relationships instead of politics.

**F**rom WHAS in Louisville,
Jane Norris rouses the rabble.

**R**onn Owens, behind the KGO microphone in San Francisco.

Fired from KGO and replaced with a divisive screamer, the thoughtful Michael Krasney moved his show to public radio.
PHOTO: HOWARD GELMAN

Paul Lyle stopped saying "Good morning, Long Island," when his radio station was sold and the new owner dumped the talk format for music.

The San Francisco billboard for Peter B. Collins

*Talkers* magazine publisher Michael Harrison sits down to talk radio with a worried President Clinton at the White House. PHOTO: *TALKERS* MAGAZINE

Jeff Kamen, a journalist who made the transition to talk show host without jettisoning his credibility, fasted over WRC in Washington, D.C., in an attempt to persuade President Clinton to change his Haiti policy.

PHOTO: RICK BLOOM

Christine Craft, tossed off television in Kansas City for being "too old, too ugly, and not deferential to men," found an alternative career in talk radio.

Robert Smith worries his Ph.D. in history may scare potential employers as he seeks a promotion from his duties on the air at WXXI in Rochester, New York.

PHOTO: DAVID FAHRER

Radio rogue Travus T. Hipp on duty in Virginia City, Nevada, before the next edition of his *Rawhide Realities Review* over KPTL in Carson City.
PHOTO: BILL GERMINO

Baltimore's "host-psychotic," Les Kinsolving.

Nikki Reed, the Virginia talk show host who decided balancing a radio career and three children was too much trouble and gave up baby number three for adoption. PHOTO: DAILY PRESS

Alan Berg, the Denver loudmouth talker who paid the ultimate price for his broadcasts. He was gunned down by listeners who wanted to shut him up. PHOTO: JIM RICHARDSON

new show as competition to Limbaugh and a platform for his own future political ambitions. The structure of the show, sent out via satellite during the same three hours as the Limbaugh show, made it initially seem a forum for fair debate. I added it to the WRC lineup, with an announcement that I considered Buchanan's politics repugnant, but felt that the format of the show created the opportunity to force-feed some alternative views on a predominantly right-wing audience.

Buchanan paraded a line of somewhat liberal cohosts—in addition to Barry Lynn—to share the microphone with him throughout his work week. The problem with this rotating structure was that the alternative hosts never had the same opportunity as Buchanan to establish their personalities with the listeners. Even the title of the show included only Buchanan's name. Consequently, Buchanan always remained in control and usually got the last word in during confrontations. Nonetheless, he sold his show as something more than Limbaugh's. And, in fact, filled as it was with newsmaking guests and at least a struggling opposing opinion, it contained more substance than the Limbaugh show.

"Rush is up in the pulpit," Buchanan told Haning, "and he's a tremendous entertainer, and a performer, and I agree with about 99 percent of what Rush says. But what we offer is something else. We offer debate and argument, controversy, both sides, interviews, call-ins." Buchanan tried to cash in on the coffee shop and bar analogy. "Ours is really a bunch of fellows that go to your house at night and maybe after dinner, and maybe after a couple of drinks, they all come from different points of view and different places and everyone presents his point of view. They're all heard and they're all given time and I represent the conservative point of view. But the other side is always there."

And, Buchanan could have added, it is actually my house and I'm in control of the direction of the conversation and in control of who gets to talk and for how long.

Buchanan is another multi-media figure. In addition to the speaking circuit and running for president, his credits include a syndicated newspaper column and CNN's *Crossfire*. "But I've always loved radio," Buchanan told Haning, "because I enjoy the long form. You sit down and can talk for three hours. If you thought of some clever line and you didn't get it out before the break, just wait three or four minutes and you can get it out after the break. It gives you much more time to really delve into an argument and a debate and a discussion."

Like most radio personalities, Buchanan understands that a special intimacy can develop between a radio listener and a talk radio host. When a host is skillful, each listener can grow to suspend the disbelief that the host is not talking one-to-one with the listeners. "There is a certain measure of intimacy that radio, I think, gives the listeners," said Buchanan, "a sense that they're really there with you."

Through early 1995, Buchanan was still dodging the question whether he was going to make another run for the White House. "Oh, I don't know," he would say, but his delight was clear whenever one of the callers to his show would remark on his 1992 campaign, especially if the comment was followed with the frequent suggestion that Buchanan would make a fine president. "I did my time," Buchanan said about his run for the presidency, "and 1992 was sort of the year when there was a tremendous vacuum there, that I think we"—he has a tendency to slip into the royal "we" when speaking of himself as a politician—"were able to fill in the Republican party, which wanted to send a message to the president that he was headed in the wrong direction, and the country was on the wrong course. And they used me as a vehicle to send that message."

Buchanan, even as he plied his journalism in print and over the airwaves all across the country, continued to try to characterize himself as an outsider—especially in regard to the media. "I think that the media in general have contributed to the tearing apart of public officials," he said, "and I think that began with the Watergate era. I think the Washington press got the taste of blood in its mouth and it has not been able to get it out. Now it's bipartisan. If you come to this city, and you're in public service, and you rise and become a celebrity, you automatically become a target. People get ripped to pieces. I think a lot of us feel that politics have become much more savage and vicious. Those who say this is a lot better than the 1950s, in a lot of ways are dead right. But in a lot of ways it's a lot worse, too."

As the 1992 campaign progressed, some of the more controversial remarks Buchanan had made over the years received widespread publicity. A detailed *Washington Post*[9] profile reminded readers that Buchanan referred to homosexuals as "sodomites" and the "pederast proletariat." The same article quoted him identifying feminists as "the Butch Brigade," and interpreting Adolf Hitler in this light: "Though Hitler was indeed racist and anti-Semitic to the core, a man who without compunction could commit murder and genocide, he was also an individual of great courage, a soldier's soldier in the Great War, a political organizer of the first rank, a leader steeped in the history of Europe, who possessed oratorical powers that could awe even those who despised him."

Buchanan has been labeled an anti-Semite by his fellow conservative William F. Buckley, Jr., who examined Buchanan's work—especially during the run-up to the Gulf War in 1990. "I find it impossible to defend Pat Buchanan," wrote Buckley,[10] "against the charge that what he did and said during the period under examination amounted to anti-Semitism, whatever it was that drove him to say it and do it: most probably, an iconoclastic temperament," Buckley quotes him as calling Congress "Israeli-occupied" territory. On *The McLaughlin Group* television program, Buchanan had said, "There are only two groups that are beating the drums for war in the Middle East—the Israeli Defense Ministry and its amen corner in the United States." Buchanan then identified four men he considered members of the "amen corner." They were *New York Times* columnist A. M. Rosenthal, former assistant secretary of defense Richard Perle, syndicated columnist Charles Krauthammer, and Henry Kissinger—all Jewish, pointed out Buckley, but with little else in common.

Still another Buchanan outburst came when he wrote that fighting in the Gulf would be done by "kids with names like McAllister,

Murphy, Gonzales, and Leroy Brown." Buckley decided that "there is no way to read that sentence without concluding that Pat Buchanan was suggesting that American Jews manage to avoid personal military exposure even while advancing military policies."

Buchanan's call for his followers to "take America back" has been interpreted as racist by many of his critics, especially when coupled with his worried query, written in 1984, about "whether the United States of the twenty-first century will remain a white nation." Buchanan revived the "take back America" theme when he made his speech to the Republican National Convention in Houston on August 17, 1992. He announced his support for President Bush and used the podium to rally his own troops one more time.

But Barry Lynn, among many others, expresses no concern about Buchanan sliding from his presidential campaign back into a talk show host chair. The synergy between politics and talk shows is as natural as that between entertainers and talk show hosts. These different roles share many characteristics, and it is understandable that the players circulate from one to another. Consequently, it should have surprised no one when Howard Stern announced he was running for governor of New York.

===

Stern's March 23, 1994, show was a news conference, attended by the mainstream New York news media. "I am dead serious," he told them. "I think people are turned on by the idea." He described his primary goal as imposing the death penalty in New York state and promised to accomplish that and the two other planks in his platform (restricting highway repairs to nighttime and adjusting highway toll taking to reduce traffic tieups) days after his inauguration and then quit, turning the government of the state over to his hand-picked lieutenant governor—a responsible politician. "Everything will be done over the radio," he announced. "When I select my lieutenant governor it will be over the radio."

Some of the reporters laughed. Stern laughed, too. "Maybe I

talk about sex too much," he acknowledged. But he refused to mock his own candidacy. "I am dead serious about this. I guarantee you I will win. I will get hundreds of thousands of votes and I will win." In a society that elected George Murphy senator from California, that put Ronald Reagan into the governor's mansion in Sacramento twice and elected Reagan president twice, just how far-fetched is a Howard Stern political career? Sonny Bono was mayor of Palm Springs and in 1994 was elected to Congress. "People think this is a stunt," said Stern. "It's not a stunt. I'm a kook with a message." He dropped out of the race when faced with the realities of the financial disclosure laws for politicians. Stern did not want to reveal how many millions of dollars he was earning. And, despite the publicity Stern's gubernatorial announcement generated, it seemed unlikely that enough registered voters would sign petitions in time to qualify him for a position on the ballot.

As the 1994 election year ripened, Stern was not alone among his talk show peers in seeking public office. Ronna Romney, daughter-in-law of the former Michigan governor and presidential candidate, was after a seat in the Senate. Known, at least in Detroit, because of her WXYT talk show, Romney told the *New York Times,* "I never could have done this if I hadn't done talk radio. Radio taught me to go head-on. I don't get rolled."[11] In Boston, WRKO host Janet Jeghelian was also after a Senate job. Talk show hosts were trying for the House of Representatives in Arizona, Arkansas, Florida, and Oregon.

The door separating talk show hosts and elective political office swings both ways. André Marrou, the 1992 Libertarian candidate for president, spent the next year trying to land himself a permanent talk radio job. "It's true that I defeated Bill Clinton and George Bush last year in Dixville Notch, New Hampshire, and nationally placed fourth behind Ross Perot," is how he began his pitch to program directors. "It is also true that I was elected to the Alaska House of Representatives several years ago." The letter proceeds to insist that Marrou no longer intends to seek any political offices, but wants to perform on the radio. "Whereas Rush, bashes liberals constantly," he writes "I am an equal-opportunity basher. I'll bash conservatives, liberals, and even Libertarians when they need it—and Lord knows they need it occasionally."

═══

"I don't think it's dangerous at all to have a Pat Buchanan on the air," says his partner Lynn. "Here's a guy who starts, in my judgment, with the wrong set of principles and draws 95 percent of the wrong conclusions. But in the middle he knows a lot of stuff; he just puts the facts and opinions and theories together differently than I do. But he knows the stuff and he's lived the experiences from his days with Richard Nixon to Ronald Reagan to running for president himself. I don't think there's any danger to that, particularly if you can say, 'Hey, be consistent. If you want government out of the lives of people, why are you in favor of sodomy laws? Why do you want to regulate what people read?' "

Another cautious compliment was paid to Buchanan by his periodic cohost Julianne Malveaux. "He tries to be fair," she told me.[12] "I think he goes out of his way on the air to be fair." She is no fan of his philosophies. With a Ph.D. in economics from the Massachusetts Institute of Technology and a distinctly liberal political and social outlook, Malveaux seeks talk radio opportunities that pit her against the established right-wing commentators. "I would say I like working with him except some of his ideas make me want to wring his neck." For Malveaux, G. Gordon Liddy, with whom she has also worked on the radio, "is a more likable fellow, although just as much of a Neanderthal." She mocked Liddy as we talked. 'Send me a picture of you with your gun in your underwear!' Are you a freak or are you a freak?" she asked Liddy as if she were talking with him in my office.

But it is Buchanan who concerned her more. "Like when he says, 'We must take back our cities.' She is convinced, despite Buchanan's denials, that the often-repeated phrase means Buchanan fears an America that is not white. "I think the language is so coded," she said. "It speaks to the number and proportions of blacks in the cities. Who is this 'we' taking the cities back and who is it we're taking the cities back from? He's sending a signal." In her book, *Sex, Lies and Stereotypes*, she writes, "You don't have to wear a hood or post a 'whites only' sign to be a bigot. In today's political landscape, all you have to do is use the carefully crafted rhetoric of taking America back.' "

Nonetheless, Malveaux backed Buchanan's radio show, especially when compared to those of Liddy and Limbaugh. "He's better than the others because he's not force-feeding people a three-hour stream of right-wing babble. At least it's punctuated a little bit." And she grudgingly admitted that he is a worthwhile adversary. "He's very smart," she said, and a debate opponent whose skills require that she does her homework.

Despite the arguments on his show, Buchanan said divisiveness is not his goal. "We do have the greatest country in the world and it is really God's gift to all of us. That means all of us, no matter where our ancestors came from or what they were doing a hundred years ago. If we lose this last best hope of earth, as it's been called, I think we lose it all. As long as we still have America and an open society, and the right to debate and argue and decide, and the chance to persuade people of your point of view, I think we can find our way back. But I think in a lot of ways America is off-track right now, and one of the things those of us who are in the world of talking about ideas and issues do is to try and see what we can do to lead it back to the way we think is right."

=====

The question remains: Why does talk radio skew to the political right wing? The Times Mirror Center for the People and the Press determined that the orientation of the medium is clearly biased. The survey analyst Cliff Zukin told me, "One of the things we found is that the talk show listeners and talk show callers are unrepresentative of the general public. They are much more conservative. They are much more harsh in their criticism of the president. There is a conservative and harsh tone to talk radio."

One raw statistic from the survey that speaks clearly to the question of bias is that Americans who identify themselves as conservatives are twice as likely to be talk radio consumers as those who identify themselves as liberals. Conservatives, according to the study, are also twice as likely to call in and get on the air. "When you compare a sampling of who is talking on the radio with the general public," says Zukin, "you find them to be anti-institutional—in other words they dislike Congress, they are more critical of the president, they are more antigovernment, they feel government should do less rather than more—they are, in fact, significantly different than the general public in some very important respects."

The *Washington Post*'s star reporter and columnist David Broder expressed either a professional fear of talk show hosts and their influence, or concern for Congress, or both, when he reacted to the defeat of the congressional pay raise in 1989. "By knuckling under to the know-nothing demagoguery of their home-town radio talks shows," said Broder, "90 percent of senators and representatives demonstrated again that they put the safety of their seats far ahead of the well-being of the Congress."

Despite Broder's worry, some wise and efficient journalists along with plenty of know-nothings, have turned to talk radio because of the increasing power they can wield with their shows—often a greater and faster-acting power than that of traditional newspaper commentators like Broder.

# 15

## "Hello, Am I on the Air?"

*Just how representative of a talk show audience and* of society overall are the callers who get on the air? Despite the cry of talk show hosts that a talk show represents the *vox populi,* a wide variety of tricks is used to manipulate the callers who are allowed to join the host on the air. A skillful talk radio host leaves the impression that an endless number of listeners are clambering for the opportunity to get on the air, but that often is not the case. Even the nationally distributed shows at times suffer from a dearth of callers.

Despite the contrived nature of so much talk radio, the medium genuinely thrives on the serendipitous. When least expected, unsolicited calls from the audience generate the raw material for the most compelling talk radio imaginable.

In the dusty pile of cassette tapes that litter my garage—evidence of years of talking on the radio—are those moments I felt compelled to freeze in time. Talk radio is an immediate medium. It is most effective during live broadcasts. Many radio stations fill the least important hours of their broadcast week with taped repeats of their stars. "You're listening to the best of so-and-so," they announce. "Don't call now, this show was recorded during an ear-lier broadcast." But true talk radio aficionados rarely are satisfied with the reruns. The spontaneity is lost. The possibility—even if it is remote and unlikely for most listeners—to join the fracas and call the show is eliminated. The material that depends on late-breaking news is dated. Listening to tapes of talk radio is a sec-ondary experience. Nonetheless, most talk radio performers keep their favorite shows around the house, not just as job-seeking tools, but also in an effort to capture some permanence from their transient work. And sometimes the programs captured on those saved tapes are so dramatic and electric that they do manage to maintain the drama of the original broadcasts replay after replay.

One of my saved tapes is labeled "Cuckolded Man." I forgot to date it, but I can isolate the period of the broadcast as 1979 or 1980. My afternoon show, *Instant Gratification,* on KXRX in San Jose was coming to a close for the day. The conceit of the show was that I guaranteed an answer to any question asked during the three-hour span of the program. For the most part, the callers rang the radio station with consumer frustrations, and we used the power of the live broadcast to attempt to facilitate accommoda-tion between the aggrieved parties and the businesses they patron-ized.

But the cuckolded man was one of the different stories.

"Hello," I started our conversation with no idea what lay ahead. "What's happening?"

"I need a little advice." The voice was strained and soft. "I did-n't know who else to call."

"Okay," I said, waiting for more material.

"Can you help me out?" Now the voice was pleading.

"Sure," I said.

"I'm hurt," he told me. "Okay?"

"Okay," I said and listened without much interest for more.

"I don't know what—" His voice cracked. He sobbed. "I don't know what to do."

I started paying attention as he cried. "About what?" I asked.

"I just came home." He forced the words out. "My old lady is with some other dude. Okay?" He was sobbing again. "And I don't know what to do," he said through the tears. "I don't know how to handle this."

Neither did I. "She's there right now?" I asked.

"I left," he cried. "I didn't know how to handle it."

"Oh," I said, realizing he had probably just caught them in the act, "you walked in the door."

"I walked in the door and there it was. Okay? So give me somebody?" It was a pleading question.

"Okay," I said. "Just relax for a second."

"I'm trying to," he said, clearly soothed just to be talking about the crisis. "I'm in a phone booth and I'm really trying." His voice calmed down as he said deliberately, "But I'm next to wild, you know?"

"I understand," I told him. "You walked in?"

"There it was!" he wailed.

"Were they actually in bed together?" I wanted to determine just how serious was the violation.

"There it was," he wailed again into the telephone, louder.

"There is no question—" I started.

"There's no question," he yelled back at me.

"Okay," I told him. "What did she say?"

"There was no chance to say anything. I just turned around and left and I'm on my way to pick up my baby at the babysitter's." He sounded so sad and confused.

I stalled while I tried to figure out what to do, what to say. "Before you get the baby, you better figure out what you're going to do."

"I don't know what to do," he said.

"Just relax a little bit," I tried. "The first thing to do is to realize—as you well do—that you have a problem on your hands." Brilliant. "And you want to deal with it . . ."

He interrupted my meanderings. "I'm trying to deal with it, but more emotion is coming than dealing. You know what I mean? I don't know what to do here and I'm trying to deal with it. But I'm just quivering, you know?" And his quivering was audible.

"Has anything like this ever happened before?" I asked him.

"Never."

"You never had any inkling that it was—"

"I thought it was together."

"How long have you guys been together?" I decided just to keep him talking while we tried to figure out what to do next. In the studios, my producers and other colleagues were scurrying about, writing me notes with suggestions of what to say.

"Five years."

"Boy, oh boy," I said. "You were coming home at an unusual time, huh?"

"I was out of town for three days, in L.A.," he said. "I just got back. My first inclination was to commit murder, and I can't do that kind of stuff because I don't want to sit in nobody's jail."

"I'm really pleased that you decided not to do that," I encouraged him.

"So I just left." He sighed. "And I don't know what to do."

I kept him talking by asking him what he was thinking. "I'm flipping out," he said. "I just want to get my baby and go, but I just had to tell somebody before I went to the babysitter. I'm flipping out."

"What do you expect you'll do," I asked, "once you get the baby?"

"I don't know," he wailed. "That's why I want somebody to talk to." He was crying out.

"I understand," was all I could think to say. I played some commercials and picked up the telephone in the studio, keeping him talking off the air—both because he was providing spectacular radio programming for us and because we really wanted to help him and keep him away from his wife.

The immediacy of his crisis kept unfolding. "I'm in panic, Peter," he said when we returned to the air. "I'm absolutely off the wall. I'm trying to deal with it and I'm having trouble dealing with it." No kidding. Ten minutes before he had come home to find his wife in bed with another man. Now he was trying to keep himself from going crazy by confiding in me—a total stranger he felt he knew intimately just because he listened to me on the radio—and he was allowing his entire community to eavesdrop.

"I don't know how to deal with it," he kept repeating. "I don't know how to deal with it. I love my wife, I love my baby, I love my life, and I love living, and all that good stuff. And I've been screwed. I don't know how to deal with it." He wailed some more, and finally asked, "Do you have a phone number for somebody who deals with this kind of thing? I don't want to hang you up, Peter. I don't want to hang you up with all this garbage." He did not realize what a captivating story he was providing for the radio listeners, as he explained how he was convinced he and his wife had already "sown their oats" before they were married, how he was convinced that theirs was a committed and monogamous relationship.

"We have lots of phone numbers," I promised him, "but it's not hanging us up. As long as this is a panic crisis for you, I just want to talk with you until I feel confident that I can hang up on you and know that you're going to be all right for a while."

"I'm going to hang in there," he said. "There's nothing else to do. I'm going to deal with it, I just don't know how to deal with it. My first thought is to go back—" He stopped, not knowing how to complete the scenario. "I don't know how to deal with it. What am I going to do with my baby tonight?" He was crying out again.

"Where are you going to go tonight?" I asked him.

"Where am I going to go tonight?" he repeated. "A Holiday Inn? And call up room service and say, 'Bring me up a couple of bottles of milk?' Christ. I don't know what to do."

We were scrambling behind the scenes, searching for referrals for him.

"Can I talk to you off the air?" he pleaded, knowing that it was almost time for the news. Bizarrely, the next commercial was for the San Jose Hyatt hotel. We provided him with professional contacts; he and I met after the show and talked more. We were able to inform the audience a week later that he was coping and divorcing. It was talk radio beyond just entertainment, but it was spectacular entertainment. Reality usually makes the best entertainment.

On a vibrant and typically warm late winter day in San Francisco in 1994, I waited at Sinbad's, a restaurant at the Ferry Building, for Peter B. Collins to show up for lunch. I ordered a drink and looked out at the sparkling bay. I ate some French bread. Collins was late. He is the consummate talk radio professional, a journeyman of the trade. We met when he held down the afternoon show at KNBR in San Francisco, before the station adopted an all Limbaugh and sports format. We worked together briefly at WRC and now he was back to his afternoon position, this time on KSFO, an upstart in the talk radio wars.

Finally Collins arrived, excusing his tardiness because of the unscheduled radio station meeting he was asked to attend. KSFO, just weeks after adopting the talk format, was announced up for sale, its future up in the air. Stability is elusive in the radio industry.

But the sudden change in his station's status made my first question for Collins even more relevant. I ask him to access the talk radio audience for me, to try to explain and describe its importance. "Who is out there," I ask, "who would listen to the drivel that so often seems to comprise talk radio?"

"Well, you know"—Collins takes off his sunglasses and slides them in his shirt pocket—"every person who does a radio show also listens to radio. I listen in my car, that's what most people do." What he is aware of are the behind-the-scenes activities. He emphasizes the long waits listeners contend with before their few minutes of stardom. "What amazes me is that people put participation in talk radio so high on their life priorities and are willing to call a show when they know they're going to be on hold from five to forty minutes, when they know they're only going to get two minutes to talk, when they know, at least subconsciously, that it's all stacked against them, that the host will win, that I control the button that will terminate their call."

Collins is convinced that the audience is sophisticated enough to be aware of what occurs off the air during a talk show. "With all that," he says, "there is this core of people who have the confidence in their views, and the desire to express them, to overcome all those obstacles."

I ask him why those determined listeners don't just sit down at lunch in a place like the restaurant where Collins and I are meeting and talk with real people.

His answer speaks to the loss of community in modern American society. "Some of them don't have those outlets," he says, "and others have worn out their welcome at those outlets." He describes many talk show callers as "hyper-opinionated," with no friends and neighbors interested in being a captive audience for their rantings and ravings. "Their wives and families have all heard it before. So this is a fresh target, kind of like a guy with a repertoire of bad jokes who's already burned everybody he knows, and finds a new victim, and unloads his greatest hits."

If the callers are just frustrated compulsive talkers, that only reinforces my concern that talk radio presentations often are vacuous wastes of time and lack any real importance to the vast majority of listeners. "Who would listen?" I ask Collins to speculate. "Why do they listen, especially in such relatively large numbers?"

"Each person has his or her own reason," he responds, and he quickly tries to convince me that he doesn't consider his shows "caller driven." Not that he ignores the traffic on the incoming telephone lines. "I'm certainly conscious of it; I know how many lights are lit; I know how many lines are open, and whether that represents acceptance of the topics that I've advanced or not. "But I don't sweat it," he insists, "when I'm not getting calls. I look at it as an opportunity to go on to that next story I've been waiting to find time for. I try to remain focused on the fact that most people are listening passively and will never call the show. And that you need to balance the entertainment value of taking a call with whether or not it really advances the program. I'll sit there with two lines up on the switchboard, and if they are people that I know are regulars, or very predictable, I'll just let them sit there, and I'll move on to another topic and get somebody else to call before I'll take the regulars."

"Who are you," I ask him, "or me, to have this soapbox and to be engaged in this pontification, let alone Howard Stern or Rush Limbaugh? There are no criteria established industry wide or in the general society for this work, other than being a draw for ratings and a blabbermouth. What gives you the credentials for this role?"

"Yeah," he says, his eyes lit with enthusiasm for his work even as he tries to act humble about it. "I have elements of humility in my approach and a certain sense of feeling very fortunate. You do get used to it, but I don't take for granted the idea that I have this outlet and that I can express my views. I try to do it in a way that isn't heavy-handed or overpowering to people, but I'm sure it comes off that way to many, or some."

I am intrigued with the self-appointed nature of the talk show host calling. Of course, employment in the business requires a willing station or network owner, but there are no schools for talk shows, no job standards other than a fast mouth. "Journalism is one of the last apprentice trades," former NBC News vice president Gordon Manning told me with satisfaction once when we were discussing the relevance of journalism schools. And talk show hosts often skip the apprenticeship, relying on their own self-confidence and arrogance as adequate training for the work ahead. In my office were hundreds of résumés from hopefuls who dream of talk show stardom.

"If you get on the bus," I say to Peter Collins, using my standard examples, "you know the bus driver takes a driving test." I point to the water. "You get on a ferryboat, the captain is licensed by the Coast Guard; the chef here in this restaurant is inspected by the health department; the lawyer passes state exams; the doctor must—"

Collins interrupts me, "Well, we take urine tests." Then, more seriously: "It's a valid point. I don't know that I have an answer. I'm just a lucky guy who has done this. I'm in a small group of people who have experience at it. I have developed a reputation and visibility for my name and my role. I assume that most people listening are fairly average, and I try to address their interests and talk to them on a level that they can access, while building in some treats for people who know more about a specific subject, and have a deeper interest or a deeper capacity to comprehend or respond. So, for example, when I talk about Oliver North running for the Senate, I try to operate on a couple of levels. I'll ask, how can you have somebody who has violated the Constitution taking the oath of office to uphold and defend it? And then I'll move to less sophisticated positions, such as, do you trust this man? When did you think he was telling the truth?"

Collins and I are good enough friends and colleagues that without insulting him, I can ask him the next obvious question. Why would somebody, especially if the audience is as average as he paints it, care what he thinks when he's just some guy on the radio? "Why," I ask, "wouldn't they listen to music tapes, or talk on their car phones to their friends, or listen to a news presentation from bona fide news reporters who are interviewing Oliver North? Why would they pick Peter B. Collins for their radio companion?"

"For most people," he tells me, "it's a vicarious connection to the discussion that is going on. There is the potential for them to participate, and even if they never exercise that, it opens the process in a way that makes them feel involved. So, if you've got half an hour between work and home in the afternoon and a sense of being involved in a discussion, as opposed to listening to Bob Seger and Fleetwood Mac on a bland radio station, there are certain people who have that active interest in vicarious participation." It is a strange choice of conflicting terms he uses: active interest in vicarious participation. "They feel as if they are going to learn something or get something useful out of listening, something that they did not expect."

"Talk radio is pornographic," is my interpretation of that vicarious participation he describes. "I feel that there is a similarity between looking at girlie magazines and listening to talk radio."

He considers my theory. "It is not a fantasy as much in talk radio, but it is a projection as opposed to a reality. It is the projection of interaction and access for average people, and I think some people listen hoping to identify with a point of view or a caller, waiting for their point to be made or for their opinion to be expressed. For some people it is empowerment. You know, they are the ones who did not raise their hands in class, but got satisfaction from knowing the answer even though they were not called on."

I concede that it is understandable why someone may choose to listen to Peter B. Collins or other talk show hosts. They usually are glib entertainers; they express controversial opinions; often they interview compelling guests. But why are so many listeners accepting of that other element of the talk show: the callers? Why do the words of those who wait on the phone for up to an hour and get on the air for a few minutes hold any appeal? "Why," I ask Collins, "is that captivating?"

"I think there is a basic social need for certain types of interaction," he says, off on the coffeehouse theory shared by so many talk show hosts. "People used to go to the saloon, or they used to go to the stable and sit around and talk horses. People have always congregated. Society really does not offer many opportunities for that anymore."

"So," I say, "if talk radio is the coffee shop or the bar, it is without touching, and without real experience and without a natural and linear continuity of the experience. As a replacement, it offers society an awful lot less than the hardware store checkerboard."

"True," agrees Collins, "but the investment on the part of the listener is low to zero. They are taking no risk. And they see it as something that potentially can give them something. At minimum, it passes the time."

"There is no risk," I say, "no threat. And so it feeds the anonymity in our society."

But Collins refuses to agree with me that the anonymity is negative. "Some of them surprise you. One out of five, one out of eight will make a point that hasn't been made. There's a sense of sharing information that has some intrinsic value that may not be obvious to others. For example, you and I don't care much about sports. But the degree to which people talk statistics, and RBIs and who's got the best average, and what the odds are on the Super Bowl, shows there is a desire to share data, or information, or just exchange. I think it fills the need for people to get put outside their usual universe. Again, without leaving that universe, without risking anything, and since most people never call, they take no chance, but they have the potential to get a reward."

"What would you have done," I ask, "were you born before the invention of radio?"

"I would probably have been a writer of some sort. I am an opinionated guy and I enjoy my verbal skills." He is studying his personality aloud, something—as a radio talk show host—he is quite comfortable doing. "I am also very curious. The combination of those three, verbal ability, curiosity, and opinions, would lead me into some similar work, perhaps just sitting in a barroom buying drinks for people so they would listen to me."

I persist with the questions, probably because in his answers I hear some validation for my own years in the talk radio trenches. "I hear you saying that there is some social worth in what you're doing—you are not just separating the commercials. But," I tell him, "the American Airlines magazine that I saw on the plane yesterday featured an interview with Howard Stern. I stopped in Dallas, changed planes, and at the newsstand I saw stacks of *Rolling Stone* with its Howard Stern cover story. I picked up the *Dallas Morning News* and the *Fort Worth Star-Telegram*. In one of them, I forget which, there was a story on dance and the headline said, RUSH LIMBO. It was about renewed interest in the limbo. Many workers in the talk radio industry are eclipsed by these new megastars. Are you jealous of them?"

"Never," is his immediate retort. "I feel frustrated because the orientation of the business has changed. And program directors are seeking imitations of these characters. But I just have kind of an old-fashioned sense that if you treat people with respect, they will respect what you're doing. I would rather have 50,000 listeners who I assume have some respect for me than 500,000 listeners who think I'm an asshole. I do not desire to be a Stern or Limbaugh." He is insistent. "I do not covet their money."

"Truly?" I push him. "You would not prefer to be on a few hundred radio stations around the country instead of one?"

"I don't have that overwhelming desire. If you put the deal together for me, I would say fine."

"You would not prefer to make a million than a hundred thousand dollars?"

"Not if what I have to do is what they do." I believe him; I agree with him. "No, I'm not interested in that. And the money—I mean, I want to live comfortably, I would like to build a bankroll, but I don't have a desire to be a millionaire. I don't expect to be a millionaire. If it happens I'll be a happy guy. But I am not striving for that. I approach talk radio on a relatively selfish basis. I love to do this and it's what really satisfies me. When I think, for example, about a network show, I think of it as confining. I listen to Jim Bohannon—who is not even allowed to say what fucking day it is because his show is run all over the place and may not air on Wednesday when he says it's Wednesday. I heard him one time fidgeting when he said, 'Now, if you want a tape of this show, you call this number and be sure to tell them the date of the show. You know what the date is, it's on the newspaper.' He was not allowed to say on the air that it originated on December 12. For me, the freedom of being in one town, and being able to do inside material about the Bay Area and being able to really be local and be relevant to my listeners, is more satisfying than to do generic radio for consumption in 50 or a 150 markets."

I ask him how he deals with the awe toward the host that often comes from the audience. "I don't have a particularly elevated sense of this calling," Collins tells me. "I mean, I think it's a job, it's a great job, an extension of my sixties and seventies activism. I consider myself an inside agitator. I have strong views on our society and our form of government and how it should be. This is my way of nudging things toward my point of view." But he claims no illusions about his power. "The biggest thing I have ever accomplished is that I helped repeal the snack tax in California. I seized on that. I led the charge. I sent Ding-Dongs to Sacramento." He laughs. "I got a lot of ink, lined up with a member of the Assembly, Dick Floyd, and we circulated petitions, and it was repealed. It was novel. Radio people love the story, but I don't think of it as very important."

He is speaking without my prompting now, analyzing his role. "I learned a long time ago that different people have different connections to the people they hear on radio and a lot of that is a function of what is or is not going on in their lives. To the extent that I can be a companion, I am happy to do so. At the point they want to get acquisitive about me as an individual or feel that they have a real interest, I draw the line. But you cannot prevent somebody from developing it in a one-way fashion."

"Is this susceptible audience," I ask him, "aware enough of the media to know that a talk show does not necessarily mean truth?"

"It is compelling," says Collins. "It is persuasive, and some people do believe everything they hear in quite a literal way."

"So does that make it dangerous? Is it propaganda of the worst kind, because it's this arrogant, self-serving, personal propaganda?"

"I am comfortable with freedom of speech," Collins tells me, "and the multiplicity of voices and viewpoints, but I do think there are some dangers. I think they're pointed up by giving somebody like Liddy a platform to espouse violation of gun laws. I do have problems with that, and the way I address them is by trying to talk to people about them."

He shrugged, smiled, looked out at the bay, pulled on his sunglasses, and was off to the KSFO studios for another afternoon as a radio demi-god.

———

At the September 1991 convention of the National Association of Broadcaster, Bob Bruno, the general manager of WOR—a New

York City talk station operating a nationwide network—offered his response to the question: What is the greatest challenge facing the talk radio?

"As life becomes increasingly more complex, sophisticated, and stressful," offered Bruno, "and with technology's ability to offer more media sources to the consumer, the talk format must protect, preserve, and nourish its unique niche as the consumer's surrogate friend, personal adviser, and general sounding board. It's our reason for being. If we lose it, we're dead."

# 16  Enclosed Is My Tape and Résumé

*Who gets the talk show host jobs? What are the* common personality traits of these people? Where did Rush Limbaugh and his brethren come from? Who trained them? Is there some way to explain just who ends up behind the potentially powerful microphones of radio talk shows?

Lucky hustlers usually get the radio jobs—lucky hustlers with raging, out-of-control egos. There certainly is no formal training ground for talk show hosts, no formal list of required qualifications. Mutual's Jim Bohannon, who transmits a show across the country in the middle of the night that is comfortable to listen to and filled with entertaining information, suggests what tools a talk show host needs. "I have a fund of trivia in my head," he told writer Adriana Chiara. "I'm one of the few people who can put trivia to use on the job. My knowledge is about 8 miles wide and a quarter of an inch deep. I can talk about anything for 15 minutes. Glib is what I am."[1]

Once on the air, the hosts perpetuate their existence by using the mere fact that they are on the air as credential enough for holding the position, especially if their shows attract a responsive audience.

It surprised media critic Norman Solomon when KABC overnight host Ray Briem waved his Arbitron ratings as evidence of legitimacy, But Briem is correct; the final arbiter in the commercial radio business is the ratings.

This self-created authority—only, of course, continuing at the pleasure of the radio stations' owners—perpetuates the egomania of so many hosts. Writes Gene Burns from his host chair at WOR in New York,[2] "Often I am asked who decides exactly what I'm going to talk about on any given program. I was taken aback the first few times the question was posed. Somewhat self-consciously I answered, 'Well, I do of course.' After all, my name is on the program. It's my reputation that's at stake. Apart from the fact that we talk show hosts rarely own the radio station and less rarely own the program, we engage in the entrepreneurial exercise of selling ourselves. This phenomenon makes us iconoclastic, wary of fellow performers, and far more shy than our detractors care to believe."

Jim Bohannon accesses his guests as mentors. "I am blessed," he told writer Chiara. "How many people can say they really like what they do? Five percent? I doubt it. I am being given a tuition-free, graduate-level course in contemporary affairs—with a nice stipend. And every day they bring in tutors—they call them guests. Essentially, I'm being paid to meet interesting people. It's really quite a scam."

Bohannon's description of his work is accurate, and his positive attitude comes across over the air. His show is usually free from strident arrogance; it is three hours a night of information, ideas, and relaxed conversation.

=====

Pat Buchanan's regular cohost Barry Lynn traces his career back to boyhood. "Some of the most interesting conversations I ever heard were on my transistor radio late at night." He remembered listening as a child to the radio in Pennsylvania and picking up Long John Nebel on WOR. And Lynn listened to Joe Pyne, "who was the progenitor of all of these conservative talk show hosts but who had, even for all his bizarre conservative theories, some level of decency—he could tell George Lincoln Rockwell to go gargle with razor blades when he finished an interview with him. I'll never forget that. Those shows to me were the most interesting things imaginable for a kid growing up in a moderate, middle income, fifties family." Lynn was transported by the magic of radio. "We didn't go many places. But there was a whole new world open to me by listening to these political and social talk shows."

=======

Christine Craft joined the world of radio talk shows after becoming momentarily famous for being fired as a Kansas City TV anchor after her boss described her as "too old, too ugly, and not deferential to men."

"Radio," said Craft from her job at KFBK in Sacramento (the station where Rush Limbaugh got his start in talk radio), "is far more satisfying than reading a Teleprompter and looking perfect. You have an opportunity to express a point of view and argue a point. You use your head. You encourage people to think critically."[3]

"Broadcasting is a notoriously nontenurial profession," Craft, in her late forties, acknowledged. Explaining why she was studying for a law degree, she said, "I want some skills for the back fifty."

You also can lose your job, even if the audience can't see you. A couple of weeks after Craft made those comments, she was fired by KFBK program director Betsy Braziel, who explained her rationale succinctly to me: "Her ratings were lousy."

=======

Remarkably few women host talk radio shows. Surveys conducted by the trade magazine *Radio and Records*[4] blame the prejudices of radio station programmers for the lack of women voices on the air. Eric Seidel, the program director at WGST in Atlanta, told *Radio and Records* reporter Randall Bloomquist that audiences are biased against women. "I had a woman on for eighteen months," he said about his test case. "She worked really hard and had great instincts, but it just didn't work out. A lot of the resistance came from women, which surprised me. They didn't like hearing a confrontational woman on the radio."

It is absurd to suggest that the gender, race, age, or religion of a host plays a role in success or failure. Success or failure is dictated by luck, talent, advertising, and promotion, not the physical being of a performer—especially on radio where so much can be hidden from the audience so easily.

═══

A few months after her dismissal from KFBK, I catch up with Christine Craft at a Sacramento natural foods supermarket café in January 1994. She is pleased for a breather from her law studies; this day she is working on material for a First Amendment class. I offer her a drink and she hesitates, trying to decide between beer and carrot juice, ultimately choosing the juice. In a year, at her current pace, she will have earned her law degree. But she is not finished with talk radio—she works as an extra at KGO in San Francisco and is anxious to talk about the business.

But first she keeps talking about the Lorena Bobbitt case. She speaks fast and with a sense of wonder in her voice. "I just think it's curious"—she smiles—"how easy it was to cut off!" She looks relaxed and full of energy. The diamond studs in her ears pick up the café's spotlighting. I cannot help but think—and she knows I'm thinking it—that she is not ugly. At her lectures, she tells me, the fact that she is not ugly is often mentioned by her questioners.

"It's a trend to listen to talk radio," she says. "In the old days, it was the kind of thing that somebody did if they really were a lonely, desperate person."

"But isn't it still the lonely listening?" I say. "Who else would call up, face repeated busy signals—"

"Someone who wants a voice," she interjects.

"What kind of voice is that?" I counter, reminding her not only how long it often takes for a listener to get on the air, but also how brief the opportunity to speak usually is for the caller. "And then adios into oblivion."

"It's almost a test," is her theory of why callers put up with such trouble just getting on the air, especially when the host often adds to the difficult experience by abusing the caller with insults. "It's almost a test to see if you can get past the screener and you can get past the abuse and make your point. Maybe some of the people who call in are just natural debaters." She draws my attention to lengthening commutes as another explanation for the growing popularity of talk on the radio.

"But Tower Records is just down the street," I say. "Why don't more commuters listen to their own choice of music or books on tape? Why do we burden ourselves with the drivel that is usually on talk stations? What is the addictive appeal?"

"Because it's easy," says Craft. "It appeals to the lowest common denominator. You have a whole generation that's been raised on easy things, quick fixes. Talk radio is a lot of generally uninformed people, spouting forth simplistic opinions with passion and fire, appealing to people's fears." She uses the Three Strikes and You're Out anticrime bill as an example of the simplistic manner in which talk radio deals with crises in society. Despite the flaws in the legislation, most talk radio hosts and callers tout the bill as an obvious answer to escalating crime in California. "We've got to do something. We're mad as hell and we're *gonna do* something about it," she says, mimicking the talk radio aficionado "I think it all starts with the movie *Network*, doesn't it?"

I agree with her, but continue to search for an explanation for what captivates listeners. "I still have a hard time comprehending why so many people would choose to listen to it, especially since it so often is—as you just defined it—lowest common denominator material, drivel, uninformed people speaking to one another."

Craft, as is the case with most talk radio performers, is never at a loss for words or theories. "We have this tabloid society," she says. "Look at the kinds of stories that really draw callers. I'm sure right now it's all the Bobbitt stuff." At the time we were talking Lorena Bobbitt was on trial for severing her husband's penis—an ideal talk radio story. I assigned a reporter to cover the trial for WRC; we ran some of the testimony live, and our talk show hosts were never without calls whenever the case was mentioned on the air. When she was acquitted, we devoted an hour of special programming to the decision.

Craft continues with a litany of similar stories, from the Menendez brothers on trial for murdering their parents, to Tonya Harding and the attack on Nancy Kerrigan, to the sexual abuse accusations against Michael Jackson. "They see the tabloid image," she says about the audiences and the hosts, "and they're going for the emotional button, a quick button."

I ask her why she thinks so many people want to be involved in something as anonymous as a talk show, where there are no relationships among listeners and callers and the hosts—just fleeting encounters.

She sees that anonymity not as in conflict with current culture, but completely in concert with it. "Everybody sits at home and watches TV. There's less of a social world in general."

"Why do relatively huge numbers of people listen to anonymous people giving uninformed opinions?" I ask.

"Well, you know what Lucy Thomas used to tell me about people who call in." Lucy Thomas was the program director at KFBK before she quit to go to art school. "People who call in," she'd say, "it's aberrant behavior. Most people will never call in a talk show."

"If we accept that it's aberrant behavior to call in, why would anybody listen?"

"Well, I listen to talk radio a lot," Craft tells me, and it's a response I hear from many talk radio hosts. Many hosts listen, not only to keep track of the competition, but because they genuinely enjoy the medium. Some even call other hosts' shows, anonymously, for sport. "If it's somebody that's really stupid, I turn it off," she says. "Sometimes I'll just listen to get the tenor of the times. It's sort of like taking the temperature of the public consciousness."

"But do you give any credibility to the suggestion that talk radio is the essence of the public mood?"

"I think it's certainly indicative of the public mood. Very often—yeah—because every talk show, every newspaper is asking the Tonya Harding question, for example, and these hot burner stories sort of polarize the public attention, then zap, they're gone, then the next one takes the place. You know how that works."

Craft elaborates on her reasons for tuning in to talk radio. "I like to listen to folks who are talking with some intelligence about the political issues of the day, because I like to see what the public mood is. And certainly I wouldn't take that as the sole index of what the public mood is, but it sure as hell is one of them. Maybe the people just feel that they are plugged in to what the public discourse of the hour is. Even if you don't call in, if someone, a caller or a host, says something that you agree with emphatically, you kind of get into it. If someone calls in and says something that agrees with you, you feel a little better." She suggests that talk radio can be an ideal device for teaching critical thinking.

If talk is so powerful and valuable, I ask, should we be concerned that there is no standardized credentialing process for the hosts?

"The big mouths aren't licensed," says Craft. "We have a society that seems to be careening more and more toward mediocrity every day." She complains that too many talk show hosts try to reduce issues to black and white. "That's not the way life is, as you know. There are five or six, seven or eight, many sides to a story."

Craft insists that the ratings for her show were good when she was on during the day and only started to slide when she was transferred to the nighttime and often preempted by sports. Her politics, her attitude, and her sex are what keep adversely affecting her career, she's sure. "I'm not always going to be saying things that support the vested, corporate powers. I'm just not." In her mind, the bosses are to blame. "I think management's pretty gutless, myself, and any time they mention the First Amendment I have to choke. They'll only put on what's selling."

After she was fired from her Kansas City television job in 1983, Craft sued Metromedia, the owner of KMBC. She won her case, but it was overturned on appeal, and the Supreme Court refused to consider it further.

Craft has her own Limbaugh story to tell. She is talking about the day the jury in Simi Valley chose not to find guilty the Los Angeles police who beat Rodney King.

"I said, 'Well, Simi Valley is a very white community.' I said, 'If Rodney King had been white and the cops had been black, and they had tried it in Simi Valley, what do you think the result would have been?' "

The general manager of KFBK pulled Craft off the air for two days, charging her with broadcasting "inflammatory" material.

"The *New York Times,* two or three days after this, came out with the same hypothetical," Craft informs me with satisfaction and irritation. "It's sort of the obvious one." But that is not what really peeves her about the episode. A week or so later, when the congressional delegation from southern California was coming to South Central, and Maxine Waters was leading the pack off that plane, Rush Limbaugh described her as looking like a gorilla in the mist." She describes KFBK executives as responding to the Limbaugh remark with a nonchalant, "what the hell" attitude. "I think they had a different standard. I guess our demographics are mostly white male conservatives over a certain age who listen to get their blood pressure going.

"I was marginalized first, then I was fired. Yeah, it irritates me tremendously because it's no marketplace of ideas. I was doing very well for them. There's no reason in the ratings to fire me at all. Or to move me to the nighttime where they knew that no one listened to talk radio in Sacramento. I'm smart. I knew that they really didn't want me there anymore." She returns to Limbaugh. "What I resent is that there's no one who's countering the crap that he puts out there. This man is a draft dodger, who got out of the draft because he had an ingrown hair on his ass. He is a marijuana smoker. So what? But he's been attacking other people for doing this, including the president. Limbaugh used to smoke dope all the time and everybody knows it." She mocks his claim that he takes hostile calls on his show. "He doesn't. If I were to call and say, 'Why don't you tell the truth about your pilonidol cyst, your dope smoking, and the fact that you didn't write either one of those books? You're pulling a fraud on the people.' That's the question he needs. He doesn't want any kind of live confrontation to bring out the truth about the fraud he's pulling on people."

=====

The most detailed published analysis of Limbaugh's draft board status suggests Craft's criticism is correct. In *The Rush Limbaugh Story,* biographer Paul Colford, who is the radio reporter for New York *Newsday,* laboriously reconstructs Limbaugh's draft history with Selective Service Board No. 16. "Records indicate," writes Colford, "that the panel acted on medical information obtained at his [Limbaugh's] own initiative, most likely from his physician, and classified him 1-Y on November 24, 1970. In the parlance of the Selective Service System, 1-Y meant that Limbaugh was 'conditionally acceptable' for military duty but would be called up only in the event of a declared war or national emergency, neither of which applied to Vietnam."

The actual medical records apparently no longer exist. On the air Limbaugh credits an "inoperable pilonidal cyst" and "a football knee from high school" for his exemption from military duty, or as Travus T. Hipp, a Navy veteran, puts it, "He had a pimple on his ass."

# 17

## The Myth of the Liberal Media

*Rush Limbaugh, Pat Buchanan, and G. Gordon* Liddy are all instantly recognizable in the popular culture as talk show hosts. Even former Ku Klux Klanner and presidential candidate David Duke hosts a radio talk show in Louisiana. Across America successful talk shows shout their right-wing message. Left-wing programs trail as a minuscule minority. The preponderance of successful shows promulgating right-wing content gives the lie to the continuing myth of a left-leaning media. Why most radio talk shows skew right politically is not clear. Perhaps advertisers feel more comfortable with a pro-business host hawking their products.

Certainly Nike would rather have a talk show host who believes in unrestricted world trade selling its shoes than hear its commercials adjacent to Jim Hightower as the talk show populist draws attention to the company's factories in Malaysia, saying working conditions there violate baseline health and safety standards and workers make in a day less than the minimum hourly wage in the United States.

Many radio station owners and operators, understandably, are more comfortable with a host who embraces the business world with no questions asked. "Can we find out what he's going to talk about in advance?" a radio station general manager I worked with asked me about Hightower after Hightower attacked Nike for the third time. It was not that he disagreed with Hightower—or even that he was upset about the effect the criticism might have on any business the radio station might do with Nike. He was worried that such direct challenges to Nike could instill fear in advertisers and make them afraid that they may be the next target.

Pat Buchanan's sometime cohost Barry Lynn agreed that commerce must affect talk show programming. "Most businesses are somewhat more comfortable being on a program that tends to be politically conservative. It's easy to sell a show where there is a conservative and a liberal because then you don't offend anyone in the audience, or maybe you offend everyone, but at least it's an equal opportunity offense and therefore it's easier to sell. But most local stations can't afford to put two people on the air. They're lucky to be able to afford to put one person on the air to fill up four hours. So I think there's a natural tendency if you're only going to have one side to have it be conservative simply because that's where the money may be."

The market-driven right-wingers rarely surprise managers and their clients with attacks on business. Yet controversial subject matter and shock styles—even coming from the political right— can scare away businesses and charities, and can result in consumers rejecting products associated with some of the more offensive hosts.

Early in 1994, the Florida State Citrus Commission decided endorsements from talk radio hosts could help increase orange juice sales. They signed up Dr. Dean Edell—the medical advice host—for a couple of hundred thousand dollars, paid half a million dollars to Larry King, and agreed to a million-dollar fee for Rush Limbaugh.

The reaction was quick and loud. "It is totally unbelievable that the Citrus Commission could possibly be so insensitive as to choose a person of such extreme views to represent the chief product of this state and by inference the state itself," was the immediate institutional response from Florida's National Association for the Advancement of Colored People. The group's president, T. H. Poole, told the *New York Times*,[1] "It would be extremely difficult to buy Florida orange juice if Limbaugh is the spokesman."

Said the president of the Florida National Organization for Women chapter, Siobhan McLaughlin, "The decision to buy time on Limbaugh's show was insulting, offensive and unwise." "There are broader audiences to reach," judged Florida Governor Lawton Chiles, "because our orange juice leaves a good taste with people and should be promoted on programs that represent good taste."[2]

On his February 17 show, Limbaugh attacked his critics. "Just keep chugging the stuff," he told his audience. "That's the single best message you can send." He dismissed calls for boycotts as "childish and embarrassing."

After six months of weathering the controversy, the Citrus Commission chose not to renew Limbaugh's deal. NOW took credit for the end of the relationship, pointing to a Florida orange juice boycott it helped organize as an important factor in the decision to drop Limbaugh.

Free speech advocate Nat Hentoff expressed disgust with the boycott attempt in his *Washington Post* column,[3] pointing out that the action was based on trying to punish Limbaugh for expressing his ideas—a dangerous precedent for a society that values free expression.

Late in 1994, Limbaugh, showed up on local New York television, this time in advertisements for the *New York Times*. In an October 13 memorandum to the paper's staff, *Times* management expressed pride in their new ad campaign, which featured not only Limbaugh but other celebrities, including Limbaugh nemesis Jesse Jackson. "We believe the cumulative effect of the commercials," said the memo, "delivered by such a wide range of well-known and unexpected endorsers, will encourage new readers to pick up a copy of the *Times*."

What the memo neglected to mention was a half-page congratulatory article about the perceived political power of Rush Limbaugh that the paper was about to publish in its main news section. Reporter Robin Toner used the profile[4] to elevate Limbaugh's stature in the nation's political and social debate without informing her readers that the *Times* had just hired him to pitch the newspaper.

Limbaugh chortled on his show that the *Times* commercial was evidence that he had "conquered the liberal media."

G. Gordon Liddy offended St. Jude Children's Research Hospital in Memphis when he solicited photographs from women listeners wearing only underwear and carrying guns. "It's not the fault of the lump of iron that someone misuses it," he said when questioned about the message he was sending when so many children are in hospitals suffering from gunshot wounds.[5] "That's like saying we can't show kids in station wagon commercials because a lot of kids get killed in station wagons." Liddy's idea was to pick his favorite cheesecake with guns and produce a calender, donating any profits to St. Jude. "Mr. Liddy is working totally independently," the hospital made clear, "and has not contacted us."

With characteristic bravado, Liddy announced that he was not interested in photographs from women who could not shoot. "It's quite obvious the ones who know what they're doing," he said. "The others just look awkward and we throw them out."

But the spontaneous nature of talk radio in general and the notoriety for controversy achieved by some hosts keep some important advertisers away. "Hartz Mountain has made a request that none of their network spots are to run in the Rush Limbaugh program on Mutual or NBC affiliates," wrote a Westwood One executive to the network's affiliates in one of a series of letters designed to separate some clients from specific shows.[6] "If you carry Rush Limbaugh, please do not air Hartz Mountain spots within the program," requests the letter. It goes on, "We apologize for the inconvenience, but Hartz Mountain has made it very clear to us that they do not wish to be associated with this program."

Johnson and Johnson was even more concerned. It requested that advertisements for its Clean 'n Clear product not air during the Howard Stern show, the Greaseman show, and all other "talk programs of any type," according to another letter from Westwood One to its affiliated stations.[7] "The advertisers have made it very clear to us that they do not wish to be associated with these types of programs."

Despite some advertisers' reluctance to be affiliated with talk shows, hosts continue to blur the traditional lines, not just between news and entertainment, but also between editorial endorsements and commercial endorsements. Bruce Williams, popular for his financial advice, slides from his free recommendations for distraught callers to paid commercials broadcast using his voice and the same homespun ("Hey, Tiger!") delivery.

"Bruce is available to record spots for your clients," says a letter from his office to affiliated stations, making a straightforward pitch for extra business for Williams. "Over the past couple of years," continues the presentation, "Bruce Williams has been recording commercials for clients of local radio stations across the country. The response from these clients has been overwhelming. Simply put, they love having Bruce advertise their business or product, and they always report increased revenues!!" Prices ranged from $600 to $2,000 in late 1993 for commercials that ran in one radio market for thirteen weeks. The top figure represented products or services endorsed on the air by Williams.

One fascinating aspect of the brochure describing Williams's availability and rates is the complete lack of any criteria that must be observed by a client (besides anteing up the $2,000) in order to receive the powerful Williams endorsement. "Radio is a commercial enterprise," Williams said, explaining his availability for endorsements to *People* magazine.[8] "If I thought endorsements were damaging, I wouldn't do them."

═══════

Although radio talk shows may be the most obvious examples of the myth of a liberal American media, examples can be found elsewhere and with ease. In an interview with Ken Kelley, *Oakland Tribune* editor-in-chief David Burgin lashed out at the myth. "That is such a crock," he insisted. "And the media-bashing based on this so-called liberalness that guys like Limbaugh get away with." He was livid. "In all the years I've worked for newspapers"—and Burgin worked for some of the best: the *New York Herald Tribune,* the *San Francisco Examiner,* the *Washington Star*—"I have never worked for a liberal newspaper. Not one. There's only about half a dozen in America!" he told Kelley. "There are some 1,700 daily newspapers and they're all run by Republicans! Why? Because Republicans are the kind of people who own things, that's why. And I don't know one of them who's going to let some off-the-wall liberal run his newspaper. Ain't gonna happen."

Burgin was on the attack and Kelley let him talk. "Sure, there are loose cannons in every newsroom who are screaming liberals, and that's fine. But they got nothing to do with the editorial page, and they don't pick the editors. That's where the power is. You can count on one hand the important newspapers who can bona fidely call themselves liberal newspapers—the *Boston Globe,* the *Washington Post,* the *New York Times,* Knight-Ridder's *Detroit Free Press* and the *Miami Herald. Times-Mirror?*" he asked rhetorically about the Los Angeles daily. "Solid Republican. Joseph Pulitzer's original paper, the [*St. Louis*] *Post Dispatch*—that's about as liberal as Attila the Hun." Burgin laughed.[9]

=====

Scapegoaters have been trying to shirk responsibility for their actions by blaming the messenger since at least the days of the ancient Greeks. So those of us who work as journalists are forced to develop a thick skin in regard to the constant chorus we hear about all the problems of the world being our fault because we bring them to society's attention. *Media* is one of the hottest buzz words of our era. "If the media would just not report it" and "the media blew it all out of proportion" are the kind of explanatory phrases we hear all the time from all types of people to rationalize away all sorts of actions.

But this scapegoating has developed into a bizarre new form with the ascent of talk radio. Just as presidents since at least Jimmy

Carter have been campaigning as anti-politicians, saying that they are not part of the inside-the-Beltway gang, so too are we now seeing major media figures—especially talk show hosts—championing their own causes by insisting they are not "members of the media."

The media has been successfully cast by these skillful charlatans as some sort of omnipotent conspiracy. And these new anti-media media stars promote themselves as being so astute and clever that they manage to escape the clutches of the monster.

For example, one of the most absurd claims on the radio was heard in Los Angeles. Shortly after he was forced out as police chief following the Rodney King verdict and the ensuing riots, Darryl Gates landed a job as a talk show host on KFI, the powerhouse AM station that also proudly broadcasts Rush Limbaugh. Gates was on the air the day that former FBI and CIA Director William Webster issued his report on why the police were unable to control the rioting. The report singled out Gates as a failure. Understandably, Gates spent his radio show that day attempting to defend his already destroyed reputation. "Clearly we should have shot a few people." Gates continued to make sure his point was clear. "In retrospect, that's exactly what we should have done. We should have blown a few heads off. And maybe your television cameras would have seen that and maybe that would have been broadcast and maybe, just maybe, that would have stopped everything. I don't know. But certainly we had the legal right to do that."

With ideas like that blasting out over KFI's 50,000 watts from the former police chief, it's little wonder that the Webster report concluded that L.A. is "plagued by hostility, rage and resentment. It could happen again."

But the sermon Gates made on the radio in the midst of all this reaction to the Webster report was typical of the skill the radio right is employing to attempt to smear journalists whose work gets in the path of their own crusade. "I am not part of the media!" Gates screamed over his prime time radio talk show. He then attempted to explain he was simply using the radio to talk about issues and explain his opinions. He insisted he was an outsider, removed from organized media liars.

Somehow Gates and his ilk (this includes Limbaugh) manage to convince plenty of their listeners that they are not part of the very system of news gatherers and printing and broadcasting companies that they themselves use to promote their own interpretations and reportings of the news. It is difficult to believe that the public can be so easily and completely snookered, but examples are easy to find.

On another Los Angeles talk radio station, KABC, a distraught listener called up to explain why she was voting for George Bush for president in 1992. "Hi, I'm Debbie. I'm twenty-nine years old. I'm calling from a car phone."

Debbie told listeners that she sold insurance to businesses. She said she was successful, happy, and worried that if Bush did not win the election she might have to spend more of her income on social services for other Americans.

But Debbie had another complaint, too, and before she hung up she explained one of the reasons she feared her candidate might lose. "The media," she said, "plays too much of a role in informing the public." I am fascinated by the bliss Debbie seeks through ignorance.

======

With such clear evidence that the media—especially talk radio— are no bastions of liberalism, how is the myth that the media in general leans left maintained? Barry Lynn believes the tactics are the same as those espoused in *Mein Kampf*. "It gets perpetrated successfully because it gets repeated so many times that people believe it," he said. "It's just like the study that said teachers were surveyed in the 1940s and the 1980s, and in the 1940s they said that the big problems in schools were gum chewing, running in the hallways, and talking, and that in the eighties it was suicide, rape, and assault of teachers. This was a completely fictitious set of non-surveys. The data didn't exist. It was all invented out of whole cloth. Yet it was repeated by Bill Bennett [former Education Secretary and frequent Limbaugh guest], by Rush Limbaugh, by every conservative, religious, or cultural conservative in the country as if it were true until the *New York Times* exposed it as a complete myth. If you hear a lie enough times," said Lynn, "you're going to start to believe it's true."

Talk radio allows those with access to the microphone the opportunity to repeat falsehoods over and over again—either maliciously or inadvertently. The medium can be easily taken advantage of by outside manipulators. Plenty of talk show hosts repeated the school survey misinformation not because they knew it was false and wanted to mislead their audience, but because it made terrific talk show fuel and they simply did not bother to check the veracity of the material fed to them. Every day talk show hosts and radio stations are deluged by material. Authors want to get on the air to sell their books, companies want to promote their products, politicians want free air time. Newt Gingrich and his Republican followers credit some of their 1994 election successes to their fax link with over 500 talk show hosts. During the campaign they deluged stations with call-generating crib sheets, which many hosts simply read verbatim. The U.S. Navy called me in early 1994 offering to hook me up (via a collect telephone call!) with a sailor on board the aircraft carrier *Saratoga* off the coast of the former Yugoslavia to demonstrate the valor of the United States military. Public relations firms call regularly with prerecorded interviews that lazy radio operators can simply add to their air product without bothering to conduct their own interview or to check the information they broadcast.

═══

In addition to the secular media, the reactionary right enjoys another broadcast forum on the thousand-plus American radio stations that consider themselves Christian outlets, a definition which usually means typical right-wing rhetoric wrapped in a Bible along with a flag. Most of the Christian programming is relatively harmless: a mixture of "traditional family values" messages with routine commercials ("Come to so-and-so's car repair shop where quality work is provided in a Christian environment"). But sharing the religious airwaves are radio stations and personalities broadcasting hate.

An example of hate radio operates in the shadow of Washington, D.C. WFAX broadcasts from Falls Church, Virginia, with the continuing message that America is "poisoned by Jewish money." Dale Crowley Jr. holds forth with a regular monologue on WFAX. His program is called *Focus on Israel,* a mixture of Bible readings and denouncements such as one monitored in early 1994 when Crowley insisted, "There has been considerable Jewish terrorism in this country." Crowley ends his broadcasts with a pitch for money, the device so many "religious" broadcasters use to generate funds. The Internal Revenue Service keeps watch on religious broadcasters, convinced that all the money coming back to them from listeners responding to the continual solicitations for cash results in many tax law violations. Joseph L. Conn, managing editor of *Church and State,* reported in the March 1994 issue of the newsletter[10] that "areas of IRS interest include excessive salaries and unreported income, extravagant lifestyles, diversion of organizational funds and property for private use, failure to pay taxes, and illegal political activity."

The National Religious Broadcasters count 1,600 so-called religious radio stations in America. But at their January 1994 convention in Washington, D.C., one of the principal speakers, San Antonio preacher and broadcaster John Hagee, made it clear that broadcasters identifying themselves as religious do not shy away from politics. "The Bible paints a portrait of the ideal woman in Proverbs 31," he thundered. "She's married and she's a mother— in that order. She's a homemaker—that means she knows how to make cookies. She's not some hip hell-raiser from an Ivy League school."[11]

For his study called "Hate on Talk Radio," Kenneth Stern cited stations in Spokane, Washington, and Portland, Oregon, that sell air time to "religious" talkers who preach that "Jews are the offspring of Satan and blacks are 'mud people' of a different species." While some of these broadcasters preach in the tradition of Father

Charles Coughlin, many others make use of the telephone and
interact with callers using the contemporary techniques of talk
radio. It sometimes can be hard to distinguish between a "religious" talk radio program and a supposedly mainstream one.

———

On the eastern seaboard and in the Southwest, the airwaves are
jammed with Spanish-language talk stations, and a Spanish-
language talk network serves the Hispanic audience. Radio Labio
(Latin American Broadcast Industry Organization) cranks out
*radio hablada en española las 24 horas.*

Throughout urban America there are stations, such as the politically powerful WOL in Washington, airing talk programs
designed to cater to the black audience. Many of the stations are
now black-owned. The hosts support their own trade organization, the National Council of Black Talk Radio. Most of these
shows make it clear that they do not expect nonblacks to be listening. Shows often are structured to suggest that there is a common black radio audience united by the black experience. "What
are we going to do about this?" a host on a black station will ask
the audience about a problem, and the inference is clear: What are
we as blacks going to do about the problem? Callers may well refer
to previous callers with language for the most part confined to the
black community, such as, "I agree with the sister who just
called."

After listening to black talk shows in Detroit for the *Detroit Free
Press,* reporter Constance Prater came up with a long list of subject
matter unlikely to appear on the city's white-oriented radio stations. In addition to ruminations about whether Michael Jackson
wished he were white, "topics included," she wrote, "how to buy
*kinte* cloth, and healthier eating habits for African Americans.
Only on black radio," said Prater, "would you hear a host tell
young listeners on a snowy morning that school will be open and
to get up and 'get yourself some grits and eggs and go to school.' "

But blacks maintain a distinct presence on radio stations with predominantly white audiences, too, although, as is the case with women, blacks are not on mainstream talk radio in proportion with their numbers in society. In a survey conducted in mid-1993, the *Los Angeles Times* found only a dozen nonwhite hosts holding down full-time weekday jobs on mainstream talk radio. Even that small group claims its right-wing stars.

One of the most popular black right-wingers is Ken Hamblin, yelling out over KNUS in Denver. Hamblin was a colleague of Alan Berg's at KOA. After Berg's murder, Hamblin mused, "Sitting in the radio booth doing my show, one thing leads to another and I get a roll going and I hear him talking to me and then it ends and I think, Jesus, this guy had more of an effect on my life than I ever realized. Sometimes, he possesses me."[12]

Hamblin told *New York Times* reporter Dirk Johnson,[13] "I'm angry, so angry I sometimes feel like I'm going to explode." Hamblin is ostracized by traditional black civic leaders in Denver for using tried and true talk radio techniques of outrage. He is famous for referring to Denver's black neighborhoods as "Darktown." But he offers a ready explanation. "I call it 'Darktown' because it is dark—dark with misery and hopelessness and despair. I use the expression because I want to get their attention."

Hamblin let loose to the *Times*'s Johnson a long litany of the type of material that keeps his ratings high in Denver:

> We are teaching black kids that they are victims—the only victims—and that everything that goes wrong in life is part of some racist conspiracy. We are teaching them to be hostile, and it's leading to a kind of xenophobia.
>
> I want to know why 60 percent of black babies are being born out of wedlock. Is that the fault of white people? I want to know why so many black kids can't speak proper English. I want to know why black people can't pass a civil service examination. The excuse is that it's culturally biased. Well, I'd like to know what could possibly be culturally biased on a test for a firefighter.
>
> Let's get serious. White people don't have time to sit around trying to figure out ways to hurt black people. They're too busy trying

to pay the bills, raise their families, straighten the kid's teeth—just like most black families.

Quotas and affirmative action are killing us. It's a system that says if you're black, then we won't expect much from you, we won't challenge you. Well, damn it, I think it's time we start demanding, challenging, expecting. If we fail, we fail. We've come to a point where every time a white person sees a black person in a job, they assume it's affirmative action. Do you know how demeaning that is?

Ken Hamblin fills up his phone lines.

# 18 The Talk Show Host As Journalist

Radio talk shows, despite their popularity and the respect a select few have managed to develop over the years and especially during the 1992 presidential campaign, usually play the same role as the supermarket tabloids. They offer frivolous entertainment, not credible news. The comparison breaks down, however, because while the tabloids clearly refuse to take themselves too seriously (witness the plethora of Elvis and alien sightings in their pages), more and more radio talk show hosts are believing their own harangues. And worse, in part because of the built-in credibility that a voice on the radio carries in our culture, too many listeners in the audience believe the unsubstantiated and undocumented propaganda now blaring out of radios across the country twenty-four hours of every day.

A close listening of just an hour or less of most any talk show on the air in America proves two dangerous points. First, hosts regularly present information as fact without bothering to rely on accepted journalistic devices for ascertaining that the information presented comes from reliable sources. Sometimes the host ignores the techniques of journalism because he or she is intent on spreading misinformation and disinformation. Rush Limbaugh's work is full of examples of such propaganda. "Do you really think the situation in the schools would turn around if we threw more money at them? What would they do with it? Buy condoms with an even greater variety of colors and flavors?" Limbaugh's setup for his coming distortion is typically flip, perhaps even comical. But then comes the lie, in the guise of a news report. "We're spending enough money per classroom today," the authoritative voice over the air proclaims, "to provide chauffeured limousines to the teachers and the kids."[1]

Most talk radio hosts attempt to create an exemption for themselves, claiming that they need not engage in the basic rules and practices adopted by credible journalists because they are simply entertainers. "I'm not a journalist," said Mary Beal proudly while wearing the credentials not only of a host on KNSS in Wichita, but also the chair of the board of the National Association of Talk Show Hosts.[2] "I don't care if I have a balanced viewpoint, because any opinion can be challenged by the people who call in." Beal missed the point. There is nothing wrong with her opinion; what she must come to terms with is that by dealing with the news on her talk show, she became a journalist by default and cannot obviate the built-in responsibilities and burdens of journalism simply by denying the reality of her role.

The second problem is worse: Some hosts are flat-out not interested in pursuing truth, but only seek to stir up the audience in hopes of generating increased ratings.

═══

Hearing the nationwide successes of the Rush Limbaugh and Larry King shows encouraged struggling radio announcers from coast to coast to throw away their music and "go to the phones." The result is an epidemic of fast-talking performers trying to woo listeners by spinning tales instead of records. I inherited one of those disc jockey–trained talk show hosts when I took over the programming duties at WRC. Brian Wilson (not the Beach Boy) had been a successful disc jockey, earning high ratings for his quick ad-libbed one-liners at stations in Baltimore and New York. But when he turned to the all-talk form of radio, he started presenting his prattle as news.

Shortly after six one morning, a caller used Wilson's Washington talk show to suggest that the Clinton administration was forbidding the military from working in uniform when at the White House. Whether the caller was intentionally spreading lies or was simply confused is not clear. Since callers to talk shows are usually allowed to speak anonymously, determining motives for calls is all but impossible.

"Let's get out there and chat with Wanda," is how the episode began.[3] "Let's see what she's up to this morning. Hi, Wanda."

"What I called about is that I was reading in the *Washingtonian* magazine last night, the new issue, and it says that the White House doesn't appreciate military men during duty hours wearing their uniforms to the White House." She paused, waiting for the response she expected.

"What," said Wilson, sounding dumbfounded. "Run it by me again. The White House—"

Wanda reiterated, "They wish that the military would not wear their uniforms during duty hours when they come on business to the White House." Her terminology has switched from "doesn't appreciate" to "wish they would not."

The verb changes again as Wilson repeats Wanda's claim. "The White House does not want military men wearing their uniforms when they visit the White House?"

"Right," says Wanda.

"On duty?" asks Wilson.

"Right."

"In other words, they want them to appear out of uniform while they're on duty when they approach the White House?"

"Right, right, right," says Wanda, "Yes, that's what it says in the *Washingtonian*."

Wilson and his sidekick question Wanda for details. She tells them the Pentagon is upset, and that the problem started when an officer was asked not to wear his uniform. She apparently is paraphrasing the article she read in the magazine. Her terminology is changing again from talking about what she read to speaking as if she has learned a fact.

"That's the mentality of this White House," says Wanda with disgust. "It's just unbelievable."

"First it's smoking, now it's uniforms," says Wilson.

"Yes," agrees Wanda.

"I'm telling you, it's unbelievable," says Wilson. "I appreciate the tip in the *Washingtonian* magazine. We ought to get a copy of that and see if we can't trace that one down." He is correct. That is exactly what he should do. But he doesn't. Instead, he turns Wanda's telephone call into a news report. "That's rather phenomenal. You can't wear your uniform at the White House."

The charge is false but is accepted as fact by Wilson, who then, acting outraged, invites the audience to react.

After his sidekick reads a newscast and the traffic reporter updates road conditions and Wilson takes a few listener calls on other subjects, he is back on the uniform story, and he adds a new charge.

"Word in from our White House source," he says authoritatively, "an individual"—now he becomes conspiratorial—"that for obvious reasons cannot and would not go on the air." He pauses. "Along with the president's consideration of a ban on military uniforms at the White House, military aides have been instructed— and this," he emphasizes, "is purely a report exclusive to *Mornings with Brian and Bob*, military aides have been instructed they must no longer salute the president." He repeats it for emphasis, "They must no longer salute the president."

"What?" yells the sidekick.

Wilson comes in with the punch line. "Because he doesn't know how to salute in return. And if any of you have seen him in those standard clips of him getting off the helicopter, there's the aide at the bottom, snapping to, you know, ripping off a nice crisp one, and there's our president giving this kind of . . ." He groans and laughs and then reiterates the "news," and by this time the qualifying terms such as "allegedly" are being abandoned. The audience, of course, tunes in and out, and those just turning the program on are hearing Wilson identify the uniform and salute issues (based so far on nothing more than Wanda's call) as the latest example of President Clinton's "loathing for the military."

As an afterthought, he muses about the story that's fast becoming his prime focus of the morning. "I wonder if anyone can substantiate that. Maybe we can call over to the White House."

In fact, the radio station's news department made the call. Deputy White House press secretary Lorraine Voles was asked if there were any orders issued or under consideration in regard to saluting and uniforms. Her response to each question was an unequivocal no. Meanwhile, the NBC radio network White House correspondent—who was listening with amazement to the non-story developing on the air—reported to his assignment editor with further confirmation that there were no such orders.

By just after seven that morning Wilson was informed that the story was false. It wasn't until half past seven that Wilson bothered to share the official information with his listeners. Predictably, in the meantime, the phones went wild. Callers were outraged, understandably accepting the story as true. After all, it had been repeated by the host and his sidekick as true, and listeners are conditioned by audio experiences going back to Edward R. Murrow and his staff of news professionals to give the benefit of the doubt to radio announcers presenting news.

"I'm just so livid about what I'm hearing," said caller Angela from Alexandria. "My husband is on active duty. He happens to be in Somalia right now. I'm waiting for him to get home in about ten days. Do you have a list of who all I call? I'll call the White House to complain, if I can get through. I'll call the Pentagon Services Committee—"

"Sam Nunn would be good, yeah," Wilson interrupts.

"I just have to express my anger," she gushes.

"I understand right now, at this point," Wilson is covering himself, "with regard to the uniforms, this is just another one of Billy's balloons—there's all these trial balloons that get floated up and if they aren't met with severe anti-aircraft fire, surface-to-air missiles, then it floats."

Angela says she's going to tell all her friends to "load the fax machines" in protest. But she expressed some confusion. "Is this true?" she finally asks. "Is it in the *Post* today?"

"If it's not in the *Post,*" mocks the sidekick, "it's not true."

"The *Washingtonian* has that story," says Wilson about the uniforms, "and according to that story, it is under consideration. The saluting order," he says, "apparently has gone out."

Both of those statements are based on nothing but hearsay. Wilson has no reference material on which to base his announcements.

"It's just totally outrageous," says Angela. "I'm livid," she says again. "I'm so proud of the people who serve and so proud of them working in their uniform. When I was watching the open house at the White House and seeing the people in uniform going by and shaking his hand and smiling and looking so happy that he was there and he was saying, 'Thank you for your service,' I was just feeling that this was kind of hypocritical. And now seeing that he doesn't even want the uniforms worn in the White House . . ." Her voice is filled with indignation, indignation caused by the misleading program she is both listening to and helping to create.

"Suspicions confirmed," says Wilson.

"I'm just beside myself," says Angela, whoever she is. "You prompted me to action. I'm going on a crusade at the office."

"Good for you," says Wilson. "Let us know how it turns out."

"I feel insulted by this," says Dave, the next caller, on the line from his car. "I was in the military ten years. I was proud of my uniform. The only way I could show respect for my commander-in-chief was to salute him and I did it proudly. I think it's wrong for him to take that away from our military."

"Maybe he doesn't want your respect," offers Wilson as bait for more angst from Dave.

"He doesn't have it anyway," says Dave predictably. "I don't respect him, I respect his rank. Last week he put a freeze on their pay. This week he says no uniforms, no saluting. What's next?"

Wilson says nothing to disabuse Dave about his conclusions.

"Here's Mark in Oxen Hill." Wilson introduces another call. "Hi, Mark."

"Listen," says Mark, "it doesn't surprise me about Clinton not wanting the officers in uniform and the no saluting, because this guy hates the military. He dodged the draft, he's an adulterer—" He then goes on a stereotypical anti-Clinton tirade, calling him "a bumbling, stupid hillbilly from Hope, Arkansas, that doesn't know what he's doing."

"Thanks a lot for the call," says Wilson.

Well after the WRC newsroom sent Wilson a computer message explaining that NBC and the White House agree that neither the uniform nor the saluting story has any merit, Wilson continues to flog them, with no foundation, as credible. "Big news making the news today," he says as he touches on some headlines before saying, "And of course the late word that we have this morning is that the orders have gone out from on high that military aides must no longer salute the president—the commander-in-chief—he doesn't know how to respond and return, of course, due to his limited experience in the military. The only real experience the president has with the military is how to avoid it. They don't really teach you how to salute in that particular department. That's the word that's gone out.

"Another consideration we have this morning out of the White House, on fairly good authority, is that the president is considering a ban on military uniforms by officers that visit the White House. If you come to the White House on official business, please do not wear your uniform." The slight hedge from identifying the material as news is revealed in the word *consideration*. "That's the latest from the front lines. I've got to tell you if you're just joining us, the early reaction from our listeners is pretty hot, pretty hot."

Calls continued from outraged listeners all morning, despite a mention during the seven-thirty newscast that the White House "vehemently denied" both stories. Wilson interrupted the newscaster to mock the White House denial.

After the show I met with Wilson. He was excited about what

he considered his success, a success he gauged by the great quantity of telephone calls he was able to generate from listeners upset about the uniform and saluting stories. But the stories were based on falsehoods, I pointed out. He expressed no remorse. On the contrary, Wilson was well pleased with the program, explaining his philosophy to me, "The purpose of the show is to strike nerve endings. As long as it gets attention, it's a success."

I objected that what he was generating was a fraud—entertainment posing as news.

"On my show," he explained, "I'm not relying on things factual. I have never had any design to build credibility." He seemed genuinely surprised and confused by my irritation and frustration with him. He told me he would air just about anything imaginable to develop interest in his show, including false news. "The show in and of itself is an entertainment entity," was his rationalization. "Credibility is never a question. You'd have to be dumber than a box of rocks not to get it."

The producer who had been on duty the morning the misinformation was spread made it clear after the show how easy it is for a caller to manipulate a talk show. I asked her how, as call screener, she made the decision to allow the anonymous caller on the air to announce erroneous information unchallenged. "The woman who called did not sound like she had an intent to give me bad information," said Sheila Jaskot.[4] She made reference to her previous job, screening calls for Bruce Williams at NBC's Talknet, saying she answered as many as 500 telephone calls there each night. "You're on the phones for years," she said, "and you pick out the phonies. I don't know what it is, but you can pick it out by some small thing in their voice." On her positive attitude toward talk radio callers, really the only attitude a call screener can adopt, she said, "I like to give people the benefit of the doubt." And with a realistic, if callous, look at the impossibility of checking the truth of anonymous callers' claims, she dismissed her responsibility to the audience casually, saying, "They'll believe what they want to believe."

Sometimes producers can pick out the phonies with that vague technique, but not always. Many skillful and calculating callers, seeking to manipulate a talk show for their own purposes, develop the techniques necessary to maneuver past the gatekeeper in the screener's booth.

Brian Wilson repeatedly explained to me that he operates in an intellectual and moral vacuum, simply as a performer. At another meeting[5] came these easy words from him about his philosophy for working a talk show: "You want me to wear the white hat, I'll wear the white hat; you want me to wear the black hat, I'll wear the black hat. I can be pro-gun on the radio, I can be anti-gun. I just happen to be pro-gun personally. My personal feelings are one thing. What you do on the air is another. It's show biz!"

His version of "show biz" was on display when, early one morning, he spoke on the air with a female caller.

"Joan, how are you?" he started the conversation.[6]

"Well, I'm pretty upset with you, Brian."

"Allright," he said.

"I'm upset with you every morning when I listen to you because of your negative and nasty remarks against this administration."

"Uh-humm," he allowed.

"Give them a chance, will you?" she asked him.

"They've had seventy-one days," he said, "and everything they do they either lie about or they misconstrue."

"Well, let me tell you, if you are so brilliant—"

He interrupts, "Why aren't I president?"

"Why aren't you in the White House?" she finishes.

They start yelling at each other at six o'clock in the morning. She barely gets a word in here and there as he insults her and President Clinton, until finally he concludes with, "Listen, Joan, I'd love to chat with you, but look, we don't have time to spend in this part of the universe anymore. If you come to the microphone, have something substantial to offer. I don't have to listen to the Star Spangled Banana. I sit here and support the Constitution every day. I talk about the Bill of Rights every day. Those happen to be the foundation cornerstones of this country." He is talking faster, his voice is rising. "Those are the ones this country was built upon.

They weren't built upon some draft-dodging, whoremongering, lying SOB that manages to manipulate enough media to get himself elected. And I've got the freedom of speech guarantee that I can stand up here to the microphone," the words are spilling out, one jammed into the next, "and I can tell you what a dork he is and the fact that he has lied to the American public. I don't need this rose-colored glasses crap that people like you throw up." His voice mocks hers, 'Oh, just give him a chance, give him a chance!' Give him a chance to what? Sell the country further down the river? Screw the middle class more? Lie on his promises? Come on, lady. Take the glasses off and get in touch with reality." Then, his voice coated with sarcasm, he sing-songs, "Thanks for the call!"

Later that morning, once he was off the air, we talked. He was pleased with himself. "It got the phones to explode," he exuded about his outburst. "My intent, was to create a confrontational moment. This is supposed to be interactive, and get people emotionally involved. Yawning is not an acceptable response." I drew his attention to the derisive words he used to describe the president. He shrugged. "I don't think there's anything wrong with calling the president an SOB."

Yawning was an acceptable response for most of the potential audience. At the time of his shouting match with Joan, Wilson's show placed twenty-first in the field of twenty-four commercial radio stations in Washington among listeners twelve years old and older.

Research commissioned by WRC showed disgust among radio listeners for Wilson's techniques. "It's clearly entertainment," said one participant in the study, "but Brian passes interpretations and opinions off as being fact."[7] Another advised, "If you put your trust in them [Brian Wilson and his sidekick], you're in trouble."

Wilson is not alone with his chameleon attitude toward his work and his relationship with his audience. "I think what I am is a performer," Mark Weaver told me as he explained his own talk show persona.[8] "I put on a good show. And what I am beyond that doesn't really matter." He, too, was trying to make me understand that personal convictions were not necessary for creation of a successful talk show, an argument I find difficult to accept. "Sometimes you have to act, that's what being a performer is all about," insisted Weaver, whose father was Jackson Weaver, a staple of Washington radio until his 1992 death.

━━━━━━

Talk programming, no matter what the contents—from the profane to the just plain wrong—is protected by the First Amendment, as well it should be. Those of us who are First Amendment absolutists long ago came to the conclusion that whatever abuses are published and broadcast are always far less damaging than censorship. In addition, the strengths of the American free press can often be traced to the freedoms we enjoy to anoint ourselves journalists. In this country anyone can be a reporter. We labor under no government or industry controls, and that, too, is as it should be.

But talk show audiences must be wary of this still-evolving new form of show business. It requires that listeners concerned with differentiating between fact and fancy learn how to sift through the growing clutter on the radio to determine which sounds coming out of the speaker need to be heard as entertainment or propaganda and which might be worthwhile to consider as reasonably accurate portrayals of the daily news.

━━━━━━

At about the same time Brian Wilson was distorting the news and misleading his audience on WRC, a Dallas talk show host was crossing and recrossing the lines between news and entertainment programming on his show. Such crossover activity has become the norm on talk shows as hosts bounce back and forth from interviewing the president to acting in mock newscasts with sidekicks and hangers-on.

As the standoff between followers of David Koresh and the Bureau of Alcohol, Tobacco, and Firearms continued, Ron Engleman jammed his KGBS talk show into the middle of the crisis. He sent messages to the Koresh followers inside the compound over the air, he gave Koresh advice, he violated requests from the law enforcement community to stay out of the negotiation process.

Criticism of Engleman's involvement in the ongoing story was immediate. "Dallas Radio Host Abusing the Airwaves with Defense of Cult," was the headline in a *Fort Worth Star-Telegram* story by Bill Thompson. Thompson summarized some of Engleman's work on the air—his calling the Branch Davidians innocent victims and his analysis of the federal agents as predatory and Gestapo-like—before concluding, "So what, you say? Who cares if some two-bit bigmouth with a microphone wants to pollute the airwaves by ranting and raving in defense of a wacko cult leader and his merry band of holy warriors?"[9] Thompson's vitriolic writing sounds remarkably influenced by the very antagonistic talk show style he criticizes. The FBI cares, he wrote, reporting that the bureau told reporters it worried that its efforts to negotiate a peaceful end to the standoff were being compromised by Engleman's intrusion into the story. And you should care, Thompson instructed his readers, "if you're a right-thinking citizen who wants to see this situation resolved without further bloodshed."

The diatribe finished with a talk radio–type flourish. "Ron Engleman embodies talk radio at its absolute worst: inane, disruptive, reckless, irresponsible. If Engleman really believes what he's been saying, he's an idiot. If he doesn't believe it, then he is exploiting a tragic situation to hype his pathetic little radio show."

As the complaints about Engleman continued, he defended himself with the assertion, "I am not part of the press. They are supposed to report without bias. I don't have to do that. I am a talk show host."

He set up a mobile broadcasting studio outside the Davidians' compound. He criticized the mainstream press for criticizing him, claiming the line he was being accused of improperly crossing— between being an observer and a participant in a story—was an artificial one. He charged other reporters with doing no work on the story other than waiting for spoon-fed information from the authorities. Although Engleman's show attracted few listeners compared with other Dallas radio stations, the Davidians were tuned in, a fact he dramatically proved when he asked them for an indication that he was communicating with them. He pleaded with them to move their satellite dish if they were tuned in, or to hang a banner from the side of one of the compound buildings. The surrounded Davidians did both.

His show was ideal for the listeners in the compound. He broadcast against gun control, against income tax, against government. At one point the Koresh followers strung another banner out of one of their buildings asking for a visit from Engleman. He wanted to go in and negotiate; the FBI refused to allow him past their perimeter. His final communication with the compound came as the federal agents began their final assault. "It's time to come out!" Engleman called to the Davidians over KGBS—the Mighty Eleven-Ninety.

After the standoff ended, Engleman was again condemned for his interference. He claimed he did nothing wrong, that he is an entertainer, not a news reporter, and consequently need adhere to no journalistic standards of ethics. His stance forced the established journalism community to study the blurring of the lines between entertainment and news collecting that has become a staple of most radio talk shows. For selfish reasons of self-protection, Engleman may not want to consider himself a news reporter, but when a bona fide employee of a radio station engages in activities that mimic the work of a news reporter, when he participates in the actual news events as they unfold and describes them and comments on them contemporaneously on the air, when he talks on the air with the principal figures involved in an ongoing news event, he is acting as a journalist no matter what he calls himself, no matter how irresponsible his actions may be.

The Society of Professional Journalists (SPJ) responded to the entire Waco debacle with an investigation, specifically singling out Engleman for attack. "The public often does not and cannot draw the distinction between a talk show host and a news reporter," the society's final report correctly observed.[10] "Even if there are distinctions," concluded the SPJ report, "all personnel who work in any capacity for a media organization have an obligation to uphold the highest ethical standards, particularly in cases of great risk to human life." While endorsing Engleman's free speech rights to criticize law enforcement, the SPJ findings were stinging, saying Engleman was "very likely interfering with the delicate negotiations," and that by sending sympathetic messages, he "was abdicating his ethical responsibility as a news media professional."

The SPJ made specific recommendations for talk show hosts finding themselves involved in similar crises in the future: "When conducting interviews talk show hosts should recognize their responsibility to adhere to accepted journalistic standards. They should set aside the kinds of biases that are freely voiced in the course of their regular shows. Talk show hosts should not attempt to manipulate the course of events; they should not take it upon themselves to conduct their own negotiations or attempt to inject themselves into the free flow of dialogue between law enforcement agencies and participants in the standoff."

The SPJ report was not universally well received in the talk show community. "Clearly, while there are similarities between radio news broadcasting and hosting a talk show, these two things are hardly congruent," protested WOR talk show host Gene Burns about the SPJ report.[11] "The performance criteria are often dramatically different. Hence to generalize enough to bring the two under the same tent of criticism is to lose all depth and substance."

Of course, the Society of Professional Journalists has no power over talk show hosts' behavior; it is merely a trade organization. And it should have no such power, even though its recommendations are sensible. Sensible, but in today's highly competitive talk show climate, probably impossible to get a consensus of talk show hosts to subscribe to and follow. Many hosts, such as the Brian Wilsons of the radio world, are not trained to make the second-by-second distinctions suggested by the SPJ task force and, of more concern, many would be uninterested in following such guidelines if they interfered with the production of an exciting, ratings-gathering radio show. Talk show hosts often are successful because they yell their opinions. To expect them to conduct themselves as journalists, especially during a vital interview in the midst of a breaking news story, may be a worthy goal but is unrealistic.

Similarly, talk show hosts live for the opportunity to manipulate events. From blocking the congressional pay raise to lonely hearts matchmaking, nothing invigorates a talk show and a talk show host like taking on a cause. To expect hosts to avoid attempts at influencing the outcome of high-profile news stories is again a lofty but unrealistic hope. And what could be better for a publicity-seeking talk show host than to negotiate the end to a crisis? As is the case with the other SPJ recommendations, SPJ's utopian ethical standards for staying out of talks between adversaries are logical, but unrealistic.

"That is a dangerous, dangerous proposition," SPJ President Paul McMasters said later[12] about Engleman's broadcasts and about a live interview with David Koresh conducted by employees of competing KRLD as the standoff was continuing. "I think that doing the interview is a legitimate tactic, but broadcasting it live lays the media open to the same vulnerability as just uncritically broadcasting whatever the authorities say." McMasters expressed disgust for Engleman's disclaimer that he was not subject to the ethical restraints of a journalist because he is an entertainer. "What we have to really rely on in that sort of situation is for the public to be more sophisticated and more critical in what it is accepting from the broadcast and the print media and to try to distinguish between those who are trying to report the news and those who are trying to raise the ratings."

Talk show hosts who consider themselves responsible entertainers, able to walk that blurring line that connects their work to journalism, expressed disgust with Engleman and his excuses. Mike Cuthbert,[13] for example, railed against him. "This is a fraudulent position taken by many talk show hosts," Cuthbert said about Engleman hiding behind the entertainer title. "It just irritates the heck out of me. Because of the fact that the radio station is involved in journalism, they use that as an entrée, and then they disclaim all responsibility by saying, 'Hey, I'm not a journalist. I'm just an entertainer,' which allowed Engleman to encourage David Koresh, take his side, and stir things up."

"Fuck them!" was Ron Engleman's response to the SPJ's findings. By the time the report was issued, he was off the air. "I am not a journalist," he told the *Star-Telegram*'s Steven Cole Smith.[14] "I guess to them, if you're on the radio and don't play records, you're a journalist. I guess to them, Howard Stern is a journalist."

Engleman quit his job while on the air. He told his listeners he was rejecting a transfer from his mid-morning time period to early morning and rejecting a management directive to engage in talk of a less strident style than what he'd become famous for broadcasting. In the relatively small fraternity of broadcasting, many of the players find themselves moving around the country from radio station to radio station, bumping into one another. Engleman's supervisor on June 18, 1993, was Morton Downey Jr.

"I can't stop it from happening," Engleman told his listeners about the switch planned for his show time and style, "but I don't have to be part of it." It was typical talk show host grandstanding—the reason why radio station program directors rarely allow talk show hosts to say good-bye to listeners when they are fired or when they quit. "Am I grandstanding?" he asked rhetorically, knowing full well that was what he was doing. "No, I'm not," was his answer. "Do I have a lot of money that allows me to do this? Absolutely not. I have nothing more than my last paycheck to my name." The questions continued. "Do I have another job to go to? No, I do not. What I do have is a loving wife, a beautiful five-year-old granddaughter that we're raising, and you, my listeners."

His speech was not finished. "There is one person I have to live with. I have to live with myself." It was the kind of personal confession and self-righteous talk that makes for fascinating radio. "If I have to knuckle under and do what is being asked of me, I would have a hard time living with myself. Therefore, as of noon today, I will no longer be employed at KGBS. I am resigning."

Engleman started the theme music that announced the end of his show, but his microphone was still on. Listeners heard the unmistakable voice of Morton Downey.

"You're resigning?" asked a shocked and surprised Downey. "Why didn't you tell management?" This from a man who developed as a stock in trade embarrassing surprises for management. Downey continued his attack. "You have the courage to tell your listeners what you think is right, but you don't have the courage to tell us?"

"I tried to tell management what I thought was right," Engleman fired back, "but management decided that they didn't want me to do what I do, so I've just resigned."

"Well, the airwaves belong to the people," announced Downey, "therefore you belong to the people, therefore you have every right to resign." Whatever that meant.

"Thank you," was Engleman's reply.

"And I thank you," offered Downey, "for a job well done."

Once Engleman was safely off the air, Downey talked with reporters, insisting that Engleman's act was not a stunt to draw attention to KGBS. And Downey, a man famous for fouling the airwaves at stations from coast to coast, complained about Engleman's antics. "It's the kind of thing kids do. After you've been in the business for a while, you learn you don't soil your nest."

Engleman left Texas for New Mexico, announcing he was publishing a newsletter calling attention to government threats to freedom.[15]

====

I know firsthand the seductive nature of breaking news stories for talk show hosts. I was on the air, for example, when the United States embassy in Tehran was overrun by demonstrators and the American diplomats there were taken hostage. And I was on the telephone immediately, trying to get a line through to the hostage-takers inside the embassy compound.

"We're standing by," I told my KXRX audience in San Jose hours after the takeover of the embassy, "because in the newsroom reporter Stan Bunger[16] is currently working with an overseas operator and apparently is relatively close to getting a hold of somebody inside our embassy in Tehran. Now that sounds farfetched,"

I teased the listeners, "but it certainly isn't impossible because earlier this morning we talked with a reporter in Edmonton, Alberta,
who was able through some telephonic wrangling to get through
to the embassy and talk to an English-speaking Iranian student
who was inside, one of the students engaged in holding those
hostages." This was exciting talk radio. "If we are able to get
through to them, it will be fascinating to talk with them and find
out what they have to say there."

Events were cascading fast as we scrambled to develop this
story. We worked on instinct: get a primary source on the air as
soon as possible. We did not sit down first for a rational discussion
of the possible ramifications of injecting ourselves into the middle
of this international incident. And even now, looking back on
those days with the luxury of hindsight and some fifteen years of
perspective, I'm not convinced we should have stopped to ponder
in detail the appropriateness of our reflexive behavior. This is not
to say that I endorse Ron Engleman's meddling at Waco or disagree with the SPJ task force recommendations. But the immediacy
of the radio medium often precludes much contemplation. Protection against abuse of the power of radio under these circumstances
must lie with the performers who execute their job, guided by constructive ethics and morals. Consequently, when the microphones
and transmitters of America's radio stations are relinquished to
selfish barkers by station owners seeking profit, with no interest
in providing public service, Engleman-like results must be
expected.

"Hello," I yelled over the noisy long-distance line, "is this the
American embassy? Is this a student in the American embassy in
Tehran?"

"Hello," came back the heavily accented voice at the other end
of the line. "This is the embassy. I am one of the students here."

"Can you tell me what is happening inside the embassy compound?" I asked.

"Everything in the embassy is under the control of the Iranian
people," he responded, "and everything is quiet and every hostage
is safe."

We talked at length and in detail about what he and his compatriots were doing and why. It was exciting, news-making radio. I asked the questions calmly and clearly, trying to keep the construction of my sentences neutral, saving the venom I expressed for the hostage-takers until we had severed the connection. After reviewing the tapes while writing this book, I remain convinced we scored a scoop that day without adversely affecting the crisis. Talk show hosts can be participatory, activist journalists without acting irresponsibly.

═══════

The distinction between talk show and traditional journalism grows fuzzier as more and more so-called traditional journalists seek fame and fortune over the airwaves. "Where the Public Likes to Really Air Views," sang out the headline in a *San Francisco Examiner* piece on talk radio reaction to the Clinton administration. "Talk Radio Hosts Kept Extra Busy Since Clinton Speech," was the subhead.[17] The article, carrying the byline of Carla Marinucci, featured the photograph of KGO talk show host Ronn Owens. The bulk of the story featured Owens and his colleague Jim Eason cast in a positive light. In italics at the close of the piece was this caveat: "Carla Marinucci of the *Examiner* staff is an occasional talk show host for KGO radio." Marinucci's news judgment, as she elevated her KGO colleagues Owens and Eason, and talk radio as a genre, just might have been tainted a bit by her desire to please her employers in that other medium where she occasionally practices.

═══════

Rick and Suds hold forth during the afternoons in southern Florida over WIOD, a broadcasting outlet that identifies itself as "news talk radio." Their trademarks include some very clever exchanges with callers who destroy their telephones (one drops his cordless from his airplane, another puts his in a blender) and a regular feature titled "Hurling for Prizes." Callers compete making the sound of regurgitation.

"Hurling for Prizes" sports its own theme song, "Lunch Is Wonderful," a song included on *The Best of Rick and Suds 1993,* a compact disc offered to the audience as both a publicity gimmick for the radio station and a fund-raiser for Camillus House, a homeless shelter.

"Want to hurl?" one of the announcers asks a caller as the song starts. "Oh, I can't right now," the caller answers. Then a big band sound that would make Frank Sinatra feel comfortable strikes up and a crooner launches into the lyrics. "Lunch is lovelier the second time around." The sound of vomiting mixes with the orchestra. "Really colorful, chunks bouncing off the ground. It's that second taste of chili, beer, and clams, makes you grab your phone, call Rick and Suds and toss it in the can." More sounds of nausea contrast nicely with the bounce of the band. "It sounds wonderful to hear the chow being blown. Makes me want to join, for no one should boot alone." A noisy burp. "Leave it to Rick and Suds to air the most disgusting thing around. But I shouldn't kick, I couldn't have missed a lick, when that guy's lunch went down a second time around." Then a flourish for the finish, the singing voice drops. "Second time around. Yeah, second time around."

It is this incarnation of talk radio that led managers of another Florida talk station, WFLA, to compose a want ad reading, "Help! ABC in New York just stole our afternoon drive personality. If you think you can fill his shoes, rush your tape and résumé to Gabe Hobbs. Young, hip, rock 'n' roll attitude a definite must. If you want to talk about the political implications of the U.N. actions in Somalia, don't bother. If you want to talk about how many dead Somalians you can stuff in a phone booth, let me hear from you."[18]

"The purpose was to minimize responses," Hobbs told me when I quizzed him about the wording of the ad a few days after it was published. He said he wanted "to eliminate those who want to talk about serious politics for three hours. This is much more about Hollywood than it is about Washington, much more about entertainment than about making the world a better place to live."

Hobbs, whose radio station is owned by the highly successful Jacor group, insisted that those who blame talk radio for creating problems are "missing the whole point." He is of the "it's just entertainment" school of explaining what he does for a living. His background is rock and roll radio, not journalism, and he found it odd that I would find the wording of his ad offensive.

"Chill, dude," cautioned many nineties talk radio operatives when I voiced concern about their antics and their tactics. "It's not art," checks in Wild 107 disc jockey Mancow Muller about his San Francisco morning radio show that makes use of many talk radio techniques. "It's garbage for the masses. But it's fun garbage."[19]

# Epilogue

This is not a kiss-and-tell book. Well over 90 percent of it was already written by the time I was fired as news and program director of WRC in Washington.

But stories of my firing and the immediate subsequent changes at WRC must be told here. They speak of the moral fiber—or lack of it—of too many of the crass business people who replaced dedicated broadcasters as owners and operators of radio stations following the deregulation of the industry. Lifelong broadcasters usually bring a sense of pride to their business work, a sense of commitment to the community, an ethic of public service that is too often missing in the contemporary arena of cutthroat radio competition. Following the deregulation of the industry, radio stations were bought and sold as just another commodity. The goal of too many of the new owners became only money.

Compare the proud history of public service that radio enjoys with the words of Andy Bloom, the Greater Media national program director, who spoke to the WRC staff the day after I was fired. Bloom arrived from the corporate headquarters in New Jersey, his speech prepared. "I don't care if you take the high road," he told the stunned employees, "or the low road. I don't care about educating people. I want to get rich and I will do whatever it takes to win. If that means getting down and rolling around in the mud, then I will get down in the mud."[1] The staff he addressed in this coarse, but remarkably honest manner, was a group I had meticulously assembled to combine life experience, intellect, and a commitment to serving society with the broadcasting experience needed to produce compelling, entertaining, and commercially viable radio. They sat shocked in the sterile eighth-floor conference room of the World Building.

"What we in New Jersey care about is excellence," said Bloom, the man who brought Howard Stern to Greater Media's Los Angeles radio station, "and by excellence I mean winning." This was not some daredevil on-the-air performer speaking, stretching the boundaries of traditional radio programming with the rationalization of entertainment and ratings. This was an officer of one of the largest radio groups in America, proudly announcing to his employees that he was representing an amoral business philosophy. He summed up his speech with a callous hybrid of H. L. Mencken and P. T. Barnum. "Nobody ever lost anything," proclaimed Bloom, "by underestimating the American people."

Many of the listening staff members were visibly offended, yet understandably cautious—Bloom was the boss and they wanted to keep their jobs. Jeff Kamen, a talk show host and news reporter who began his career in the sixties covering the civil rights movement in the American South, was among those repelled by "nobody ever lost anything by underestimating the American people."

"Try Nazi Germany and Imperial Japan," he called out. Kamen told friends later that he realized he had "blown it, but I guess I couldn't stand to sit there and suck up."

Bloom invoked the industry catchall that "entertainment, not education, is what talk radio is all about." That guidance provoked Dr. Jane Fishman Leon, a practicing veterinarian and host of a show called *Pet Talk,* to risk a question. Would her show be more entertaining, she wanted to know, if it opened with discussions of "sex with your pet"? Bloom dismissed her, but concluded his speech with a final instruction to the staff. "Read *USA Today,*" he explained. "It's what you need to read. Everything you need is in there."

The new general manager of WRC was in lockstep with Bloom. "We don't give a shit about Bosnia," he told his employees when asked to define the radio station's programming policies. "We want to hear more about Lorena Bobbitt." This at a radio station that broadcast hunks of the Bobbitt trial live and dedicated an hour of postverdict air time to a talk show discussion of the case.

Were Andy Bloom and Robert Longwell really speaking Greater Media company policy? Without a doubt. Just a few days before, I had been on board the *Spirit of Washington* tour boat for a dinner cruise commemorating the retirement of a Greater Media manager. I ate with the chief operating officer, Tom Milewski. We exchanged talk radio philosophy that evening. "The formula for a successful talk show these days," he insisted throughout the meal as he expressed company policy, "is to find out what your audience's bigotry is and play to it."[2]

Talk radio's future is loud and pornographic and perhaps even of periodic value to its listeners.

- Talk radio will continue to grow as an economic success and popular cultural influence.
- Cyber experiences through the medium of talk radio will continue to replace real-life human experiences. More and more listeners will turn to their radios for companionship, education, distraction, and sexual gratification.
- Sex talk on the radio will move from lectures, instructions, and randy stories to nonphysical sexual interaction between the host and listeners for the sexual gratification of audience members. Variations on phone sex will be available over the air for interactive talk radio orgies.
- More and more Americans will confuse what they experience through the radio speakers with real-life circumstances.
- The chatter on the airwaves will be corralled only by the limits of the imaginations of the hosts and their producers.
- Unsuspecting shills will always fill the audience, aiding the hosts with endless calls.
- Previously acceptable limits of obscenity and privacy invasion will erode further as the medium seeks greater sensationalism in the

face of increasing competition. Howard Stern will look tame compared with whoever is waiting, watching, practicing, and scheming to replace him. "The next Howard Stern is jacking off tonight in his socks," said longtime radio station programmer Julian Breem during the same business cruise on the Potomac that his boss used to reflect on the concept of playing to the audience's bigotry.

• Cable-delivered talk and talk that interfaces via modem with personal computers will allow for censor-free programs, out of the grasp of lingering Federal Communications Commission restrictions.

• Low-power and obscure radio stations, with nothing much to lose, will be forums for alternative talk shows testing the limits of taste and decency—both social and political.

• Service talk shows teaching skills and offering advice, along with shows fostering interpersonal relationships, will attempt to compensate for an increasingly dysfunctional American society.

• Habitual talk radio listeners will resort to increasingly longer periods spent listening to talk radio—while they're stuck in traffic, stuck at home, or stuck in the office.

These enticing or disturbing developments mean more talk radio stars will be using and abusing their podiums to advance political and other careers—carving out talk radio as an arena where Americans can rise to celebrity, business, and political zeniths based only on a gift of gab.

The precedent is already set. Limbaugh is a college dropout and Liddy a federal felon. U.S. Representative Robert Dornan launched his career as a talk show host and often uses talk show tactics from the House floor, like when he was officially reprimanded in early 1995 for yelling that "Clinton gave aid and comfort to the enemy during the Vietnam War." Pat Buchanan ran for president. All reasons enough to, at least periodically, turn down your radio!

# Appendix: How to Get Yourself on the Radio

If you want to use talk radio as a soapbox for your own ideas, there are some specific techniques you can use to get on the air and to reduce the time you're forced to wait on hold.

Most talk shows use a call screener who asks a few questions to help determine which calls get on the air and in what order. As a caller, you have a few seconds to make it clear to the screener that you will be exciting and interesting.

Speak clearly and coherently in response to the litany of questions. You won't get on the air without answering, so don't antagonize the screener with complaints like, "Why do you want to know how old I am?' or "What difference does it make where I live?" Remember, though, there is no way for the radio station to confirm the claims you make. So, if it doesn't bother you to adjust reality, you can radically increase your odds of getting on the air and getting there quickly.

Make yourself relatively young: At least twenty-five suggests some maturity, and under forty keeps your age in the range that talk shows consider most valuable. Next comes your location. The bulk of calls come from major cities, so pick as your hometown a quaint little crossroads.

Alternatively, try a distant city. Ego drives talk show hosts. If you call a show that's based in San Francisco and say that you're calling from Los Angeles, the host and the screener will be impressed that you picked an out-of-town show to listen to and invested long-distance charges to make the call. They'll probably bounce you to the front of the line.

The car phone gambit still works to get on the air quickly. Hosts and screeners know that calling even the shows with toll-free phone numbers can run up time charges for listeners using car phones.

More important than your location is what you want to talk about. If the host announces that only one or a select few subjects are up for grabs, don't try to change the subject. Instead, pick one of those topics. Make it clear to the screener that you have something specific, different, and exciting to say about it. Give the screener examples. If you stress that you have had a personal experience with the subject and want to add information to the show, you'll be considered a more valuable caller than those who may be ahead of you but just want to ramble on with loose opinions.

Once you're on the air, quickly—you often only get a minute or two—say something succinct about the subject of the hour. Then change the subject to get out whatever it is you really want to say. The best device for changing the subject is to appeal to the host's ego with a line like, "There's something else that's been bothering me that I'd like your opinion about." Few, if any, radio telephone jockeys can resist being put up on that kind of pedestal.

If the show is open to any topic, your job is to titillate the screener with your subject matter. Again, you can use one subject to get on the air and then change to your real message once you've captured the frequency. To initially intrigue the screener, pick something unusual and controversial, but mainstream. The screener wants your call to trigger follow-ups.

And—to avoid unnecessary feedback—don't forget to turn down your radio.

# Notes

## CHAPTER 2     LIVE FROM THE WHITE HOUSE LAWN

1. Fox's comments were in a December 30, 1988, *Washington Post* article by Bill McAllister dealing with the opposition to the pay raise.

2. Drier was quoted in a September 1989 article in *California Journal* by Chico (California) State University political science professor Charles Price.

3. Quoted in *New York* magazine, February 27, 1989.

4. *Talkers* is available from Goodphone Communications, Inc., Box 60781, Longmeadow, MA 01116.

5. Aaron's op-ed piece was in the February 19, 1993, *San Antonio Express-News*.

6. March 8, 1994.

7. The Ailes exchange with Imus was excerpted the next day by Lois Romano in her *Washington Post* column "The Reliable Source."

8. Translated by the U.S. prosecutor at the Nuremberg trials, Alexander Hardy; in his book *Hitler's Secret Weapon* (Vantage Press, 1967).

9. Translated by Joachim Remak in his 1969 Simon and Schuster book *The Nazi Years: A Documentary History*.

10. The Limbaugh broadcast was collected and criticized in my April 3, 1991, media column "News Real" in the San Francisco tabloid *SF Weekly*.

11. The Limbaugh transgression was quoted in a March 12, 1994, *Washington Post* article by Howard Kurtz criticizing the general media response to Whitewater.

12. Davis, who talked on WRC between nine and noon at the time,

took the day off to attend the briefing. Six months later he moved to WBAP in Fort Worth. I hosted his show that day; he reported on the antics at the White House as they were ongoing, using a cellular telephone, and later made notes about his experiences.

13. Kinsolving's ratings remarks were quoted by Lee Green in his ode to talk radio published in Southwest Airlines' March 1994 *Spirit* magazine.

14. *Open Line* is available from the association at 134 Saint Botolph, Boston, MA, 02115.

15. January 15, 1990.

16. July 29, 1991.

## CHAPTER 3     THE STRETCH TOWARD CREDIBILITY

1. The survey is available from the Center at 1875 Eye Street, Washington, DC 20006. I spoke with Zukin on September 23, 1993.

2. The telephone interviews of hosts were conducted between May 25 and June 11, 1993 by Princeton Survey Research Associates.

3. Princeton Survey Research Associates are responsible for the at-large survey too; it was conducted May 18–24, 1993.

## CHAPTER 4     THE GENESIS OF TALK RADIO

1. Duff was program director of KLAC from 1963 until 1967 during its talk heyday. His memos and musings from that time are collected in the 1969 self-published volume *The Talk Radio Handbook*.

2. "Hate in Talk Radio" was published in the July 1992 *USA Today* (the educator's magazine, not the Gannett newspaper).

3. Professor Munson's analysis of talk radio is assembled in his 1993 book *All Talk*.

4. Wolfman transcripts are cited in Gene Fowler and Bill Crawford's *Border Radio*.

5. Quoted by David Armstrong in *A Trumpet to Arms*.

6. In an interview with *Radio and Records* writer Randall Bloomquist, February 19, 1993.

7. March 30, 1994.

8. Cited by Kurt Andersen in a "Spectator" column in the October 11, 1993, *Newsweek*.

## CHAPTER 5    THE MECHANICS OF A TALK SHOW

1. Some of Berg's choice dialogues with listeners—including this one—are documented in *Talked to Death,* the Stephen Singular book about Berg's murder.

## CHAPTER 6    STERN AND LIMBAUGH: HOUSEHOLD NAMES

1. All collected by the *Flush Rush Quarterly.*
2. In *Newsweek,* August 16, 1993.
3. In an unpublished essay describing his encounter with Limbaugh titled "Pestilence in Broadcasting."
4. January 10, 1993.
5. February 20, 1994.
6. For its February 10, 1994, cover story.
7. March 27, 1994.
8. October 28, 1993.
9. This Stern excerpt was chosen by *Atlantic Monthly* writer Nicholas Lemann for an op-ed piece that ran in the January 13, 1994, *Washington Post,* in which he opposed the FCC's actions against Stern, maintaining, as do many free speech advocates, that what is said on radio and television should be free of any government-mandated restrictions.
10. September 6, 1993.
11. April 2, 1993.

## CHAPTER 7    TALK RADIO IN THE SHADOW OF THE STARS

1. October 10, 1994.
2. March 25, 1994.
3. The broadcast was September 21, 1993, on WRC, Washington, D.C.
4. August 23, 1991.
5. In *Newsweek,* October 28, 1991, and to me when we met in 1993.

## CHAPTER 8    HOWARD STERN ONLY TALKS ABOUT SEX

1. This stunt was broadcast on WJFK in Washington, D.C., in mid-1993, at a time when the capital was in the midst of an epidemic of mindless street slaughter—most of it perpetrated with guns.

## CHAPTER 9    LARRY KING: TOO BUSY FOR HOMEWORK

1. *Washington Post* radio columnist Jeffrey Yorke reached King at home later that week for an explanation of his failure to broadcast from the scene of the earthquake.

2. From an interview with the author on January 20, 1994. The producer requested anonymity.

3. *Christian Science Monitor,* June 25, 1992.

4. January 25, 1994.

5. April 12, 1994.

6. September 29, 1993.

7. Courtesy of Tyler Cox, the program director at WBAP in Fort Worth.

8. The questions about Limbaugh and Stern came during the November 18, 1993, King show.

9. December 1993.

10. December 1993.

11. November 12, 1993.

12. By John Zmirak in the June 1993 issue.


## CHAPTER 10    THE LISTENER PROFILE

1. The ones I cite were collected from Krasney by *San Francisco Chronicle* critic Gerald Nachman for his January 17, 1993, column.

2. The ad runs on the same page as San Francisco's radio schedules in the Sunday combined *Chronicle* and *Examiner*. The one I clipped ran April 10, 1994, adjacent to a picture of a tough-looking blonde. "Nasty Babes 24 Hours!" reads the copy on that ad along with an 800 number. The juxtapositioning seems fitting.

3. From Stephen Singular's book on Berg's murder.

4. In the *National Review,* June 29, 1991.

5. Kevin McManus collected the Harris and Bouvin comments for a piece that ran in the July 17, 1992, *Washington Post.*

6. April 28, 1994.


## CHAPTER 11    BROADCASTING HATE AND SLEAZE

1. Broadcast on WRC on August 19, 1992.

2. The Stuttering John questions were collected for an April 28, 1994,

*Washington Post* feature. The *Post* chose to delete the specific epithet Downey used against Melendez.

3. From the Downey show that aired August 18, 1992, on WRC.

4. The "hard-on" ad lib occurred June 20, 1992, over WRC.

5. Downey's airport adventure was covered in detail by the *San Francisco Chronicle* on April 26, and 27, 1989.

6. A story carried nationwide on the Associated Press wire in April 1994.

7. The "minor domestic tiff" was thoroughly covered by reporter Indira A. R. Lakshmanan, December 23, 1993, in the *Boston Globe*.

8. Leykis's commentary was message number 168981, S/5 on the Compuserve Radio/TV Talent bulletin board on December 31, 1993.

9. All collected by Kenneth S. Stern for his "Hate in Talk Radio" essay in *USA Today* in July 1992.

10. October 24, 1994.

11. November 4, 1994.


CHAPTER 12     THE WORKHORSES OF AMERICAN TALK RADIO

1. From a spring 1991 interview.

2. This meeting with Hipp was in January 1994.


CHAPTER 13     POLITICIANS AND ACADEMICS PONDER THE TALK RADIO THREAT

1. March 2, 1991.

2. From a November 12, 1993, interview with Todd Diamond in the *Christian Science Monitor*.

3. In an August 25, 1987, editorial by the vice president for news and public affairs, G. Donald Gale.

4. *USA Today*, September 7, 1993.

5. Prato wrote the piece for the February 1994 *Communicator*, the magazine of the Radio Television News Directors Association. Prato was RTNDA treasurer at the time. The association was a leader in the fight against the Fairness Doctrine.

6. In the 103rd Congress the Senate version (S. 333) was introduced February 4, 1993. The same language was used on May 5 when the House version (H.R. 1985) was offered.

7. The program was sent out over the Mutual Broadcasting System on February 1, 1994.

CHAPTER 14      TILTING AT THE LIMBAUGH WINDMILL WHILE BUCHANAN TRIES TO TAKE BACK AMERICA

1. In an interview for a *San Francisco Examiner* story by Craig Marine.
2. Spring 1994. *Flush Rush* is available through P. O. Box 270525, La Jolla, CA 92198.
3. Cited in the *St. Louis Post-Dispatch* on August 14, 1994.
4. The poll results are available from the Benchmark Company, 611 South Congress, Austin, Texas, 78704.
5. On the National Public Radio program *Talk of the Nation,* November 23, 1994.
6. *Mother Jones,* January–February 1994.
7. March 22, 1994.
8. February 6, 1994.
9. February 15, 1992.
10. In his book *In Search of Anti-Semitism.*
11. April 16, 1994.
12. March 25, 1994.

CHAPTER 16      ENCLOSED IS MY TAPE AND RÉSUMÉ

1. From a profile by Chiara in *Crystal City Etc.* magazine, Spring 1994.
2. In the December 1993 *Open Line,* the National Association of Radio Talk Show Hosts newsletter, about a year before Burns and WOR severed their business relationship.
3. These Craft remarks were quoted in an August 15, 1993, *New York Times* profile by reporter Jane Gross.
4. The samples were taken in June 1991 and January 1994.

CHAPTER 17      THE MYTH OF THE LIBERAL MEDIA

1. In an interview with reporter Larry Rohter, February 18, 1994.
2. *Inside Radio,* February 11, 1994.

3. August 13, 1994.

4. November 3, 1994.

5. Lois Romano dug up the Liddy story for her "Reliable Source" column in the February 25, 1994, *Washington Post.*

6. Westwood One—a subsidiary of Infinity Broadcasting—operates the Mutual Broadcasting System and owns the rights to the name NBC for one of its network radio news services. The July 27, 1993, letter was from vice president of station relations George Barber.

7. July 6, 1993.

8. October 9, 1989.

9. Kelley's detailed interview with Burgin about newspapers and journalism was printed in the April 8, 1994, *East Bay Express.*

10. *Church and State* is the newsletter of Americans United for the Separation of Church and State, the think tank and lobbying group headed by Barry Lynn. Literature is available from the organization at 8120 Fenton Street, Silver Spring, MD, 20910.

11. *Church and State,* March 1994.

12. Cited in Stephen Singular's *Talked to Death.*

13. January 2, 1994.

## CHAPTER 18        THE TALK SHOW HOST AS JOURNALIST

1. This example of Limbaugh's technique was collected by *New Yorker* staff writer David Remnick for his attack on Limbaugh in the *Washington Post* op-ed pages on February 20, 1994.

2. *Columbia Journalism Review,* November/December 1992.

3. Wanda called Wilson on February 25, 1993.

4. We talked February 25, 1993.

5. March 16, 1993.

6. April 2, 1993.

7. The study was conducted in July 1993 by Spectrum Research of Cherry Hill, New Jersey. Participants were paid a nominal fee to listen to WRC for a few days and then join a discussion group about the radio station and their radio listening habits.

8. We talked on December 20, 1993. Weaver worked at WMAL in Washington, another news and talk station.

9. The Thompson story ran in the March 12, 1993, edition of the *Star-Telegram.*

10. *Waco: What Went Right, What Went Wrong,* was released November 15, 1993, by the Society for Professional Journalists and is

available from it at P.O. Box 77, Greencastle, IN 46135. The report was prepared by a special SPJ task force as "a reflection on some substantive issues of journalism ethics."

11. In the February 1994 *Open Line* that he edited.

12. January 17, 1994, on WRC's morning show with Pat Korten and Mike Cuthbert, the show which replaced Brian Wilson after he was fired.

13. Cuthbert's career includes work at the Washington, D.C., public radio outlet WAMU, Boston's important talker WRKO, and WCKY in Cincinnati, in addition to the talk duties he has performed over the years at WRC.

14. Smith's piece ran in the October 2, 1993, edition of the paper.

15. Called *Freedom Report*. Engleman said his newsletter is available from P.O. Box 2858, Edgewood, NM 87015 for $35 for twenty-four issues.

16. Bunger went on to further career success at KCBS in San Francisco and then KRLD in Dallas, where he found himself in the midst of the Waco story.

17. February 20, 1994.

18. The ad ran in the trade paper *Radio and Records* in the fall of 1993.

19. From an April 7, 1994, *San Francisco Chronicle* interview with Muller, who infuriated thousands of San Francisco commuters when he mocked President Clinton's haircut at the L.A. airport by blocking traffic for hours on the Bay Bridge.


Epilogue

1. Several employees with journalism backgrounds were in attendance at the April 1, 1994, meeting, and it was from their notes that these quotes were gleaned.

2. March 29, 1994.

# Select Bibliography

*Hip Capitalism* (Sage, 1979) is based on Susan Krieger's doctoral dissertation submitted to the Stanford University Department of Communication in 1975. She spent time in the early seventies observing developments at KSAN in San Francisco, and her book includes documents resulting from the complaint against the station because of the discussion of oral sex on one of its talk shows.

*Natural Foods and Unnatural Acts* (Delacorte Press, 1974), by one-time KSAN talk show doctor Eugene Schoenfeld, includes the transcript of his "Dr. Hip Pocrates" radio show on KSAN that dealt with sexual themes in a manner that motivated one listener to complain to the Federal Communications Commission.

*Confessions of a Raving Unconfined Nut: Misadventures in the Counter-Culture* (Simon and Schuster, 1993), is Paul Krassner's autobiography, where he describes his unique manner of dealing with sex on the radio.

*Private Parts* (Simon and Schuster, 1993) is Howard Stern's print version of his radio show, absent the influence of what few Federal Communications Commission restrictions may restrain Stern's broadcasting persona.

*Rush Hour* is a superficial, sycophantic look at Limbaugh by Southern Methodist University journalism professor and *Dallas Morning News* columnist Philip Seib (The Summit Group, 1993).

*Rush!*, by *Los Angeles Times* writer Michael Arkush, is a straightforward history of Limbaugh (Avon, 1993).

*The Rush Limbaugh Story,* by *New York Newsday* radio critic Paul Colford, is the most complete study of Limbaugh (St. Martin's Press, 1993).

*Rush! The Way Things Ought to Be* (Simon and Schuster, 1992) and *The Rush Limbaugh Story: See, I Told* You So (Simon and Schuster, 1993), both by Limbaugh, are written for his fans.

*The Big Broadcast* by Frank Buxton and Bill Owen (Viking, 1972), catalogs radio shows broadcast from 1920 to 1950.

*On the Air: Pioneers of American Broadcasting* (Smithsonian, 1988) is the catalog of a National Portrait Gallery show on the history of radio.

*All Talk: The Talkshow in Media Culture* (Temple University Press, 1993) is Wayne Munson's scholarly study of talk radio and television.

*Too Old, Too Ugly, and Not Deferential to Men* (Prima Publishing and Communications, 1988) is written by Christine Craft, who gets her revenge by comparing KMBC general manager R. Kent Replogle to Roddy McDowall made up for *Planet of the Apes.*

*Censored! The News That Didn't Make the News—and Why* (Shelburne Press, 1993) is Project Censored director Carl Jensen's look at 1992 news stories he, his students, and a panel of experts considered underreported.

*Radiotext(e)* is an anthology of literature dealing with radio. It is issue 16 of the journal *Semiotext(e),* published in 1993 at Columbia University.

*Talk Radio and the American Dream* (Lexington, 1987) is an attempt to use two Boston talk shows as sources for an oral history of the sixties and seventies. The author and collector is Murray Levin, a Boston University political science professor.

*Talked to Death: The Life and Murder of Alan Berg* (William Morrow, 1987) is the book by Stephen Singular that the movie *Talk Radio* was based on.

*Mort! Mort! Mort! No Place to Hide* is Morton Downey Jr.'s autobiography, written with William Hoffer (Delacorte, 1988).

*Right From the Beginning* is Patrick Buchanan's autobiography (Little, Brown, 1988).

*A Trumpet to Arms: Alternative Media in America* is David Armstrong's thorough study of the traditions of alternative media (Tarcher, 1981).

*Border Radio: Quacks, Yodlers, Pitchmen, Psychics, and Other Amazing Broadcasters of the American Airwaves* (Limelight, 1990) is Gene Fowler and Bill Crawford's romp along the Mexican border as heard over the radio programmed by the border-blaster stations on the Mexican side.

*Media Circus: The Trouble with America's Newspapers* (Times Books, 1993) is *Washington Post* press critic Howard Kurtz's look not only at newspapers but also at the role talk shows play in providing Americans with news and information.

*Strange Bedfellows: How Television and the Presidential Candidates Changed American Politics, 1992* (Hyperion, 1993) is *Los Angeles Times* correspondent Tom Rosenstiel's contribution to the debate.

*The Roar of the Crowd: How Television and People Power Are Changing the World* (Times Books, 1993) comes from Michael J. O'Neill, a former *New York Daily News* editor.

*Tell Me More* is one of Larry King's several books about himself and his shows, this one written with Peter Occhiogrosso (Putnam, 1990).

*On the Line: The New Road to the White House* (Harcourt Brace, 1993) is Larry King's analysis of the influence of talk shows on the 1992 presidential campaign.

*In Search of Anti-Semitism* (Continuum, 1992) is William F. Buckley's investigation, which includes a chapter on Pat Buchanan's bigotry.

*"Slick Willie": Why America Cannot Trust Bill Clinton* (Annapolis Publishing, 1992) is Floyd Brown's diatribe against Clinton the candidate.

# Index

# About the Author

Peter Laufer's talk radio career began while he was still in high school producing shows in the sixties for the Metromedia station in Oakland, KNEW. He went on the air at KSAN during that San Francisco station's underground heyday, cohosting the station's talk show. After talk show stints in the 1970s on ABC's KGO in San Francisco and KABC in Los Angeles, he joined NBC News in the 1980s as a correspondent in its Washington bureau.

Laufer has a master's degree in communications from American University in Washington and was the winner of several major broadcasting awards, including the B'nai B'rith Edward R. Murrow Award for his work producing and hosting a nationwide NBC talk show on the AIDS epidemic. He writes and lectures on issues in journalism and contemporary culture.